CHINA IN AFRICA

China
in **AFRICA**

ARTICULATING CHINA'S AFRICA POLICY

Jean Kachiga

中非合作論壇

AFRICA WORLD PRESS
541 West Ingham Avenue | Suite B
Trenton, New Jersey 08638

Book and Cover design: Saverance Publishing Services

Library of Congress Cataloging-in-Publication Data

Kachiga, Jean.
    China in Africa : articulating China's Africa policy / Jean Kachiga.
        pages cm
    Includes bibliographical references and index.
    ISBN-13: 978-1-59221-941-4 (hardcopy)
    ISBN-13: 978-1-59221-942-1 (paper back)
    ISBN-10: 1-59221-941-1 (hardcopy)
    ISBN-10: 1-59221-942-X (paper back)
    1. China--Foreign relations--Africa. 2. Africa--Foreign rela-
tions--China. 3. Investments, Chinese--Africa. 4. Economic
assistance, Chinese--Africa. 5. China--Foreign economic rela-
tions--Africa. 6. Africa--Foreign economic relations--China. I.
Title.
    DT38.9.C5K33 2013
    327.6051--dc23
                          2013015963

TO SARA: THE LOVE OF DAD!

CONTENTS

China in **AFRICA**

LIST OF TABLES AND FIGURES

TABLE

FIGURES

PREFACE

This book, like many others, was inspired by an observation of the manifest various expressions of Chinese interest in the African continent. Like many books, it started with an idea or a question, or an idea engendering a question deriving from observed phenomena and asked questions. The idea and question constituted the contour within which the book was initiated and guided its first steps. Just as the idea and the question at the beginning of the project morph in the course of a closer examination of the phenomena in question, so do the steps envisaged. In other words, a closer examination of the initial idea or question almost undoubtedly reveals angles and facets that prove to be compelling enough to warrant a reevaluation, reassessment, or adjustment. Often, the book takes on a contour, shape, and focus that the author did not anticipate.

Books have a way of imposing their rhythm, of bringing to the surface what the focus should be. They engender their own dynamics and sometimes they give the feeling of being self-propelled. As a result, in the course of my exploration and research, the subject of this book gradually gravitated toward the rationale of what makes China's approach singular.

The book therefore is not a chronological account of China's activities in Africa. At least four books have done just that: J. Cooley's *East Wind over Africa*, B.D. Larkin's *China and Africa: 1949-1970*, Ogunsanwo's *China's Policy in Africa 1958-1971*, George Yu's *Africa in Chinese Foreign Policy*, and more recently, Ian Taylor's *China in Africa*, all of which are referenced herein.

These authors have documented with great scholarly care the history of China's involvement in the continent since the Afro-Asian Bandung conference of 18–27 April 1955 almost until the advent of globalization, at least in the case of Ian Taylor's book. I have quoted and alluded to these works in this book for the great insight they provide.

This book and some completed recently pick up from the reform-success era of 1978 and shed light on China's path to Africa. This book nevertheless has the vocation of providing the historical, cultural, ideological, economic, and strategic rationale whose respective end goals China harmonizes while exercising its foreign policy. This book therefore aims to elucidate China's rationale vis-à-vis Africa and, in the process, China's vision vis-à-vis the strategic reconfiguration of the hierarchy of world powers.

This last dimension justifies the focus on the singularity of the Chinese approach. China's approach contrasts with the Western approach, which has been prevalent in the African continent until now. In the same vein, this view justifies the interest in Africa's response to China's solicitation.

This book also contributes to the study of international relations of non-Western nations. Long neglected in the field due to its insignificant ability to influence or affect processes and outcomes in the international arena, the non-Western world, also identified as the developing world and more recently as the global South, was just a footnote in the arena where the elephants play. The number of elephants is growing, some of them now located in the South and the non-Western world. Furthermore, the arena itself has ceased to have a unique focus and a unique center of interest and therefore has seen the emergence of enough multiple factors, actors, identities, and issues to distort the traditional structure of power processes. In this transformation, the non-Western world is increasingly becoming less marginal as the core or center of influencing capacity has shifted. In this context, the non-Western world is claiming more than just a footnote space in the international system and its order. Foreign policies of these nations of the global South have deserved attention and are now been given it.

In the case of China and Africa, a possible triangulation between them and the West may very well constitute one of the gravitational dynamics for the near future of world politics as Africa's mineral resources, known and unknown, become even more essential for the economic growth of the elephants in international relations.

China's genuine and commercial interests in Africa also constitute possibly the last of such a massive interest in the continent by a foreign entity. After the West and colonization, of Africa, China is now seeking access to Africa's raw materials. The pool of important nations interested in Africa's natural resources is not unlimited. A time may very well come when Africa's raw materials will have no takers. It is therefore imperative that Africa finally figures out how to form, save, and invest its own capital. Efforts undertaken so far have been only a prelude to that.

Acknowledgments

It is appropriate at this spot to express in a few words my thanks for The Dale Scholarship Grant. Established by Simpson University in Redding, California in 2005, the grant seeks to encourage projects by faculty members and ultimately stimulate their professional development and participation in the debate of their respective fields. Scholarship, it is believed, in turn will inform their teaching. This particular project was the recipient of the grant in question in spring of 2007, to help cover costs.

My acknowledgments go as well to my senior class of spring-fall 2007. As I was scheduled to teach a course on any given selected topic in non-Western history, I endeavored to develop a course about the rise of China. My focus was going to be an exploration of the unraveling shift in the hierarchy of powers and wealth and their implications and the so-called going-out policy that subsequently led China to Africa. The course was entitled *China in Africa*. With my class of seniors, I explored China's reform successes in the context of globalization and China's approach to entering African markets, trading, investing, and providing development aid to the continent. I also knew that I wanted to explore the topic and write a manuscript as I realized the growing significance of China's involvement in the continent as little attention has been paid to this particular development, which has potential to upset traditional order of business in the continent. As always, a number of questions arose in my mind. Often, these questions lead to the decision to start a manuscript project.

I decided to enlist my students in the book project and divided them in groups after they registered for the course. I gave them themes to explore, sources, and reading materials to use, and encouraged them to seek additional information and data. I also gave each group a matrix with ten to fifteen questions to which they had to find answers, which they were to report to the rest of the class. The other students had to read the same material to critique the presented reports, which prompted discussions based on the report, which I recorded. As I graded the reports and listened to the recorded class discussions, I profited from my students' insights and contributions. I was inspired and stimulated to approach this book in the form presented here.

I trust that my students have learned a thing or two in the course of the semester with respect to the substantive information. Moreover, they have been initiated in the art and methodological process of approaching an academic project. The students who participated are: David Martinson, Benjamin Shipman, Alyssa Bess, Tristen M. Myers, Joel Slaegle, Ken Bias, and Ryan Swan.

My short-term consolation is in their written evaluations submitted the end of the course.

INTRODUCTION

In 1973, Alain Peyrefitte (1973), a French foreign minister, wrote a book whose title was a quotation by Napoleon I. Translated from French, it reads: when China rises, the world will tremble.[1] Since 1978, thanks to the open-door reform policy expressed in modernization objectives initiated by Deng Xiaopeng[2] in agriculture, industry, science, and defense, it seems that China has been rising indeed. China's awakening has since reverberated throughout the world as it took and continues to take advantage of global liberal economic policies made possible by the leading proponent members in international economic institutions. Peyrefitte, in the meantime, encouraged and comforted by the accuracy of his first prediction, wrote a follow-up book in 1997 with a predictable title that translated from French, reads: *China Has Finally Risen!*[3]

Observing China's past and present; any observer can see a nation whose civilization and historical timeline never receded to oblivion, not even during the three hundred years of the Dark Ages or during foreign rule by the Mongols and the Manchu dynasty of Qing, who, for the most part, assimilated into Chinese culture. The dynamism of the Chinese civilization has been constant since the earliest account of its history by the historian Sima Qin[4] in second century B.C.E. (145-87). During that time, China developed a bronze culture that predated today's Chinese porcelain, early Chinese writing during the Shang Dynasty (700-1027), and later in the same era, the iron culture, trade with Rome under the Han Dynasty (206 B.C.E.-220 C.E.) mastered structural engineering, possessed maritime know-how, produced double-deck ships that allowed a voyage to the African east coast between 1405 and 1433 by the explorer Zheng He, also known as Ma Sanbao. China has invented products that accelerated the advent of modernity: compass, paper, gunpowder. The country was well on its way to a global leadership position in a time when Europe was slowly emerging from the Middle Age. A self-imposed containment policy by the Ming Dynasty (1368-1644) in reaction to piracy and certainly driven by xenophobia and egocentrism implied in the designation "empire of the middle" explains why such a vibrant, dynamic, resourceful civilization became less prepared to face the West. This era of retraction and self-imposed isolationism can be metaphorically considered the dormant phase of the Chinese historical trajectory.

However, considering how historically continuous the territorial geography of China has been since the Qin Dynasty (221-207 B.C.E.), its cultural patrimony, scientific know-how, and worldview, it was only logical for Napoleon I, quoted by Peyrefitte, to imagine that, given the right leadership and a modern vision, China could easily reemerge. It was therefore only a matter of time before China tapped into its resources and woke up.

No historical process is detached from the social, political, and cultural dynamics from which it emerges. Historical phenomena therefore are not generally generated spontaneously. They are either a manifestation, a continuation, a deviation, or a rupture from a preceding state of affairs. Historical phenomena therefore can be described, localized, and timed. In the case of China, the phenomenon to which we refer is the reform course that constitutes the historical start of China's awakening. This reform course constituted a reaction to the meager successes during Mao's era since 1949 (failure of the Great Leap of 1958 and the abuses of the Cultural Revolution from 1966 to 1975. The meager successes, of course, justified the need for change and explained the necessity of reforms that ensued. Deng Xiaoping, the man by whom reforms were to arrive, sealed the end of Mao's era. In the process, Deng responded to the need to adjust to a new context of a dawn of a new era in the region where China's neighboring nations (Singapore, Malaysia, South

Korea, and even Taiwan), all of which have either a dominant and huge Chinese population or an important chunk of resident minorities, were showing signs of emerging. Conditions were ripe to allow a new reform policy to take hold and even to succeed. These conditions are as follows:

First, the capacity of Chinese people to mobilize once called to duty is a trait, as many authors (e.g., Khan, 1998) have pointed out, very much in agreement with the code of ethics of Confucianism. Historians have argued that the Chinese are obedient and persevere in their endeavors, sense of duty, honor, and civic pride as a result of the Confucian worldview. Speaking of mobilizing capacity of Chinese, Michel Jan (2006) wrote,

> *Une mobilisation, politique ou economique selon la periode, d'une population intelligente, docile, courgageuse, entreprenante et laborieuse, ayant tendance a confondre conviction et conformisme.*

> A mobilization, political or economic depending on a given period, docile, intelligent, fearless, entrepreneurial, hardworking, having the tendency of confusing conviction and conformism.[5]

The second condition was the presence of Chinese businessmen and entrepreneurs of the Diaspora and Chinese extraterritorial enclaves (United States, Canada, Hong Kong, and Taiwan) and their capacity to mobilize capital. They were soon to take advantage of the open-door policy. They participated enough to make a difference in foreign direct investment (FDI), joint ventures, as the increased flux of capital into Asia in the late 1980s and the 1990s evidenced, to the detriment of other parts of the developing world such as Africa. Indeed throughout the 1980s, the flow of FDI, according to the World Bank (2002), fell from 25 percent in 1970 to 5 percent in 2002, with a net FDI of $63 billion; constituting two percent of the GDP was all Africa could count on.

The third condition was that the implementation of the open-door policy coincided with the successful push by conservative governments in the United States and Great Britain for liberal economic policies that would induce globalization in the aftermath of the collapse of the Soviet empire, after the International Monetary Fund (IMF) and World Bank succeeded in recommending or imposing structural adjustment programs (SAPs) on their client developing nations of the global South.

Like Japan since the Meiji restoration in 1886, another Asian nation was on its way to using reforms to catch up with the West. Unlike Japan, China started an unprecedented experience not of attempting to move from feudalism to capitalism but rather of rendering compatible communism and market economy. China has been doing just that by keeping a two-track economy wherein the public sector remains predominantly statist with profit incentives while the private sector remains free-market oriented.

The experience so far has produced palpable results such as China becoming the fourth economic power since 2003, and by all accounts, based on current trends, will become the first economic power in the world sometime between year 2015 and 2020. China has become the second energy consumer, which implies a rapid industrialization pace, an **annual economic annual growth-rate averaging 9 percent,** year after year since the late 1990s. China has been able to **move 400 million people out of poverty since the late 1990,** shrinking their Gross Domestic Product (GDP) gaps with the United States from 1/10 to 1/7 and Japan from 1/4 to 1/3 in 20 years. The trend shows no sign of deceleration. China has become the largest exporter to Japan, surpassing the United States and becoming the third biggest economic partner to Africa.

With such an emergence, China has increasingly articulated a voluntarist and sophisticated foreign policy goal to reflect its new interests. This contrasts in many ways, as we shall explore, to that of the current undisputed superpower, or hyperpower to borrow the terminology coined by former French Foreign Minister Huber Vedrin. In fact, the official Chinese press agency, Xinhua, used the term "golden age" to refer to the successes of Chinese diplomacy in 2005. This intense diplomacy has paved the way for China's offensive in the quest to access world resources. Since 2003, China has been aggressively investing to sustain both its energy consumption and its bourgeoning private sector.

How does all this pertain to Africa? In what way is Africa of interest to contemporary China? Four reasons link Africa to the emerging China: raw materials, investment, foreign aid, and China's vision of contemporary and future international relations. The need for raw materials, both mineral and non-mineral, is neccessay for any industrializing economy. China is such an economy and is no exception to the fate of newly industrialized nations. The Chinese seek access to raw materials and new markets, which explains its interest in a continent rich in such products. As for investment, China must invest in both state and private sector venues to access new markets for its own mass consumption and increasingly high end or high technology products. Capital available in China seeks investment opportunity and Africa constitutes an outlet. Regarding aid, China understands and identifies itself as a developing nation and sympathizes with struggling nations of the African continent. China claims to have authentic and pure motives with respect to genuine aid, contrasting its understanding of it with that of Western nations.

Development aid therefore is a venue through which China seeks to provide development assistance and has been taking the leadership role among developing nations on issues beyond economic development in the name of South-South cooperation and the promotion of antihegemonic international relations. To emphasize that vision, China has called its relations with Nigeria a *strategic partnership*. China's intent to lead developing nations of the South has been manifest in international fora such as the United Nations (UN) and the World Trade Organization (WTO).

This book therefore envisages presenting, articulating, and analyzing China's presence, activity, and discourse with respect to Africa, based on foreign policy, economical interests, and available aid data.

The idea for the book was inspired by following two factors. First, the manifest growing presence of China and its increased economic activity in a time when Africa seemed to become insignificant, a mere footnote, to use the terminology of Howard French ("China In Africa: All Trade, With No Political Baggage, *New York Times,* 8 August 2004), in the aftermath of the end of the Cold War and the subsequent loss of strategic significance and considering Africa's share of global trade volume from 4.7 percent in 1995 to 1.7 percent in 2005 (according to the World Bank). Africa had become a scar on the consciousness of the world, to paraphrase former British Prime Minister Tony Blair. Second, the idea of this book has been fueled by the realization of how little research and exhaustive work has been done or written in the area of China and Africa in the field of International relations. As a discipline, International relations has been more or less trapped in the prolific political science literature from the United States in particular and the West in general. This literature characteristically deals with the elephants in the room, namely the biggest and most influential international actors. This focus scrutinizes the behavior of countries such as the United States, rendering almost irrelevant the international relations of other nations that had become for the most part the décor of the international scene, wherein the acts of the principal actor dictate the path and the pace of the play. New developments have been pointing to a more complex constellation for the 21st century, which has already forced an adjustment of that attitude.

In the early 1960s, in the aftermath of the Vietnam War and with the anticolonialist sentiment of that time, the entire field of social sciences in general, and political science in particular, had already been criticized for being too focused on the Western world. The criticism pointed to the concepts and notions conceived and thought out in the West and described the realities of non-Western cultures and civilizations. The Western-centric perspective has certainly led to inaccurate accounts of realities in these notions. In the meantime, empirical realties have demonstrated the degree to which they were misconceived. Criticisms ensued. These earlier criticisms, which were well taken, allowed the emergence of area studies in the 1960s. Comparative politics took on the task of sorting things out. Since then, works on subjects such as Africa or China were to be found in library sections listed under area studies. There has been, however, a body of work that cut through the regions and did not involve the United States or Western Europe. Such literature is today still probably found in the non-Western sections of libraries. In the meantime, the emerging international community, and the synergy resulting from international interactions and intersections between global and local forces, have been gradually eroding the clear distinction between area and international studies. Now a new consensus on the validity of multiplicity of cultures and civilizations has de-emphasized Western centrism and such works are increasingly classified under international relations or at least imbedded in international studies sections of libraries. The historical beginning of international relations in the politics of Western European nations and its later domination by the United States explain a certain understanding of the discipline as driven by the paradigm of realism and explains as well in the process, the neglect of harmless or less menacing nations.

European power politics since the mid-1800s and the principled and normative terms of the Versailles Peace treaty as well as subsequent accords such as the Locarno Pact (October 1925), the Stresa conference (April 1935), and the concept of collective security have been subject to Bismarck's Realpolitik until the arrival of Hitler's National Socialism in the 1930s.

The post-World War II era and the subsequent order of the Cold War have only cemented this understanding of international relations issues driven by the realist perspective. This perspective rendered irrelevant, or at least omitted from the picture, the foreign policy of many nations. These nations also have interests and design rationales to pursue them. We have now entered a Post–Cold war era of globalization whose dynamic processes have allowed a new international order whose contours have yet to be clearly defined. The international relations of some nations with increasing influential capacity and capabilities are bound to gain more respect and interest as those of others shrink. Tomorrow's international relations may find attention drawn to exactly such states. India comes to mind for tomorrow but China has already commanded such attention today.

China is emerging as one of those elephants in international relations: when they sneeze, everyone else hears. China has started to make waves and has been positioning itself as a nation poised to have a say in the establishment of the contours of the next international world order. In the shaping of those contours, two concepts are already competing. On one hand, American neoconservatism articulates a notion of a sole, unchallenged superpower whose vision of the world ipso facto constitutes a referential source from which universal norms shall derive. On the other hand, the Chinese approach envisages a multipolar world with certain principles to guide its actions. It is a vision of competing dualism between global hegemony and multipolarity. The outcome of such a conceptual dualism as a foreign policy goal will depend on resources, energy, and will be brought to bear by respective protagonists. Irrespective of the commitment of each, however, both global hegemony and multipolarity as foreign policy goals pertain to a world in transformation. This transformation has shown so far that no one state, big or small, is guaranteed success.

Thomas Friedman's (2005) notion of a flat world comes to mind. This transformation may produce a world wherein China and India will be the closest and biggest economic partners and therefore allies, leaving the European Union a third-tier role, as argued recently by Thomas Barnett (2005). These transformations will certainly have repercussions, and the contours of the unfolding world order will then depend on the new configuration of emerging nations and the balancing they will induce. In other words, they help determine which vision, that of the United States or that of China, will prevail.

The United States and China may work toward a given future functional international political and economic order, but their respective capacity to bring it about does not depend solely on them. In the quest to see its vision of the international order prevail, China has been planting the seeds in its foreign policy articulations and behavior. This book's scrutiny of China's presence in Africa should be seen in such a broader context.

CHAPTER 1

THE RISE OF CHINA

Much has been said and written about the economic rise of China and its newly acquired top-tier status in the world economy. Economic wealth is a factor of power as it can be translated into political influence. Consequently, this realization begs the question, how will China use the power it has been acquiring from economic wealth? Here is where the notion of intention proves important in international relations. It is evident that the missing ingredient to link economic wealth to political influencing capacity is the intent or the will to want just that. One way to find that out is to look at China's foreign policy pronouncements and behavior in the international arena.

The perception of Chinese foreign policy so far, based on pronouncements from Beijing and its behavior in the international arena (i.e., voting record at the UN and the Security Council, stances in international institutions and fora), is that it was enigmatic, pragmatic, and sometimes diffusely articulated. Bergsten et al. (2006) criticized China's foreign policy for lack of vision and long-term strategy. This perception was echoed in Bergsten (Bergsten et al. 118) who wrote, "Rather than offering an explicit outline of a long-term national security strategy, China often characterizes its foreign policy and national security goals in terms of series of principles and slogans"

Supporting this view, Xinning Song and Gerald Chan in Hu, Chan, and Daojing, (2000, 19) wrote, "Chinese leaders have articulated many strategic viewpoints on international issues but offered no theoretical framework or theory" Chan, however, explained why. Xinning and Chan stated that China did not have nor teach international relations theory until the 1980s.

Others, such as Kornberg and Faust, have suggested that China's attitude in the international arena was that of an overly cautious nation that has lived through a century of humiliation. This era left marks, leading China to emphasize the notions of independence, territorial integrity, and sovereignty. Kornberg and Faust (2005, 140) stated, "Mao and Zhou remembered the era of unequal treaties all too well, so much so that autonomy and a fierce defense of Chinese sovereignty became the basic tenets of the foreign policy of the people's Republic of China."

Most nations learn from their past. France, for instance, was intransigent and almost paranoiac vis à vis the Germans from 1871 (Prussia's invasion of France) to 1945 (German's invasion of France) until François Mitterrand and Helmut Kohl, in May of 1992 symbolically and psychologically started a new era.[6]

Indeed Chinese pride, the collective sense of self-consciousness, and the civilization they created were shattered three times in a dramatic fashion, first, during the Mongol invasion and subsequent reign (1279–1367), the second time in the Manchu domination (1644–1911), and third by Europeans, who were already in the region around the seventeenth century and were rejected and expelled (Tokugawa Japan) only to come back in the nineteenth century. A hiatus of a Japanese invasion between the two world wars can be counted as an additional shattering event. The first two invasions occurred when China was temporarily divided and politically and militarily weak; the last two invasions took advantage of the invading countries' technological superiority over China.

NINETEENTH CENTURY

The nineteenth century, which combined a double threat of Manchu Dynasty of Qing and Western menace, was an era when China had to jump when foreign masters said so, which resulted in a number of treaties (more than eight), granting among other things the status of extraterritoriality to port cities where expatriates ruled and where, in some areas of Shanghai, Hong Kong, and Macao, Chinese were not allowed to have residency, after the Opium War of 1840. Although these invasions and conquests were experienced by China as an open wound to its psyche, Chinese culture never subsided.

The latter part of the nineteenth century also was a time during which old and new ideologies (nationalism, anarchism, socialism, liberalism, and communism) competed for constituency. Two diametrically opposed ideologies emerged as political forces in China: the Chinese Communist Party (CCP) led by Mao, and the pro-Western Kuomintang (KMT) led by Sun-Yat sen and later Chiang Kai shek. Both were nationalistic vis à vis foreign presence and therefore tolerated each other at first, as they combined forces against the foreign invader, Japan, whose defeat and surrender in World War II left the two Chinese protagonists with no immediate external enemies. They turned against each other as their ideologies entailed mutually exclusive fundamentals. After early successes by the KMT and a strategic retreat by the communists in the long march, eventually Mao's Communist Party prevailed against Chiang Kai shek's pro-Western nationalism.

FROM 1949 THROUGH THE 1960s

A communist state since October 1949, China strengthened the communist bloc alongside Russia. Soon, as early as the same year, at the conference of the Moscow-led World Federation of Trade Unions (WFTU), President Liu Shao-chi presented China's revolution as a model for all underdeveloped and semi-colonized nations (Cooley 1965). China expressed its intent to lend international support to the communist movement and its bloc, in supporting independence struggles in Africa and denouncing imperialism in Latin America.

From 1949 and throughout the 1950s, China's view on world politics was dominated by the theory of "two camps" (*lianggezhenying*; Wang 2000), which emphasized China's alliance with the communist brother and neighbor, the Soviets, who sought to undermine the imperialist West. China sought to escape its diplomatic isolation in the 1950s in a string of attempts to position itself as a viable and vital supporter of all those nations struggling to rid themselves from the grip of colonial and imperial powers. With the support of these nations, China ultimately, overcame its isolation with its membership in the UN in 1971, the apotheosis in the Cold War era. Since the mid-1950s, the honeymoon between China and the Soviet slowly and progressively became tense because of ideological disagreements as stated earlier. In addition, discordance emerged over the Soviet invasion of Czechoslovakia in 1968 (Kornberg and Faust 2005); and last but not least, the clash on their common borders in 1969. In the mid-1960s, China clearly had not conceded its second-in-command-status vis-à-vis the Soviets.

In a speech in September of 1965, Lin Biao offered a version of what might very well have been called the Chinese Truman doctrine entitled, "Long Live the Victory of the People's War." In the speech, Lin expressed as a duty to all socialist nations to lend support to those fellow socialists faced with the task of defending themselves against capitalist world ideals. After proclaiming the worthiness and universal validity of its revolutionary model, China articulated ideological differences with the Soviets and sought to demonstrate its independence. The Sino-Soviet clash was about disagreement over respective visions of world communism and the means to ensure its affirmation. The Soviets emphasized an international proletariat whereas China emphasized the struggle against imperialism and the developing world as the theater for that struggle. The Soviets, next to the United States and the West, advocated a disarmament policy in developing nations whereas China sought to empower those under the yoke of imperialists and enable them to achieve independence with revolutionary means. China viewed revolution as the only and foremost goal, whereas the Soviets were willing to put issues of development and food security first.

Despite China's efforts to emerge from under the Soviets shadow, however, it remained second in command in the communist camp. In the international arena, the Soviets spearheaded the communist movement and had the potential of affecting and responding to the needs of satellite nations better than China at that point in time. Next to the experience of the century of humiliation in determining the course of Chinese foreign policy sensitivities, however, that nation's stature as second in command in communism, as well as its ideological and historical natural aversion to the United States as an imperialist force, determined a second feature of China's foreign policy sensitivity. Indeed, China sought to portray its independence vis-à-vis both the Soviets and the United States. Dealing with both, China engaged in a game of tension and détente with the Soviets and rapprochement with the United States.

In the 1960s, China emphasized what it called a theory of "opposing imperialism, revisionism, and reactionaries" (*fanduidixiu fan*, Ho Wang 2000). The 1960s were as well the time of dissonance with the Soviets.

THE 1970S AND 1980S

The 1970s were a decade of the theory of the three worlds (*sange Shijie*; Ho Wang 2000). In April of 1974, during a speech at the UN, Deng Xiaoping presented his "Theory of the Three Worlds." A not-so-original look at the world based on the ideological and economic statuses of constitutive elements, the theory saw the world as made of three blocs of actors. The first world comprised the United States and the Soviet Union: The second world comprised Canada, Europe, Japan, and Oceania; and the third included Africa-Asia and Latin America. The theory described world affairs as characterized by the struggle of the third world against the first, the latter being essentially hegemonic.

The same decade was that of rapprochement with the United States. This came about during the tension phase with the Soviets and culminated in 1971 with President Richard Nixon's visit to Beijing. China's rapprochement mode extended elsewhere. The significance of the UN as a locus of postcolonial, residual-issues debates, the universalist character of the organization, the comfort in number enjoyed by newly developing nations in that body, and finally the legitimizing role it played justified the need for China to belong. After years of resistance by that international body's most influential members to see communist China become a member, and since their support was given to the de facto declared Republic of China led by Chiang Kai shek, which enjoyed a seat, and the end of the Korean War in 1952, the adoption by the UN of the universality clause in 1955 (Le Pere and Shelton 2007), China was poised to seek membership. With the unrealistic intransigence of Chiang Kai shek to recognize his victory and its appeal to many other nations outside of the West, the time finally arrived in October for the UN to vote on Resolution 2578 on the question of representation of China. The vote resulted in an overwhelming victory for the People's Republic of China, the communists, 76 to 35 with 17 abstentions.

China became a member of the UN Security Council in 1971. The nation found a niche as an advocate of the cause of the developing nations to which it proudly claimed to belong. Kornberg and Faust (2005, 16) wrote, "Now the people's republic was not only supporter of third world aspirations, but also powerful voice in the United Nations system in which the non-aligned nations of the third world exerted their power most effectively."

At the end of his time in 1976, Mao was running out of ideas. The debacle of the Cultural Revolution made matters even worse. The coming to power of Deng turned the situation around. As his initiated reforms became successful and vindicated in the late 1980s, China started to accentuate peace and development (*heping yu fazhan*; Ho Wang 2000). Wang pointed to the end of the use of terms such as *imperialism* and *hegemony* in that era.

THE 1990S AND BEYOND

In the 1990s, China no longer looked suspiciously to the West but became an advocate of a multipolar world and opened itself to participating in multilateral organizations after determining that was where its interests were best considered. Indeed, China doubled its per capita output ten years after the reforms were implemented, foreign trade increased more than thirteen times, with surpluses in bilateral trade with the United States, and these trends continue. China opened up to multilateral institutions and the whole architecture of world trade mechanisms, which it now needs. China has since partnered with many international institutions. To that effect, Bergsten et al. (2006, 139- 140) wrote,

> Previously, China had been suspicious of multilateral structure that could potentially constrain Beijing's sovereignty and independent action, but its perspective changed as Beijing interests in multilateral environments, and it gradually came to appreciate the international system's benefits in addressing transnational challenges such as piracy, drug trafficking, terrorism, and infectious diseases.

China started to rub shoulders with the rest of the world. Indeed, Chinese foreign policy soon became more sophisticated. In 1980, China signed the most favored nation (MFN) agreement with the United States. By 1994, President Bill Clinton demanded that annual renewal no longer needed to be linked to Beijing's domestic and foreign policy attitude, providing a push to that integration process. China's openness march did not stop because its own economic reforms dictated the pursuit of such a path. China became a WTO member in 2001. China's economy slowly created links to the rest of world's economies.

The dormant giant, to use the metaphor of Napoleon I, was finally rising up. Unlike Mikhail Gorbachev, whose *glasnost* (reform) and *perestroika* (restructuring) have been encompassing and drastic in scope, and like Japan in the reform era in what Michel Jan (2006) called selective *appropriation of means* such as ideologies, science, and techniques, Chinese modernization efforts and reforms have succeeded in holding the structure together and facilitating a less communistic flow of internal economic activity and processes. Deng's political structure remained intact while internal economic processes were reformed, whereas Gorbachev's structure came tumbling down, making it impossible for processes of reform to flow and run their new course.

This course led China to increasingly becoming a full member of the world's nations with membership in more than

130 intergovernmental organizations and a signatory of more than 250 multinational treaties (Bergsten et. al. 2006). As such, China started to profit from international regimes' services and advantages such as transparency rules, information, infrastructure, and other facilitations. The increasing quantity and quality of international organizations and the increasing interdependence and integration process they imply justify the existence of international regimes whose regulatory mechanisms and efficacy require a juridical competence that was chipped away from national governments. They are in many ways factors of vulnerability and sensitivity. All along, China was aware of the danger of opening the door because flies were expected to enter, to paraphrase Deng Xiaopinmg. China has a history of looking suspiciously at all things foreign (Peyrefitte1996). Such has been the case historically because of its sense of superiority and in the modern era because of communism. The potential dangers that emanated from opening China were of internal social, political, and economic nature.

Socially, the Chinese value system could have been endangered by phenomena such as sexual revolution, gay lifestyle, divorce practice, and so on (Peyrefitte 1996). Politically, China could have maneuvered itself into chaos or revolution due to ideas of pluralism, individual and press freedoms, and certainly democratic aspirations incited by the West. The 1989 Tiananmen Square incident illustrated eloquently the groundedness of the notion of anticipated danger. Economically, it was a perilous endeavor for a communist country to do business with capitalists. First, it presented *per se a contradictio terminus*. Moreover, China was aware of the linkage often established by the West between economic agreements with conditions such as human rights, structural adjustment programs, and various expressions of quid pro quo that often tilt the balance in the West's favor.

China's View

To avoid potential venues of vulnerability, China ensured that the domain of economics was distinctively addressed apart from that of politics. China used the history of the nation-state and dug out principles and norms of the 1648 Westphalia Peace

Treaty that have served to regulate interstate behavior. Autonomy, national sovereignty, territorial integrity, noninterference in internal affairs, and self-determination have since become China's set of parameters, which allows the country to keep business issues distinct from the political concerns of potential and actual partners. It seems that China has been succeeding with that approach.

As China continues to emerge, it seems to reject and even condemn attempts from any given nation to influence the internal political course of any other. Given the realistic nature of international relations wherein political power and economic might determine international leverage with incentives, threat, and voting power in relevant international institutions, China has realized that only a few nations have that capability. Because they do not shy away from using it, China has not hesitated to condemn any hegemonic behavior in the international arena.

China therefore has been promoting an antihegemonic and a multipolar international order wherein individual nation-states can pursuit their self-interests peacefully, with respect for the norms and principles of international diplomacy as inherited from the Westphalia Peace Treaty and rejecting an international relations system based solely or predominantly on the power factor. China favors what it calls a democratic world system. All in all, China has been developing, since its ascension to global visibility, a Kantian approach to foreign policy that assumes that adoption of reasonable behavior by individual states was conducive to international norms that promote mutual gain in contrast to antiquated power politics that cultivate mistrust. China advocates international relations with a vision of a harmonious coexistence and, thereby, still in Kantian tradition, of a so-called perpetual peace.

As such, it is China's wish to dissociate itself from hegemonic aspirations and behavior. Consequently, China's foreign policy and diplomacy are expected to articulate antihegemonic intentions and use antihegemonic goals to attain them. So far China's intentions and goals seem limited to issues around its own security, the Taiwan question, and the promotion of its economic development. China's means seem to be the preference of dialogue and cooperation in mutual respect to solve world problems and promote mutual gain.

How Will China Use its Capabilities?

However, China's policy must furthermore reflect both the changing times and its own newfound global status. Returning to the question asked at the beginning of the chapter, we must ask, How will China use its increasing capabilities?

This question underlines how new expectations and responsibility require, almost beg, for an articulation of a Chinese worldview that will provide paradigmatic parameters by which to anticipate and evaluate China's moves. Along with its neighbor---Japan, India, and Taiwan--, reassurances were in order. Various scenarios are possible. This worldview in light of the new context in which China finds itself will be articulated based on defined strategic and interest calculations of that nation. China can choose a hard line and assertive attitude with Taiwan and many believe that it has, after voting on the military option should Taiwan move toward declaring independence. Others believe that China has not chosen that line as it was content with the status quo provided Taiwan did not seek just that, because only such a move could dissipate the hope for a future unification, which China may very well count on, given increased economic interdependence as argued by Barnett (2005).

With India, China has been engaging in dialogue and cooperation, and both these nations certainly are more interested in sustaining their economic surge than fueling tensions. India, for instance, does not need tension east of its border, having already one to the west with Pakistan.

With Japan, various options are possible as well; from political rapprochement to economic cooperation and promotion of a regional security regime that would provide a certain degree of assurance against a possible arms race that would otherwise ensue, and to guarantee a peaceful regional economic regime that has all the potential to make Eurasia the next pole or the new core of global trade, to use the terminology of Barnett (2005). The historical context and the volatile North Korea call for such a security regime.

The lack of a viable security regime has been seen by current observers of Southeast Asia as a reason to worry and a deficit. One such observer is Zbigniew Brzezinski (2004, 107) when he wrote, "Asia is thus at once a rising economic success, a social volcano, and a political hazard." Efforts have certainly been undertaken to remedy that deficit. Asian security and/or economic multilateralism do exist. The Association of Southeast Asian Nations (ASEAN), the Asian Pacific Economic Cooperation (APEC), the Shanghai Cooperation Organization, the Conference on Interaction and Confidence Building in Asia (CICA), the Council on Security in Asia and Pacific Region (CSCAP), and the Northeast Asia Cooperation Dialogue (NEACD), which comprises China, Russia, India, Kazakhstan, Kyrgyzstan, Tajikistan, and Uzbekistan, are proof of such a need for multilateral cooperation in both security and economic issues. However, they remain, by all accounts, underdeveloped, and the level of commitment by members remains to be tested.

Should these regional cooperation alliances blossom into fully developed regimes, China is likely to become the regional hegemon and would, in the process attempt to marginalize the security balancing role played by the United States. Such regional regimes would also lessen the chances of a potential direct confrontation with the United States, which is still committed to protect Japan, even though commitment in favor of Taiwan has been recently nuanced in favor of China. As if China were doing just that, regionally it has been engaging its neighbors to conceive a security regime based on trust and common interest, as argued by Hongying Wang (2005). Internationally, China so far is proposing an antihegemonic, multipolar world and a subscription to Kantian internationalism. Are these reactive, almost defensive measures enough? How aggressively will China push for antihegemonic behavior and in favor of Kantian internationalism in the international system? China spoke for a peaceful rise (*he ping jue qi*) in October 2003 in speech by Zheng Bijian at the Asian Forum annual meeting at Bo Ao (Hainan)[7] Is that statement enough to dissipate questions or even fears about its rise? Or should China articulate a more positive, voluntarist vision? Is there any Confucian-grounded thinking that can translate into a Chinese vision of global politics? Hongying Wang (2000, 145–51) argued that indeed some tenets of Confucianism had already found their way into Chinese foreign policy behavior. Among these are the notion of Chung-yung: the spirit of Chinese pragmatism and the aversion to use force (i.e., be strong but know how to win without using force), which prompts a preference for defense over offense, and the emphasis on moral conduit and rule of propriety.

Great powers have always formulated overarching ideals and visions to underline and morally justify the exercise of their acquired influence. The Romans created *pax romana*; European colonial powers spoke of the white man's burden; the Soviets are believed to have fought against the exploitative nature and forces of capitalism; the United States has articulated the innate and inalienable rights of the individual, leading to the notion of human rights and liberty and subsequently to self-determination. These have found their way into U.S. foreign policy goals since Woodrow Wilson.

Maybe a peaceful rise is in itself a good enough goal for now and a more visionary worldview will follow. These may be good enough, since, as a matter of historical evidence, rising nations at the peak of their dynamism have sought to expand the realm of their influence by conquest. This need for *lebensraum*, to use the terminology of the late nineteenth and early twentieth century German geopolitical theorist Friedrich Ratzel, explains the expansionistic behavior that can be indirectly exercised with hegemonic influence or undertaken directly from physical presence such as with colonization, occupation, or annexation. In modern history, the rises of both Russia and the United States have resulted respectively in the annexation of neighboring countries and territorial expansion (e.g., the war with Mexico 1846–48, through which the United States aggrandized their territory with part of Texas, New Mexico, Arizona, Colorado, Nevada, Utah, and California). The rise of the National Socialist Party in Nazis Germany and imperial Japan has as well been characterized by expansionistic wars. Most important, China has been a direct victim of the expansionistic zeal of the mentioned nations. The last one was Japan in 1921. With this in mind, the concept of peaceful rise by China suggests a demarcation from that historical pattern. Of course, we can argue that China had its thirst for expansionism quenched earlier. If the era of territorial expansionism is now behind us, as we hope, will China resort to the use of indirect hegemonic influence? China's size (country, people, military, and economy) would allow it just that. If there are concerns and worries about China's rise, as implied by the use of the term "yellow threat",[8] which is still in use in European literature and media today, like communism was disparaged by the use of the term *red menace*, China so far has been reassuring.

The concept of peaceful rise is therefore not a vain concept but rather a message. Such a message is designed to suggest China's good intentions, which ought to count for something in international relations. Next to good intentions are of course deeds and behavior. Chinese intellectuals such as Gong Shaopeng (2006) have been making the case by pointing out that indeed China's peace-mindedness has been in fact translated into true policy. To illustrate the case, consider the following examples: the active role played by China in the six-party talks to diffuse the North Korean nuclear crisis; the suggestion by China to establish a China-Asian Free Trade Area; declaring itself to agree to a code of conduct with respect to the island dispute in the South China sea; and the signing by China of the Treaty of Amity and Cooperation. Territorial disputes that have poisoned its relations with neighbors such as Laos, Russia, Vietnam, Kazakhstan, Kyrgyzstan, and Tajikistan have been proactively and peacefully addressed.

Mark Leonard (2005, 114) lent support to this argument:

> Certainly, the Chinese have gone to great length to communicate their desire for peace. In recent years, they have resolved virtually all land border disputes with their neighbors. They signed a non-aggression pact with ASEAN, which means that sovereignty disputes over flashpoints such as the South China Sea would be shelved indefinitely in the interest of joint economic development. They are working earnestly to help resolve the North-Korea nuclear issues. Through means that include free trade agreements,

the Chinese leadership also pledged to boost import from, and economic aid to ASEAN countries. They have conducted joint military exercises with Russia, Kyrgyzstan, India, and Pakistan to build trust with their neighbors.

Bergsten et al. (2005), as mentioned earlier, like many others, deplored the lack of strategic vision of Chinese foreign policy pronouncements. Does the underpinning of China's current international policy really lack vision, or is it just a misreading, reflecting instead earlier phases of Chinese global diplomacy? After all, our understanding of China must be attempted using Chinese lenses and not by subjugating Chinese logic to that of the observers. The next chapter attempts exactly that as it explores China's worldview.

CHAPTER 2

ADJUSTING TO NEW STATUS

Foreign policy projects a state's interests and/or ideals. Whereas ideals usually are less flexible, interests may shift. Political and/or economic interests can be pursued using tactical or strategic maneuvering, as these interests may be achievable in the short or long term and therefore may necessitate adaptation or adjustment. They may morph as the need, reasoning, or circumstances that underlie their relevance and raison d'être increase or dissipate. Interests are dynamic by nature. All foreign policy formulations that are based on interests are consequently dynamic, adjustable, and adaptable. So far, Chinese foreign policy has shown a high degree of flexibility and pragmatism based on the relevance of currently identified interests. Chinese foreign policy very often articulated in slogans that unequivocally and plainly state its desires, tends to reflect China's contemporary and concrete need. China has avoided backing itself into a corner by using normative, long-term visions that often are informed by and the product of ideals.

China's foreign policy pronouncements have been practical and unpretentious. Though seen by many as simplistic, they have had the advantage of clarity and coherence. Complex foreign policy formulations indeed tend to get trapped in that moral dilemma that often emerges from the pursuit of flexible utilitarian interests alongside idealistic and normative values. Indeed, incoherence appears due to the uneasy exercise of attempting to reconcile flexible and self-centered interests (such as winning the war) with less flexible and normative ideals (such as human rights). U.S. foreign policy, for instance, has more than once found itself trapped in such contradictory maneuvering and has been therefore called on many occasions hypocritical and inconsistent as it selectively chose to accommodate, depending on circumstances, one over the other.

China usually does not even pretend to seek a moral higher ground; and one could argue that there is value in that humility. China sees pretentious, long-term, strategic foreign policy as a feature of ambitious and hegemonic powers. China considers itself antihegemonic, and the simplicity of its foreign policy is seen as testimony to that.

China's political worldview so far seems to promote a more harmonious and peaceful coexistence, conflict-free cooperation, a rejection of power politics, which it believes carries the seed for international conflicts by exuding an attitude of "my way or the highway," as illustrated by President George W. Bush's declaration regarding the September 11th 2001 terrorist attacks: "either with us or against us." China has declared its good intentions and its preference for peaceful coexistence and multipolarity over hegemonism to anyone willing to listen.

CHINA AND HEGEMONY

It will be interesting to uncover whether China rejects hegemonism as a matter of policy choice or as a matter of fundamental cosmogonic difference with the West. A positive use of hegemonic power does bring about an efficient organization of international public good. Hegemonic power is driven by either a normative/philosophical goal such as promotion of democratic rule, self-determination of human rights; or an empirical goal, such as fostering prosperity. In both cases, the determinant of a good use or bad use of hegemonic power is not the pursuit of these goals but the manner in which they are pursued. An aggressive, self-centered, intransigent, nonconsultative use of power by the hegemon turns it into an imperialist. If the United States is viewed as a negative hegemon or imperialist, China has been distancing itself from that model, which is based on power. A self-centered use of hegemonic power, however, is almost necessary to hegemony when the hegemon's increased interests compel it to design a policy and create a structure and system that ensure a smooth run of its interests. More interesting here, therefore, is the question of whether China can or will remain forever antihegemonic in light of increased, amassed interests that require protective infrastructure of logistic, military, and political nature, or will China eventually find itself in a position that forces it to defend its interests? Given its power, such an urge to defend its interests could turn China into an active hegemon.

China's antihegemonic stance calls for a democratic international order based on equality among sovereign nations. We must then ask whether this is realistically, in international relations, a legal fiction, to reiterate the thought expressed by Brzezinski (2004). These questions will remain open until China's power is undisputed. Now China voluntarily restrains itself and exercises external prudence (Brzezinski 2004).

The Chinese notion of peaceful coexistence is more in agreement with its traditional philosophies of Confucianism, Buddhism, and Taoism, whereas hegemonism reflects a certain historical tradition of modernity inspired by Charles Darwin and liberalism and whose historical rationality is about competition, efficiency, maximization of profit, acquisition of wealth, and power-seeking. Inductively, the rationality of the modern West leads to a logical consequence of instrumentalization of power for preferred political goals and therefore explains hegemonism, imperialism, and colonialism from the West since the nineteenth century, as China has argued. Will China insist on its anti-Western hegemonism as it acquires a preponderant role in the world system to reflect the harmony-seeking Confucianism, reappropriated by the Chinese establishment as the communist ideology fades?

Contrary to the perceived lack of vision, China has explicitly articulated its intentions throughout the years, which seem to have one leitmotiv, namely to respond to its currently identified need and to formulate a foreign policy to that effect. On many occasions, in speeches and policy papers, China has done just that. In chapter 1 we have identified three key policy pronouncements that articulate China's intentions. The speech by Liu Shao-chi in 1949 at the Moscow conference offered China's approach to revolution as a model to the developing world that was facing subjugation by Western imperialism. At the Bandung conference of 18–27 April 1955, China essentially sympathized and identified with the struggle of the colonized and imperialized world, as a communist country eager to counterbalance Western capitalist imperialism and lend support to the struggle they faced. In the 1960s, discord with the Soviets was a reality as Mao disagreed with Nikita Khrushchev's idea of peace and détente, which he felt would happen to the detriment of China in Africa, for instance, in addition to many other ideological and policy issues. China was on its way to developing an independent foreign policy. The 1965 speech on the victory of the people's war by Lin Biao was an expression of such a political will. Gaining confidence in its access to most influential African nations then, China even attempted to organize a second Afro-Asian conference in Algiers in 1965 and actively sought to exclude the Soviets for this very political, strategic reason by advancing the argument that the Soviets were neither Asian nor Africans (Cooley 1965).

The 1970s were the era of the three-world theory, and China attempted to galvanize the support of the entire developing world in Africa, Asia, and Latin America against both superpowers. Chinese antihegemonic and anticolonialist argument pitched to African did not resonate with respect to the United States as it did with respect to Europe as a colonial power. The United States was anticolonialist, and its imperialism was not felt firsthand in Africa. African foreign policy sensitivities throughout the 1960s and 1970s were essentially anticolonialist, antiapartheid, pan-Africanist, pro-self-determination, and nationalistic. The most nationalistic arguments from the African continent did not call into question the United States nor even the Soviet Union. African foreign policy goals were in unison and in agreement with key principles of the U.S. foreign policy mantra as inherited from Woodrow Wilson, namely idealism, self-determination, and a free and liberal society. The United States even shared with both the Soviet Union and Africans anticolonialist sentiment to the detriment of the Europeans, the sole colonial powers.

Despite the lack of attraction of its vision of the three worlds, China remained in anti-imperialist and militant mode until 1974 and still committed to the ideas expressed by Lin Biao. Since the 1970s, China has manifestly articulated its foreign policy independence vis-à-vis both the United States and the Soviet Union and continued to incite the developing nations to revolt against both those members of the first world.

CHINA'S NEW WORLD POLICY

In September 1982, at the 12th National Congress of the Chinese Communist Party, China unveiled a new world policy, which stated that Chinese foreign policy was to be independent, putting into practice that which was already in existence. The context of international politics of that time is noteworthy. Indeed China had completed its rapprochement with the United States but reiterated its independent voice from the Soviet Union with less virulence. Overall, Sino-Russian relations were also about to improve during that decade. The second part of the 1980s was characterized by a number of changes in international politics as the reforms in China were visibly albeit slowly bearing fruit, the flux of foreign investment in Asia increased, the Southeast Asian tigers were emerging, and the Soviets were preoccupied and caught up in a pas de deux with the United States as the Reagan administration turned up the heat on the "evil empire." A product of its reforms, a dynamic China was emerging. In the 1990s, an engaging and multilateralist China was being fully integrated in the world community. In the same process, China was making bold moves and making waves in Africa with investments, trade, and proactive aid package deals. By then, China had caught the attention of the entire world.

Principles of Peaceful Coexistence

In 2004, commemorating the 60th anniversary of Zhou Enlai's Eight Principles, Chinese premier Wen Jiabao announced a new frame of reference of Chinese foreign policy. It was called the *Five Principles of Peaceful Coexistence.* Drawn from the eight minus three, these principles are:

1. Mutual respect for sovereignty and territorial integrity
2. Nonaggression
3. Noninterference in each other's internal affairs
4. Equality and mutual benefit
5. Peaceful coexistence

So when Bergsten et al. (2006) spoke of a Chinese foreign policy expressed in slogans rather than in long-term strategic discourse, although that indeed reflected the reality in form, it did not imply lack of substance but reflected a rather pragmatic approach designed to allow the change of policy course at a moment's notice, without becoming trapped in entrenched rationale and mechanisms implied by a long-term visionary and normative foreign policy.

China also has been careful not to project any ambitious foreign policy goals that may suggest an aggressive rise of a new superpower that would anger others and encourage them to brace against it, and thereby create a context that would jeopardize the country's economic surge. Throughout history, the rise of any nation to superpower status has almost forcefully implied a certain degree of either territorial expansionistic tendencies or at least assertive policy articulation that mirrors that nation's newfound position. That explains the aggressive and assertive foreign policy of the so-called elephants in the arena of international relations. However, such a phenomenon, though historically verifiable, presupposes political willingness or intent. Capabilities alone do not turn a state into a hegemonic bully, just as political will or intent alone, without capabilities, will not transform an ambitious state into an influential actor in the international arena.

It is exactly that political will and intent to exercise hegemonic power politics that China has explicitly repudiated in its many foreign policy white papers and publications. Again Bergsten et al. (2006, 121) noted, "Chinese leaders explicitly state China's lack of interest in regional hegemony or international leadership." China seems to have organized its foreign policy around the needs of its emerging economy. With the fourth largest economy in the world, China, according to Zweig and Bi Jianhai (in Pam 2005), already "has been able to adapt its foreign policy to its domestic development strategy." It will be interesting, however, to observe how long China will continue to hold onto a humble foreign policy formulation exclusively based on supporting its economic development as its interests grow, diversify, and become complex enough to warrant an encompassing and visionary foreign policy. After all, complex interests need complex approaches.

THE GROWING CHINA'S SHADOW IN EAST ASIA

How long will China pretend to be just another nation in the South Asia, Central Asia, and in the rest of the world for that matter? China's membership in the Shanghai Cooperation Organization, for instance, confers a certain status it can hardly escape. With such growing capabilities, China could easily, some resistance not withstanding, be tempted to propel itself to the status of regional hegemon and articulate regional goals such as pushing the US military presence outside. "In Southeast Asia, China has skillfully positioned itself as a central player, to the extent that the Americans are beginning to feel a little left out" ("Aphorism and Suspicions" 2005,24)

In the Association of Southeast Asian Nations (Laos, Brunei, Myamar, Malaysia, the Philipines, Thailand, Indonesia, Cambodia) and their most significant neighbors, South Korea, Japan and China, which Australia, New Zealand and even India join in the context of East Asia summit, China's economical significance makes it ipso facto an elephant. Some scholars, such as Samuel S. Kim (1997) have argued that such a Chinese regional hegemony was in fact already a reality as it had started, since the post-Cold-War era, to develop a space-conscious policy of lebensraum, called in Chinese *shengeun kongjian*, which includes the sea as a national territory (*haiyang quotu guan*). This policy has induced a shift of China's naval military doctrine. Of course, China's modernization of the army, its increase in defense spending, and its opacity in the matter reinforce Kim's assertion.

Kim is not alone but is backed once again by Bergsten et al. (2006), who argued that, alone, the need to transport and secure China's energy imports will lead to a stronger naval force and induce a more proactive role. China's defense spending has increased up to 17.8 percent of the budget in 2007. China has been building five strategic nuclear missile boats and adding several nuclear-powered submarines ("China Expends Sub-Fleet," *The Washington Times*, Gertz 2007, 2 March), acquiring antiship missiles (Moskit), anti-aircraft missiles (Grizzly), and Soviet destroyers (*somennys*) and intends to build an aircraft carrier, which Davis (2000) called the centerpiece of a real blue-water navy.

These illustrations of a more significant Chinese role in regional and global affairs that call for a more visionary and encompassing Chinese foreign policy approach -à la Monroe, Truman, or Brezhnev doctrines- contrast with an unpretentious, utilitarian, and relatively humble Chinese approach driven so far predominantly by the desire to accompany and accomplish its industrialization process. China has rather concentrated on bilateral and multilateral trade and investment agreements and on smoothing tensions to gain access to world markets, minerals, and nonmineral raw materials.

Indeed, as evidenced by the case of its relations with Russia and India, China seems to live up to its intent of a peaceful rise. At this juncture, as suggested by the Council of Foreign Relations task force report (CFR 2006), China may not have a choice but to behave as it does, considering the latent potential for domestic uprising, as all authoritarian regimes inherently breed, and therefore is interested in appeasing potential external sources of conflict. The same analysis was expressed by Avery Goldstein (2003, 60- 61), who wrote,

To cope with the challenges posed by a preponderant U.S. and suspicious neighbors, the strategy
combines a subtle realpolitik effort at developing
national capabilities and cultivating international
partners (one designed to avoid the provocative
consequences of a straight forward hegemonic
or balancing strategy) with a level of international
economic and diplomatic engagement designed
to maximize the benefits of interdependence (one
designed to avoid the vulnerability consequences of
bandwagoning or opportunity costs of isolationism).

A Prudent Machiavelian

This Machiavellian approach by the Chinese leadership,
which Goldstein characterized as neo-Bismarckian,[9] and the
promise of better welfare for the population have the advantage
of raising the threshold for volatile, potential, internal tensions
and may very well create a sense of pride, cohesion, and belonging among the Chinese, and may ultimately benefit the communist leadership. Signs of such an evolution are now manifest.
The general assumption has always been that once issues of
basic survival have been addressed, the Chinese will develop
a taste for a more pluralistic and liberal state. For now, China
works hard not to antagonize economic partners and jeopardize the success of its economic reforms. Although politically
and ideologically still communist, China no longer blows that
horn; and even if it did, it would not resonate. China has ceased
to be authentically communist. It has embarked on an unprecedented experience of blending communist politics with market
economy. So far, the experience has been successful. Such a
success has been possible because its underlying reforms could
not have come historically at a more propitious time.

Indeed, the open-door policy of the late 1970s has capitalized
on essentially three distinct facts. First, the era of a worldwide
market has been rendered possible since the iron curtains have
been lifted and the works of various international trade regimes
have produced liberalized economic conditions the world over.
China has been part of this worldwide market since its membership in the WTO in 2001. Its abundant cheap labor will soon

earn China the nickname of the "world factory" as foreign firms and corporations have started outsourcing or relocating there to take advantage of the huge Chinese pool of cheap labor. The availability of venture capital and the willingness by the Chinese Diaspora to reconnect with their home nation have fueled FDI and joint-venture enterprises. The result has been almost three decades of double-digit annual economic growth.

Second, the collapse of the Soviet Union has left a void which the neoconservatives in the United States have not wanted to see filled. China may just stumble into it. The growing economic forces may propel China into the status of the next in line, and its view of a multipolar world offers an alternative to the aggressively hegemonic, reductionistic, and Manichean foreign policy of the United States since the George W. Bush administration, which one issues of *Time Magazine* cover (July 2006) referred to as "cowboy diplomacy."

Third, the erosion of moral authority and clout of the United States, since its aversion to collaborate with international initiatives and new regimes such as the Kyoto protocol and its carbon dioxide reduction goals, the international justice regime via the International Court of Justice, and since the invasion of Iraq on 19 March 2003, the many incidents such as the images of abuses of the Abu Graib prisoners in Iraq, all have provided an opportunity for China to display and emphasize the notion of soft power and an argument to fend off attacks against its own human rights records. As a consequence, in the intersubjective perception of international opinion, China's positives are starting to outweigh its negatives. In the mind of some institutional agents, some congressmen in the United States, and Pentagon operatives, the perception of a friendly China has not yet been resolved in China's favor. Barnett (2005) recently warned China not to remain entrenched in the Cold War mind-set and has argued for China as a core partner with whom soon the United States may have more and more interdependent relations than with Europe. As the balance of power between the emerging power and the status quo and current power still have to be established, so does as well the entire rules of the game of the near future of the world order.

In the meantime, China has been promoting an international vision wherein international actors are not heard or respected based on their power status and wealth. This is not only because such a model can be used to court African countries but also because China needs allies to see its vision prevail. International relations should be based, according to China, on mutual respect. With such an identified and formulated foreign policy goal from Beijing, Africa and many disfranchised, economically poor and weak nations, and those less accepting of the hegemonic pressure from the West (Cuba, Zimbabwe, Venezuela, Nicaragua, Bolivia, Iran, Sudan, etc.) have found an alternative. Beijing argues that the predominant Western influence in international development aid has been abused and instrumentalized to keep poor and weak nations in chains..

Beijing further argues that the Western preponderant role in the decision-making procedures of international institutions is essentially power, and resource-based, and therefore marginalizes weaker nations. Last, Beijing argues that reliance on power in the international system, making the system hegemonic by its very inception, has been rendered less critical of the need for dialogue and mutual respect and has produced an imbalanced payoff matrix that disproportionately favors the powerful. The remedy proposed by Beijing is a multipolar world order wherein the principle of one nation one vote really is abided by and a practice of official development assistance not linked to para-economic conditions. Such an international relations goal is substantially in agreement with the demand and aspirations long formulated by developing nations since the distribution conflicts of the 1970s and their attempt to create a new international economic order. China has been presenting an alternative to the West with respect to Africa and structurally[10] winning friends/partners in Angola, Zimbabwe, Nigeria, and Sudan to name just a few.

Of course, it does not help when the United States, the international finance institutions, and the European Union persist with the Manichean approach of either-or toward African nations, which those entities justify by the need for efficiency but which in fact is made possible because of their weak bargaining power. As a result, China has been making waves and strides as it carves itself a sphere of influence to enhance the prevalence of its foreign policy goals and objectives. In 2005, for instance, China upgraded its relations with Nigeria to strategic partnership. This means that their relations will go beyond the realm of economic cooperation as they agreed to consult and coordinate their moves in the international arena to support and promote the interests of developing nations. Had such an agreement taken place between China and Gabon, for instance, it would not have meant a great deal. With Nigeria, however, the agreement implies special attention to a large oil producer, a member of the Organization of Petroleum Exporting Countries (OPEC), regional leader of the Economic Community of the West African States, a continental player, and candidate for an African representation to the UN in a time when its restructuring is becoming increasingly unavoidable. China sees this enhancing cooperation with Africa as an expression and a need to consolidate South-South cooperation, with a higher objective of balancing the structure of international power and wealth.

CHAPTER 3

A LONG HISTORY OF
ENGAGING AFRICA

Having been subjected to foreign rule since the end of the Ming Dynasty in 1644, and after becoming officially communist since 1949, both of which were responsible for the rise of Chinese nationalism and anti-imperialism, have justified China's sympathy to countries of the African continent. China's intentions were articulated in 1949 by President Liu Shao-shi, as mentioned in the previous chapter, at the Conference of the Moscow-led World Federation of Trade Union, offering China as a model for nations under imperialist oppression. Africa, with a pool of such nations, became as a matter of consequence a potential client to China's offer. After making contact with African leaders in Bandung in 1955, Zhou Enlai capitalized on it in 1956 by establishing its first diplomatic relations with Egypt. Throughout the 1950s, during the theory years of the two camps, China was resolutely militant for the communist cause in Africa. Once its first diplomatic relations were established with Cairo in 1956, China used its presence on the continent to pursue an agenda that soon was revealed as different from that of the Soviets. As a matter of fact, China has developed its own rationale vis-à-vis Africa that turned anti-Soviet over time, convinced that the Moscow approach toward the specifics of the African political and economic contexts was inadequate.

Cooley (1965, 5) noted, "Peking has set out to do what Moscow failed to do between 1956 and 1960: to promise the Africans disinterested aid, deny their strategic commodities to the West, and capture what it needs for itself."

The twenty-first century began with a Chinese consolidation of a process already under way, which consisted of restructuring and reconfiguration its relations with Africa. In this process, China carved itself a new role. That nation has become essentially an economic partner to Africa. Chinese economic agents and state, provincial, city, and private enterprises were the main actors, sent out to ensure a competitive China's quest for economic glory. Princeton N. Lyman (2005, para. 4) wrote, "China returns to Africa in the 21st century with not only a need for economic resources but with the cash to play the game dramatically and competitively." It was only then that the rest of the world started to notice the increase in China's presence on the continent.

From Zheng He to Bandung

This new development, however, did not start *ex nihilo* but was built on a long history of China's involvement in Africa. China's interest in Africa can be written with an historical overview that encompasses three distinct periods. First, was the time of Zheng He's expeditions (1405–1433). The second period waited until the Asian-African Bandung Conference in 1955 and lasted until the last African nations became independent (Zimbabwe in 1985). The third phase coincided with the modernization reforms whose successes started to manifest in the mid-1980s and are still in progress.

The seven expeditions of sixty-two ships and 28,000 men, 500 troops, plus cargoes (exporting silk and porcelain and importing tropical woods, spices, and exotic animals) by the Chinese explorer Zheng He to Africa served as the first China-Africa encounters. These would not transform the culture of the African coastal Swahili city-states of Kilwa and Malindi because the Ming Dynasty soon after withdrew from maritime expeditions. That withdrawal ended what might have constituted a viable link between Africa and the flourishing trade in

Asia, which has attracted European interest and justified their expeditions and expansion into that region. Historians have suggested prior encounters between China and Africa, of China most precisely with Egypt, before the Christian era, which may not be far fetched as the Chinese Han Dynasty commercial relations with Rome and Egypt were in between (Aicardi de Saint-Paul 2004).

There are indications that Arabs and later the Portuguese introduced Africans to East Asia between the fourth and fourteenth centuries. Aicardi de Saint-Paul further suggested a Chinese presence in eastern Africa during the colonial era and after the abolition of slavery as workers in various mining companies, plantations, and construction. These encounters were driven by diplomatic and commercial interests and almost presaged the motivation of today's China in Africa.

These interests faded as a result of a policy shift during the Ming Dynasty (1368–1644) only to reappear in the aftermath of the communist victory in China and the proclamation of the Peoples Republic of China in October 1949. This proclamation was the dawn of the second phase of the China-Africa encounter, although the Qing Dynasty dealt with South-Africa early in the twentieth century. This phase of the China-Africa encounter was the period of struggle against expressions of imperialism, namely colonialism. The postcolonial era was characterized by China's attempt to provide development aid to newly independent and developing nations. In this era, therefore, the Chinese encounter with Africa was driven by the ideology of the Communist Party. Prior to 1949, Mao had already conceived regions such as Africa as buffer zones between capitalism and communism (Taylor 2006). With that concept in mind, a communist China was not going to be indifferent to Africa. Even before China had established diplomatic relations with African nations, its ambition and interest in the continent were increasingly clear between 1949 and 1951 (Cooley 1965).

The Chinese presence in Africa, although it seems to surprise many, is therefore not an act of opportunism or a reflex born out of the germs of globalization. It is by all historical accounts a prolongation of an early communist vision with respect to oppressed, colonized Africa by colonial, capitalist, and Western powers. In China's eyes, it shares common oppressors with Africa. China's own century of humiliation has served as a point of reference, informing its foreign-policy attitude. China has therefore ventured beyond the ideology in addition to the sympathy factor to tie it emotionally to Africa. Both China and Africa are non-western; they both are cultures with a long history predating the West, and both have been disrupted and colonized by the West. On 25 June 1951, the Chinese official Lu Ting-yi reiterated the content of Liu Shao-chi's speech and announced it to be the "dogma to the Chinese communist code" (Cooley 1965, 10).

China, whose politics, culture, and mannerisms seem to be laid back, has indeed an assertive and ambitious political and foreign-policy vision that has been almost overlooked, given its third-tier status in the political context of the Cold War. Between 1949 and 1954, China had not yet established diplomatic ties with African states. That was going to change. In 1954, Zhou Enlai visited Nehru in India and articulated the Five Principles of Peaceful Coexistence, which signaled China's interest in international affairs. On 10 April 1955, China was finally invited to attend the Afro-Asian conference, after attempts by Russia to isolate it had failed.

At the Bandung conference, the original five principles became seven

1. Respect for sovereignty and territorial integrity of nation
2. Abstention from aggression and threats
3. Noninterference in internal affairs of nations
4. Racial equality and nondiscrimination
5. Equality of all nations
6. Respect for the freedom to choose a political and economic system
7. Mutual beneficial relations between nations

FROM BANDUNG TO CHINA SHENYANG INTERNATIONAL ECONOMIC AND TECHNICAL COOPERATION CO. LTD

China has used the presence of Zhou En lai at the conference to sympathize with Africa's struggle against colonialism and, most precisely, the French grip on the Maghreb and the Egyptian struggle to ensure the sovereignty of the Suez Canal. In addition to Egypt, which led the African delegation, Sudan, Ethiopia, Liberia, Libya, and the Gold Coast (Ghana) were the other African nations present at the conference.

Zhou En lai met President Gamal Abdel Nasser in Bandung a year later on 20 May 1956 when China established its first diplomatic tie with Africa. Egypt was the stepping stone into Africa. For a diplomatically isolated China in a quest for international recognition, the first African recognition by Egypt was a cornerstone upon which to build a truly influential position. The significance of this date for China became clear on 12 January 2006, when the Chinese assistant foreign minister Lu Guozeng issued a China-Africa Policy Paper to commemorate fifty years of China-Africa relations. Also in September 1956 the West Asian and African Department was created by the Ministry of Foreign Affairs and has since become an influential component of China's Africa relations.

In December 1957, the Asian Solidarity Committee organized the nongovernmental Afro-Asian People's Solidarity Conference in Cairo. The meeting produced a permanent secretariat committee and a council that was chaired by Anwar el- Sadat. China capitalized on its presence in Egypt. In 1960, when its relations with the Soviets went sour, China no longer desired to instigate actively against both Western and Soviet interests. The split with the Soviet came about because of many ideological and strategic disagreements as mentioned, a split that was becoming an embarassment for the communist world.

China also actively acted against the nonalignment movement and tried to get Africans to seek their brand of socialism. To that end, China enlisted Radio Peking in many African capitals and the New China News Agency for propaganda purposes.

Between 1957 and 1963, China continued to consolidate its relations with African countries, creating a Chinese Commission for Cultural Relations with Foreign Countries in 1957, supporting the liberation movement of Antoine Gizenga, Alfonse Nguvulu, and Patrice Emery Lumumba in 1958 in the Democratic Republic of Congo, and supporting the Union de Population du Cameroun (Larkin 1971). A year later, China attempted to get involved in Rwanda, offering support to the exiled Tutsi King Kigeli V Ndahindurwa (Larkin 1971) and elsewhere in various liberation organizations, such as between 1957 and 1962, when China supported Algeria against the French colonial empire. China's effort was soon rewarded on the diplomatic front as official relationships were entertained with Morocco in November 1968, Algeria in December 1958 with the interim government, Sudan in February 1959 and so on.[12]

This is still the era of the struggle for independence by various African political movements. China is not the only communist power that has offered support to these movements as they have declared their resolute will for revolution and antipathy to the procapitalist economic system. The Soviet Union was part of the support alternative against the West. Reasons mentioned in the previous chapter prompted China to demarcate itself from the Soviet Union. Africa had become the theater of Sino-Soviet rivalry during the 1960s, most particularly, Algeria, Somalia, Tanzania, Malawi, Zimbabwe, and the two Congos (Cooley 1965).

Although China's offensive in Africa did not surpass in influence that of the Soviets, China continued to build on its momentum. A Chinese diplomatic delegation's visit to a number of African states in 1959 was followed by the visit by the eminent Zhou En lai between December 1963 and February 1964. Between 1963 and 1965, Zhou made three trips to Africa to reinforce China's interests in the continent on issues of anti-imperialism, economic and technical aid, and the Taiwan question.

In January 15, 1964, in Ghana, Zhou Enlai delivered the Eight Principles of Economic and Technical Aid speech, emphasizing China's intent to support Africa's development effort.

China's diplomatic offensive, a shift away from the revolutionary content of the 1950s, reflected the shift in the political status of most African nations that had become independent. Chinese involvement in Africa was about remaining vigilant against new venues of domination (i.e., neocolonialism). By then, the Soviets were potentially part of foreign domination. Furthermore, any diplomatic recognition of China by African nations occurred to the detriment of Taiwan. China needed international recognition, which in turn was possible only with the contribution of African nations. Any such diplomatic success by China was in reality a threefold success: for anti-imperialist engagement in the continent, containment of the Taiwan's aspirations for independence, and the inducement of the legitimacy of communist China. Regarding Taiwan, China, ever since the 1960s, has not practiced a foreign policy based on conditionality (Larkin 1971). China has, however, always had one such condition attached to its involvement: exclusivity. China applied something of a condition to its aid that linked to support of its one-China policy, which was designed to induce African nations not to support Taiwan's secession. China indeed felt strongly about that particular policy, which underlines the interest of maintaining China as a unitary state in the context of other tendencies with respect to the legal separation of Macau and Hong Kong from Beijing.

China gradually succeeded and still is making progress in doing just that. In 1963, thirteen Africa nations officially recognized China. This number became fourteen by the end of 1965. During 1963, nineteen African nations recognized Taiwan. By the end of 1975, thirty-seven African nations had recognized China (Yu 1988). Today, forty-eight of fifty-three African nations[13] recognize China. Burkina Faso, Chad, Gambia, São-Tome, and Swaziland still do not support China's Taiwan policy. Most African nations were independent after 1960 (thirty-five as of 1965) and therefore had become members of the United Nations, constituting 30 percent of UN membership in 1993 (Yu 1988).

In September 1965, Lin Biao's previously mentioned speech offered support to revolutionary struggles in Asia, Latin America, and Africa. This was an ideological rationale for involvement in Africa. However, between 1965 and 1970, China's activity in Africa seemed to be at its lowest. Internally, China was going through the phases of the Great Leap and Cultural Revolution, both of which consumed its political energy and economic resources and turned out to be unsuccessful. Despite the Great Leap, China has remained predominantly agricultural, and the Cultural Revolution incapacitated, exorcised, and branded the most productive members of Chinese society with the label of antirevolutionaries. The consequences to China of the African involvement were that, among others, Chinese ambassadors, with the exception of Egypt, were recalled. China's activities in Africa were to be observed only in a few capitals and nations, such as Congo-Brazzaville, Guinea, Mali, Tanzania, and Zambia. These happen to be African countries under Marxist regimes. This focus on African Marxist regimes, more than a necessity, was designed to curtail the African influence of Russia, with whom China was still in disagreement.

Such rivalry was manifest in Africa in the distinct support by either the Soviets or China for various African liberation movements and parties. Two prominent cases are Angola and Zimbabwe. In Angola, China supported the Uniao Nacional Para la Independencia Total de Angola (UNITA) whereas the Soviets supported the Movimento Popular de la Liberacao de Angola (MPLA). In Zimbabwe, China supported the Zimbabwe African National Union (ZANU) led by Robert Mugabe, whereas the Soviets supported Zimbabwe African People's Union (ZAPU), led by Joshua Nkomo (Cooley 1965).

Feeling more and more at ease with its international standing since 1971, China renewed its engagement in Africa, focusing on the few remaining independence struggles in Angola, Mozambique, and Zimbabwe and on limited economic assistance. China had become an official member of the United Nations and had secured its UN seat with the support of seventy-six nations, of which twenty-six were African. During th 1970s invitations were issued by Beijing to encourage African heads of state to visit China. Many heeded the call and did just that. "Between January 1970 and December 1975, no less than sixteen African heads of governments visited China, including president Nimeiri of the

Sudan in 1970, Emperor Haile Selassie of Ethiopia in 1971, and President Nyerere of Tanzania in 1974" (Yu 1988, 855). These African visits were not limited to Marxist leaders on the continent. Presidents Kwame Nkrumah of Ghana and Mobutu Sese Seko of Congo, a resolute pro-Western politician, visited China in 1976 and returned with some of the communist approaches to mass indoctrination and economic development goals based on objectives to be met within a given time span.

The climate of détente with the United States in the 1970s and President Richard Nixon's visit to Beijing made it acceptable for pro-Western leaders to sit in the vast foreign dignitary reception hall on large, seemingly comfortable wooden chairs and white cushions next to Chairman Mao, having their pictures taken with the interpreter in between. Many other visits to China followed. "From 1978 through 1997, forty-two African sub-Saharan leaders performed thirteen trips to the Great Wall of China, while Chinese politicians made 154 trips to forty-one African nations" (Gattamorta 2004).

The persistent and relentless Chinese anti-imperialist and anticolonial messages were making waves. Sekou Toure of Guinea, Marien Ngouabi of the People's Republic of Congo, and later Thomas Sankara of Burkina Faso succumbed to the political charm of the Chinese. However, given the context of the Cold War, and given its limited economic capacity to compete with the Soviets in the era of economic assistance, China contested but never succeeded in evicting the Soviets from their premier influential role among African socialist and communist movements. China has, however, succeeded in positioning itself as an alternative to both superpowers.

China vs Soviets [margin annotation]

Despite its limitations, China's new ideological initiatives kept coming. The speech of April 1974 by Deng Xiaoping unveiled a *Theory of the Three Worlds,* which attempted to reconceptualize communist China's vision of the current political landscape and in the process redefine the place of Africa. It did not capture the African imagination. The Soviets seemed to maintain their influence in Angola and Mao Zedong died in 1976. Exhausted by the years of Mao's ill-advised policies, his successor, Deng Xiaoping, changed what he perceived as a self-destructive course upon which China had embarked. The later part of the 1970s is characterized by a reasoned China, conciliatory vis-à-vis all, including the Soviets and the United States, and urged those in Africa who still struggled for independence to try other means to obtain victory than violent revolution and guerrilla warfare.

The true reasons for this change of heart vis-à-vis Africa is China itself. Deng initiated reform policies aimed at modernizing China in 1978. This momentous endeavor necessitated resources, time, effort, and new allies. Africa slid behind in the prioritization of Chinese politics. This prioritization envisioned economic prosperity at home first, to remedy the damages caused by years of unsuccessful policies, and then abroad, to seek the company of those who had succeeded in the same modernization effort and had become prosperous. In the midst of these changes with respect to Africa, China continued in the late 1970s and early 1980s to try to reassure its partners politically.

obstacles

Part of that reassurance in 1979 involved a visit by Vice Premier Li Xiannian to a number of China's friends: Tanzania, Zambia, Mozambique, the Democratic Republic of Congo (formerly Zaire).

These changes within led China to proceed in 1982 with the normalization of its relations with the Soviets. African Marxist parties or movements no longer had to prefer one or the other leading communist nations. In September 1982, during the 12th National Congress of the Chinese Communist Party, China unveiled the new rationale for its foreign policy.

It reiterated China's independent foreign-policy tenet, which were now guided by the 5 Principles of Peaceful Coexistence. These principles regurgitate previously documented themes such as Zhou Enlai's eight principles. They are: opposition to hegemonism and power politics, international cooperation based on equal footing, non-interference in each other's internal affairs, promotion of world peace, and the promotion of friendly relations between world nations. China then found a generic formula to guide its policy attitude regardless of the counterpart. With respect to Africa, China dealt with its partners on an equal footing and with mutual respect; which was certainly a jab at the face of the Western attitude toward Africa.

China's attitude vis-à-vis foreigners has historically not been driven by conquest if we take the example of Zheng He's explorations as suggested by Le Pere and Shelton (2007).

Contrasting Chinese attitude with that of the West Le Pere and Shelton (2007,47) wrote that it was justified by following reasons:

> Firstly, their explorations were not motivated by conquest. Their raison d'être was simply to enhance the prestige of the emperor, to extract profit through trading and bartering and to exchange imperial favors for foreign "tribute" and tokens of allegiance. Secondly, for Europeans, an assault on Africa was seen as useful for feeding their impoverished countries, but also their growing industrial and commercial machine. And solely for its raw materials, Africa was seen as a worthy prize to be conquered. For its part, China had enough gold and many other forms of wealth, and any notion of conquest or subjugation of other people would have been alien to the Confucian temperament and its sinocentric metaphysic, which still saw China as the hub of the universe and all other countries as part of an inferior periphery.

Such a nonbelligerent attitude, informed by Confucian temperament, seems to have informed the cultural psyche of the Chinese.

As reform implementation progressed, China needed new approaches to deal with both its friends and its perceived enemies. China needed to rethink its overall strategy. With respect to Africa, despite its receding economic support, China continued to press on with its diplomatic effort in Africa. Between 20 December 1982 and 1 January 1983, Premier Zhao Ziyang visited eleven African countries (Algeria, Congo, Egypt, Gabon, Guinea, Kenya, Morocco, Tanzania, Zaire [Democratic Republic of Congo], Zambia, and Zimbabwe. By then, themes of the Chinese African foreign policy had become repetitive: economic support, third-world unity, and the struggle for liberation as South Africa was still under the yoke of apartheid and Namibia still colonized.

On the economic front, on 13 January 1983, a policy paper was presented by Premier Zhao Ziyang on Sino-Africa economic and technical cooperation in Tanzania. Zhao identified four principles upon which such cooperation ought to be grounded: emphasis on mutual benefits, practical result, diversity in form, and common development. Zhao was in fact recognizing the new realities both in China and in Africa and framed the new policy direction to suit China's own changing fate on the world stage.

The principles, like many others in the past, were vague, evasive, and in no way original. According to Yu (1988), this vague and generic framing of China's foreign policy in Africa with respect to economic and technical assistance reflects China's own limited resources and domestic need in the first part of the 1980s. Africa was in the midst of exacerbated social political and economical conditions. In 1986, job insecurity, corruption, inflation frustration, and disappointments in the population forced a revision of China's Africa policy, resulting in reduced activity on the continent. In Africa in the meantime, the 1980s were in so many ways a terrible decade. Coup d'états were still commonplace, endemic diseases, civil wars, bad governance, and a diminishing flux of FDI seemed to have spurred resignation vis-à-vis the continent.

In the meantime, economically, China had to readjust its economic foreign policy on Africa. Aid hence was to benefit both partners. Joint ventures were encouraged and good economic results were sought. Means of investment were to be diversified. Third-party foreign donors were expected and the Chinese bids on construction and other projects funded by African states were demanded. In short, the objective of Chinese aid was to contribute to the enhancement of the self-reliance capabilities of both Africa and China (Yu 1988). Note that at this juncture of Chinese internal political development, Deng Xiaoping's reforms were already under way and the new approach and spirit of daring to think about efficiency, profitability, gain, success, and results were entering the vocabulary and the political discourse of the official party line.

Changes induced by Deng's reform policies have also brought about the last and current period of Chinese-African encounters, which evidently started in the mid-1980s. This era has provided China with a new rationale that necessitated a concerted effort to combine trade, aid, and investment initiatives to affect both economic development in Africa and respond to its own pragmatic needs.

FROM CSYIC TO 2007

In 1984, China established the China Shenyang International Economic and Technical Cooperation, a limited corporation (CSYIC), to "undertake international contracted projects, state aided foreign projects, export of labor and services, export and import, and to establish overseas single-proprietorship and joint venture enterprises" (China Facts and Figures, 2002). How the areas of trade, investment, and economic assistance have found expression in contemporary China's involvement in Africa is the subject of upcoming chapters.

China's Africa policy had been driven by commerce and business considerations until 1989. China had been forced to reevaluate its stock in the international arena after witnessing the fury against it in the aftermath of the Tiananmen Square massacre (Taylor 2006). Friends in need are friends indeed. China had to count on its friends to counter the diplomatic fallout of an isolation attempt by the rest of the international community. Political Africa, traditionally not excited about international claims about human rights abuses, was such a friend to China. In light of such an event, China's official visitors to Africa, such as Qian Qichen between 1989 and 1992 to fourteen African countries were quite telling. In July 1992, Yang Shankun's visit summarized what have now become the prevalent tenets of the China-Africa cooperation, basically stating the same themes as those on the official China-Africa Policy Paper issued in 2006, as we shall explore next.

In 1992, a new person, Jiang Zemin, took charge in China. He rekindled the process of modernization. The repositioning of China's rationale for its Africa relations and the signaling of a new era occurred in light of both global liberalism and its supportive institutions, of which China was becoming a member, and the palpable successes of its open-door policy. China was now, without scruple or discomfort, feeling comfortable with reforms and catching up to a history of forces for counterreform. Indeed, as many times before, since the Manchu Dynasty or the Qing, in the nineteenth century, and during Mao's communism, delayed reforms were finally a reality.

This new dawn of China-Africa relations became handy for both China and Africa as the latter struggled to escape its marginalization in the world economy and China finally acquired the ability to take advantage of the continent's natural resources with demand justified by its industrialization phase. China's newly redefined context of its interests in Africa explains the renewed and subsequent high ranking of China's official visits in Africa. In May 1996, President Jiang Zemin visited six African states (Kenya, Ethiopia, Egypt, Mali, Namibia, and Zimbabwe), and suggested a fifth proposal that updated Sino-Africa relations to reflect current conditions. These five points were: sincere friendship, equal treatment of each, unity and cooperation, common development, and looking into the future. By then, in the 1990s, China had become assertive in its foreign policy, as signaled by military buildup, only to change course and retract between 1995 and 1996 so as not to antagonize the international community that it needed for its own ascent.

In the meantime, China politically recalibrated its leading elite at the top of the Communist Party. New, younger, and loyal members to both the politics of reform and the party revitalized the party, the government, and the country. After Mao Zedong, Zhou Enlai, Zhao Ziyang, Deng Xiaoping, and Jiang Zemin, names such as Hu Jintao and Wen Jiabao who embodied the new China now had command of the destiny of the country at a crucial time. Even "for them, the party remains the apotheosis of a resurgent China abroad and the standard-bearer of stability at home" (Le Pere and Shelton 2007, 39). Under their leadership, and with the successful wind of the reform propelling them from the back, they seemed in charge, competent in their grasp of the pace of change, and knowledgeable about the path to navigate.

In 2000, a confident China proposed a new institutional framework within which its relations with Africa were to find a more structured home. On 10–12 October, a China-Africa Cooperation Forum was established in Beijing as a multilateral and political consultation forum wherein broadening of consensus, increased mutual understanding, friendship, and promotion of cooperation were to be sought with the goal of achieving long-term stability, equality, and mutual benefit. First on the agenda was the question of how to push ahead with the establishment of a fair and just new international political order and to safeguard the common interests of the developing countries. Second on the agenda was the question of how to promote China-Africa economic and trade cooperation. This meeting produced two documents: "The Beijing Declaration" and "The Program for Social and Economic Development and Cooperation between China and Africa." This China-Africa forum gathered eight high-ranking officeholders from forty-four African nations alongside Chinese businessmen. The forum meets every two years to assess and evaluate previous goals and establish new ones to be pursued and evaluated two years hence.

Two years later, in 2003, a second meeting was held in Addis Ababa, on 15–16 December.[14] Subsequently, Hu Jintao visited Cairo,(29 January to 1 February), Gabon (1–3 February 2004), and Algeria (3–4 February 2004). Honoring the tradition of high-level visits, President Hu Jintao visited Africa in April 2006, his third visit. The frequency was remarkable considering he had been head of state for three years. He emphasized long-term stability, equality, and mutual benefit. In November 2004, the China Business Council met with the UN Development Program. In 2004, Premier Wen Jiabao visited the Central African Republic and Liberia. Ever since, a certain routine has been emerging to cement a long history of China's involvement in Africa. As expressions of China's interests in Africa increase, these routine visits are bound to intensify. Table 1 lists the Chinese official visits to African nations in 2006, the fiftieth anniversary of the inauguration of diplomatic relations between China and Africa.

TABLE 1. *Chinese Official Visits to African Nations (2006)*

Visitor	Countries Visited/ Meetings Attended
President Hu Jintao	Nigeria and Kenya
Premier Wen Jiabao	Ghana, the Republic of Congo, Angola, South Africa, Tanzania, Uganda
Wu Guanzheng (Member of Standing Committee of the Political Bureau of the Central Committee of the Communist Party of China, Secretary of the Central Commission for Discipline Inspection	Rwanda, Madagascar, Botswana, Gabon
NPC Vice Chairman Ismail Amat	Seychelles
NPC Vice Chairman Cheng Siwei	Gabon, Inter-Parliamentary Union Conference (Kenya)
CPPCC Vice Chairman Wang Zhongyu	Senegal
Foreign Minister Li Zhaoxing	Cape Verde, Senegal, Mali, Liberia, Nigeria

Source: UNcomtrade

In addition, China hosted visits by the presidents of Togo, Madagascar, Gabon, Senegal, Benin, Liberia, Guinea-Bissau, Seychelles, and South Africa, three vice presidents, one prime minister, six speakers of parliament, and eight foreign ministers from the region (Department of Policy Planning 2007). As a result, today multilateral and bilateral agreements and supporting institutions are in place to envision a long haul of such China-Africa history.

All in all, an argument can be made that China's contemporary attitude toward Africa has kept a fairly pragmatic and yet constant rationale and mind-set throughout the years. China has, for instance, vowed to respect African nations' choices of political systems and developmental paths. This policy preference, which will remain one of the recurrent elements of Chinese foreign policy, reflects China's commitment to and agreement with the old terms and principles of the 1648 Westphalia Peace Treaty alongside others, such as the commitment for mutual

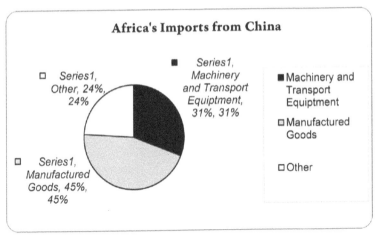

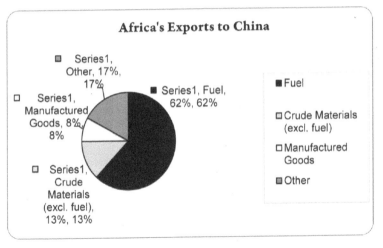

Figure 1. China-Africa Imports and Exports

respect, noninterference, and self-determination in addition to the already expressed support for independence struggle and promotion of development of society and economy. From the African perspective, there was nothing in China's foreign policy intentions that African nations would not like.

CHAPTER 4

CALIBRATED APPROACH
TO AFRICA

Throughout the history of China's interest and involvement in the African continent, a certain pragmatism seems to have guided and characterized its approach. This pragmatism is reflected in the constantly adjusting of China's policy toward Africa to reflect the former's own immediate historical, economic, and political circumstances.

China's foreign policy toward Africa, therefore, reflects China's own immediate interests, which first were aimed at lending support to anti-imperialism and nationalist movements around the globe.

From 1949 to 1956, the dates of the triumph of the Communist Party and the implantation of the first Chinese embassy in Africa, China developed a self-conscious understanding of communism. From that self-conscious approach to Communism China was not willing to play second fiddle to the Soviets and had developed through the 1960s and 1970s an independent foreign policy approach toward both the Soviets and the United States in the most contested decades of the Cold War era. It is both China's anti-imperialism and support for nationalists and its desire for independent foreign policy that explain its early Africa foreign policy attitude. Against the Soviets in Africa, China started to argue in the early 1960s, in terms of similar experiences with Africa. Both have experienced foreign rule and both were ancient civilizations assaulted by the West. China has even added a racial dimension to its analysis, referring to the White race of the West and to our brown brothers of Africa also non-whites as the Chinese are. The same race card was "played" since 1963 in China's effort to undermine the Soviet influence in the continent, describing the latter to whites (Cooley 1965, 7). In 1965, China became bolder as the speech by Lin Biao, as mentioned, simply articulated the proactive role it intended to play in assisting anticolonialist struggle by not shying away from proposing a different, more radical, and less conciliatory approach than that proposed by the Soviets.China has continued to argue from the ideological perspective until African countries have become entirely decolonized.

Economic difficulties in the 1970s forced China to retreat somewhat from its commitment to development aid programs in Africa, only to reemerge in the early 1980s demanding efficiency from recipient African countries and some possibility of a payoff for China to lessen its financial burden, and it undertook to link its aid to trade and investment. In the late 1980s, the reform policy initiated the previous decade was bearing modest fruits. Indeed, by 1993, China had become a net oil importer and had consequently become aggressive in seeking supply of energy needing to propel its economy. One way of sustaining the momentum from China's perspective was to encourage its own nascent industry and corporations to take advantage of the influencing capacity that economic aid renders possible. The influence is exercised to facilitate China's investment and market entry into Africa by way of implementing a package deal model that combines China's financial aid to take over by outbidding the competition, needed infrastructural projects, among other needs reimbursed in kind by Africa's raw material, primarily oil.

China secures reimbursement in kind by utilizing its own corporations with exploration and exploitation rights. With this foot in the heart of Africa, immense needs and potential China further secures additional investments, market entry, and access to nonenergy resources for its nascent manufacturing sector.

As a result, China-Africa relations pragmatically adapted to the new context of globalization.

Therefore, the second phase of China-Africa relations was driven by the implications of the open-door policy. Entering a phase of mass industrialization, China needed raw materials that were abundant in Africa but that China never was able to tap into in its early involvement with the continent. The efforts undertaken by China in its early involvement in Africa, to spare Africa's resources from the industrial West, had not gone anywhere as China itself could not replace the West as a client. That was to change. China was reorganizing and creating institutional infrastructures, enterprises, and policy, as we will explore in upcoming chapters, to tap consequentially into African markets and resources.

The need for mineral and nonmineral raw materials from oil, cobalt, nickel, copper, aluminum, bauxite, and iron, for which the public and the new private sectors in China long, could be found in Africa. The rising status of Africa as a producer of non-mineral raw material (gas and oil),[11] decade after decade since the 1970s, coincided with the rising of China's demand, which had become increasingly important since 1993. Nicollo Pedde (2004) pointed to this date as the starting point of Chinese aggressive foreign interest acquisition deals in exploration and production sites. Worried about the concentration of demand in the Middle East, China preventively sought to increase its supply sources from everywhere, included Africa.

Such exploration and production rights and interests were acquired in Gabon, Nigeria, Sudan, Angola, and Algeria. This diversification of supply sources is rational but also a product of a number of factors such as the predominant Western access to Middle East oil, to political volatility in the region, and increasingly to fear fueled by reports of diminishing oil reserves in the region kept secretly by the leadership. This eventuality of diminishing or even depletion of oil reserves is simply possible because, as noted by Matthew Simons (2005, 135), "Like people, oil and gas fields age. A fundamental part of their aging is the drop in reservoirs pressures." Because of that, oil "peaks, declines, and depletes" (P. 262). Simons was not alone in pointing to that eventuality. Pedde (2004, 96) concurred: "Saudi oil-fields could not be able to increase output in the next decade given the reaching of the structural peak and with an effective possibility of increase in spare capacity production only for limited period of time."

Simons warned against the rosy estimates from the Saudis, pointing to the acknowledged challenges and difficulties of estimating oil reserves and predicting their longevity. Under this scenario of guessing at the longevity of the aging oil fields of Saudi Arabia, a game Simons (2005, 278) compared "to trying to predict how long an aging person will stay productive," Africa's newly discovered oil fields and the quality of its low sulfur content became attractive to the Chinese.

In 2004, China had become the second largest oil consumer after the United States (J.Y.Wang 2007). China's need for oil and other raw materials continued to increase, allowing China to become the second largest trade partner of the continent after the United Sates. In February of the same year, Angola became the first supplier of Chinese crude oil, surpassing the Saudi Kingdom with 1.33 million tons of oil (Pam 2006). Currently China imports one-fourth of its oil from Africa. In 2005, Pam stated, Chinese companies invested a total of $175 million in African countries primarily on oil exploration projects and infrastructure. J.Y. Wang (2007) noted in turn that since 2000, 6,000 km of roads were built, 3,000 km of railroads, 8 large and mediumsized power plants, and 31% of China's offshore contracted projects in 2006. In this context, Africa's place in China's strategic alliance linkages will not cease to grow.

In light of such a development, China's foreign policy is evidently designed to serve its national energy interests. Here is where Africa's strategic importance to China derives. Indeed, there is a national security dimension in the access—or lack thereof—to available energy sources. If there were ever doubts about what China gained from its relations with African nations and if the doubt were justified in the 1950s, 1960s, and 1970s as some scholars have debated, according to George T. Yu (1988), that doubt has surely dissipated given this new context.

Many authors, including Chietigj Bajpaee (2005), have suggested that such a quest for oil and its overall importance has become China's only interest in Africa and that it has been willing to do anything in exchange for oil: "China's political, economic and military relations with Africa have been subordinated to its quest to secure energy resources" (p. 25). This interpretation of the Chinese approach in Africa is limited to a myopic view that takes into account only the current development and overlooks both the long history of China-Africa relations for which we have accounted here and the complexity of China's involvements in the continent, equally to be documented here in coming chapters. Finally, the recalibration of China's foreign policy approach toward Africa occurs in light of China's own claim to superpower status, a realist consequence of its economic surge. In this recalibration, China must realistically reflect its new interests and the willingness to define them with increasing clarity, which traditionally will lead China to fall into the logic of power politics, which it resents. The challenge or dilemma, therefore, to China's foreign policy beyond its Africa vision consists of dealing with the imperatives and implications of an unpredictable world, which necessitates the threat or use of power while wanting to be a force whose vision of international relations differs from that of the West. The subtlety of Chinese diplomacy so far suggests that they may very well be on course to successfully navigate that challenge and dilemma.

China's economic wealth is bound to produce political power. Economic influence capabilities inherently induce political power in the self-help institutions of the international system. This means that China's economic wealth will potentially or ipso facto produce its rise of status and prestige as an international actor. This explains why the rest of the world and most precisely China's neighbors have been watching and listening to signs of the flux in that country's international relations intentions.

Both with respect to Africa and to the rest of the world, China has taken a great deal of care to reassure the international community of its peaceful coexistence objective and project the notion of a peaceful rise. China has been producing documents that articulate its intent to democratize the international system, promote dialogue and respect in international relations, create a multipolar world, and express its antihegemonic position.

China's Africa's policy today is the culminating expression of China's pragmatic approach to Africa reflecting China's own need as the next chapter details its articulation.

CHAPTER 5

ARTICULATING CHINA'S AFRICA POLICY

The raison d'être of foreign policy resides in and emanates from the anti-autarkical nature of nation-states. Even if they were economically not self-sufficient, nation-states still need to cooperate both to promote peace and to allow exchanges whose distributive benefits have historically been proven. Foreign policy therefore is articulated to seek the benefits that can be extracted from a willing partner when the bottom line of that in the payoff can be documented. In this exercise, it is legitimate for each actor to look after his own advantage and interests, preferably not to the detriment of the partner (zero sum) and ideally to a mutual benefit (non-zero sum). In the case of China-Africa relations, as in any other cooperative context, their foreign policies meet in the arena of diplomacy where each actor seeks to secure its utmost preferable outcome.

In the case of Africa, realistically and historically its structural vulnerability (due to the dire state of the economy of the continent in general and lack of international institutional influential capacity) has resulted in a bargaining weakness that has allowed cooperation outcomes to be imbalanced to the detriment of the continent. In this light, it becomes imperative for Africa to look at any foreign policy formulation toward the continent through the lens of whether it is directed toward exploitation of the continent's weaknesses and therefore its exploitation or whether there is a real quid pro quo proposition. This has not always been the case. Even though Africa is not responsible for the formulation of the foreign-policy rationale of third countries, Africa owes it to itself to evaluate foreign-policy formulations by their capacity to allow a give-and-take process as they seek implementation in agreements negotiated at the bargaining table. Africa must find ways to overcome its historical and current lack of bargaining leverage and structural and political inefficiencies that allow it to persist.

A China-Africa foreign policy therefore ought to be examined for its degree of fairness, or win-win proposition as China's Africa policy document claims (See Appendix A for full text of the document). Furthermore, China-Africa foreign policy claims to have the purpose of aiding Africa to overcome the hardship of underdevelopment and its structural weakness. Seen from that perspective, China's Africa policy has a moral dimension for which it consequently must account.

THE POLICY PAPER

Since the 1950s and throughout the years, China's Africa policy formulation has been articulated in a typically communist style of verbiage and slogans full of good intentions, bordering on platitudes, with terms such as equality, solidarity, mutual respect, win-win, learning from each other, and so on.

These good words announce intents and objectives, as do most diplomatic papers and communiqués, and were driven at first by ideological considerations and underpinnings. A closer look at the document issued 12 January 2006, reveals an evolution from those attitudes and an approach that reflects China's own internal transformation and changes. Encompassing and comprehensive in scope, this policy paper moved away from the ideological underpinnings of the 1950s and 1960s, the uncertainty of the 1970s that led to the need for reforms in China, and the adjustment and readjustment of its policy in the 1980s. This process reflected the discomfort of adapting to the transition into a market economy, during which period China, facing its own need for capital, vacillated between assisting Africa economically and seeking some kind of return or efficiency to justify its engagement during the modernization era. Nascent Chinese capitalism demanded that Africa, in addition to receiving Chinese aid, also must open its development projects for bid to Chinese businesses. Africa was becoming a business opportunity for China and a market. Since 1987, Chinese enterprises have spread into well over twenty Africa countries (China Facts and Figures 2002).

Indeed, after turning capitalistic, China, the self-declared champion of communism and anticapitalist imperialism, had to rely less and less on ideological mantras and arguments. The emphasis shifted to economics and the capacity of Africa to play an important role in a nascent China's industrial capitalism. This reckoning by China materialized in the 1990s, when China realized the potential of its economy, the advantages of a globalized trade context, and the need to sustain its growth. China also realized its vulnerability and fear of what Pierre Antoine Braud (2005, 2) called "energy containment" . The potential to use limited access to oil as a weapon by nations such as the United States, which had already secured access to Middle Eastern oil, to contain both China's economic and political rise was far too menacing to contemplate.

This reckoning prompted a need for strategic and geopolitical diplomatic restructuring. Braud (2005) retraced this process, which led to China's foreign policy restructuring as follows. In 1993, the success of the reform policy turned China to a net oil importer. This momentum should have been sustained. Between 1994 and 1996, Chinese oil companies (the National Petroleum Corporation, CNPC) and Sinopec were restructured to facilitate their international operations capacity. For China's energy needs, these companies became the key players, acquiring exploration and production rights as well as joint ventures overseas, as illustrated by the cases of Nigeria, Sudan, Angola, Algeria, and Gabon. As financial capacity is always needed to accompany foreign investment, a Chinese export-import bank (Exim Bank) accomplished that task, as "the sole state-owned entity that Chinese government uses to dispense official economic aid worldwide, including Africa" (Gill and Reilly 2007, 43), whose operations we shall explore later.

This restructuring allowed a gradual reduction in dependency on Middle Eastern oil since 1995 (from 56 to 40%). The trend will not deflate because in 2007, 30 percent of China's oil is supplied by sub-Saharan Africa. Even more telling is the fact that Angola has replaced Saudi Arabia as China's biggest supplier.

By 1997 the CNPC, in a joint venture, acquired exploration and exploitation rights in Sudan. Deserted and marginalized by globalization and by its own doings, including civil wars and the plagues of failed states, bad governance, and endemic diseases, most important African oil producers were affected in various ways that have allowed a loosening of Western investment.

In the case of Sudan, the embargo, which led Chevron to withdraw its activity in the 1980s, and the charges of terrorism by the United States in the aftermath of September 11th 2001 Angola was dealing with a civil war and Nigeria was subject to international criticism through the 1990s (Braud 2005).

China made its move into Africa. In January 2006, China issued its Africa policy paper in light of the above-described context. This policy paper did not come *ex nihilo*. It reflected the following factors: China's own political identity, China's current needs, the current international political landscape, and Africa's special situation. The policy built upon the history of diplomatic relations between these two actors.

Because of that, the policy paper appears to address almost all relevant and various venues and channels through which relations among nations are made truly comprehensive. As a matter of consequence, in every area covered, the paper spells out China's intentions and objectives and therefore provides a frame of reference and parameters of expectations for China's engagement in Africa beyond 2006.

The elements of China's Africa policy (see Appendix A) encompass the following areas of interest: politics, which speaks to the state of African political landscape; China's intent to relate to African states at that level; and the role of Africa in what China considers to be the order of international relations. The second part speaks to issues of economic cooperation, namely trade, investment, financial cooperation, agricultural cooperation, infrastructure building, tourism and resources cooperation, debt reduction, and development aid. The third part deals with what we can refer to as issues of soft-power domains, as it addresses education, science, culture, health, and social aspects such as media, people-to-people relations, the environment, and humanitarian assistance. We refer to these as *soft-power domains* as they allow China, away from the concerns of politics, peace, security, and economics, to rub shoulders with Africans, allowing them to experience China and Chinese firsthand. From a China perspective, the hope is that they will gain the hearts and minds of Africans and build goodwill. The fourth part of the policy paper speaks to issues of peace and security, most precisely matters of military cooperation, conflict settlement, and peace-keeping. The fifth part deals with institutional support as vessels that facilitate consultation, discussion, decision making, and implementation of Chinese policy objectives in Africa. The sixth and last part addresses China's behavioral intentions vis-à-vis existing African regional organizations and institutions.

Active in the above-mentioned domains, China's policy toward Africa is driven and built upon a rationale of give and take. On the giving hand of the Chinese policy choices are these operative intents: to cooperate, to assist and support, to trade and invest, to win the hearts of Africans, to build, and to educate. *who has it better?* ←

On the taking hand of China's Africa policy, the operative intents are: to access and acquire (resources and markets), to export, to secure and diversify (supply sources), to win strategic allies, and to increase China's influential capacity and status in international politics.

NAVIGATING THE AFRICAN POLITICAL LANDSCAPE

Relying on a history of involvement in and experience dealing with Africa since 1956, China has capitalized on old friendships in the cases of Algeria, Angola, Zimbabwe, Egypt, Tanzania, Zambia, Benin, Burkina Faso, both Congos, and so on, and on some kind of fatigue of Western involvement in the continent, the frustration and entanglements with Western international finance institutions, and the disillusionment of many African leaders vis-à-vis the West. Lindsey Hilsum (2005) best captured the expression of such frustration by an African official in her article quoting Sahr Johnny, Sierra Leone's ambassador to Beijing, while hosting a Chinese delegation preparing to invest in hydroelectric power and agriculture: "The Chinese are doing more than the G8 to make poverty history. . . . If a G8 country had wanted to rebuild the stadium, we'd still be holding meetings! The Chinese just come and do it" (para. 19).

However, even though driven by the need for energy since the early 1990s, China realized that its goals in Africa would be better served in a greater context of a transforming global politics. China's African strategy therefore must include a political dimension that is attentive to the needs of the continent on both bilateral and multilateral levels and beyond. On the continent, China operates bilaterally using a set of principles such as noninterference in internal affairs of host nations, respect for territorial integrity and sovereignty, nonpolitical strings attached, and the adherence of the one-China policy to the detriment of Taiwan being the exception. China also as a matter of principle or political realism contributes to the promotion of the stability of friendly regimes by using military aid. Between 1996 and 2003, 10 percent of all conventional arms sold to Africa came from China.

Zimbabwe and Sudan are the most notorious cases. China sold, despite the embargo, Shenyang fighter planes, twelve supersonic F-7s worth $100 million, and built three weapons factories near Khartoum in Sudan. In Zimbabwe in 2004, China sold, despite the U.S. and European Union arms embargoes, twelve fighter aircraft (FC-1) and one hundred military vehicles worth $200 million, and provided a military-strength radio-jamming device. Similar agreements have been signed with Equatorial Guinea, Ethiopia, Eritrea, Burundi, Tanzania, and Nigeria.

China further encourages closer ties from consultation and exchanges of officials at a higher level and on a local governmental level with parties, legislative bodies, and so on. Indeed if China's growing influence had not been noticed earlier, one of the reasons that it finally received attention was the frequency and the high level official visits made by Chinese authorities to Africa. We recounted in Chapter 4 a number of visits made by various Chinese officials since Zhou Enlai in 1963 up to the one made by Hu Jintao in April of 2006, the last to date (2007) of his three visits to Africa in the three years of his tenure. As for governmental-level visits, in 2004 alone, Chinese Vice President Zeng Quinghong visited Tunisia, Togo, Benin, and South Africa. More than a dozen exchange visits have occurred between China and Africa. In October and November of the same year, the National People's Congress Chairman Wu Bangguo visited Kenya, Nigeria, and Zambia. In January 2006, the Chinese foreign minister visited Cape Verde, Senegal, Mali, Liberia, Nigeria, and Libya. Reciprocally, many African dignitaries, from Kenya, South Africa, Zimbabwe, Cameroon, Namibia, and Rwanda, have likewise visited China. The trend is not slowing down.

Multiple bilateral agreements, as noted in following chapters, have been signed with various African states that have entertained relations with China, with the exception of those that still recognize Taiwan. Even there, signs of flexibility have been noticed in West Africa, in the areas of trade, health, military, education, science, infrastructure-building, and professional and medical assistance. Alone in the area of trade protection, China has signed agreements with twenty African nations. Strategic global partnerships have been extended to some, such as South Africa and Nigeria.

China's nondiscriminatory and nonconditional relations practices with African states have been the subject of abundant criticisms. Chapter 11 herein is devoted to an examination of their merits or the lack thereof.

Multilaterally, China has paid attention to the collective African effort to tackle issues that plague the continent. Economic challenges are being better met regionally by an integrated structure, which has led Africa to adapt and revitalize its former Organization of African Unity (OAU) structure. Since January 2002, the continent has created a new institutional structure called African Union (AU), and a number of previously existing regional organizations have been revitalized to deal with issues of economic development as well the twin issues of concern for the continent, namely peace and security. China has recognized that for both Africa and itself, no sustainable development will ever take place without true peace, just as lack of peace would jeopardize Chinese interests.

To counter that eventuality, China has vowed to support the goals and endeavors of multilateral organizations such as the AU and its offspring and initiatives such as the New Partnership for Africa's Development, the Peace and Security Council (May 2004), the Pan African Parliament (March 2004), the African Development Bank, and subregional organizations such as Economic Community of West African States (ECOWAS), South African Development Community (SADC), and so on.

China's own initiative to create a supporting institutional infrastructure has produced the China-Africa Cooperation Forum. This forum has become, since its first meeting in Beijing in October 2000, a conduit through which issues, projects, and consultations between China and the whole continent are channeled in a way that reflects the objectives of the AU, the New Partnership for Africa's Development (NEPAD), and various integrative regional organizations. The forum deals with issues of technical assistance, trade and investment, peace and security, development aid, and consultations. The forum's implementations are monitored and evaluated every two years. As for issues of peace, security, and stability on the continent, to affirm its commitment, China has participated in peacekeeping missions such as in December 2003 with 550 troops and 200 vehicles and water-supply trucks in Liberia, deployed about 4,000 People's Liberation Army (PLA) troops in southern Sudan to protect the oil pipeline, participated in a peacekeeping mission in Darfur/Sudan, and sent 175 PLA troops and a 42-member medical team to the Democratic Republic of Congo (Brookes and Shin 2006). In 2004, via UN missions, China contributed 1,500 peacekeepers across Africa (Pam 2006).

Beyond Africa, this South-South cooperation has, in China's mind, an objective whose ramifications should reach beyond the Africa continent. Addressing the delegates of a seminar in Beijing on 23 September 2004, the keynote speaker, Mr. Fola Adeola (2004), saw China-Africa cooperation as aiming to "promote the effective participation of developing countries in the formulation of international rules and better protection of their interests to reverse their global marginalization in the face of globalization" (para. 9). Such cooperation should be about the unison articulation of the views of the developing world and the projection of a united front to upset the individual limits of developing nations in international institutions and fora. These institutions are nominally the United Nations and its Security Council, the WTO, and of course, although China is not affected, the International Monetary Fund and the World Bank. Within the WTO, the first success has been checked, namely in Cancun, Mexico, in September 2003, where the developing world en masse, the G23, and China, being a prominent member thereof, pushed onto the agenda issues of primary concern to them and successfully contained the desiderata of the United States, Europe, and Japan.

In the context of the United Nations, China's veto power made it possible, in September 2004, for the UN Security Council resolution 1564, driven by the United States and the European Union seeking the imposition of sanctions against Sudan over the situation in Darfur, not to prevail. In July 2005, Great Britain, with the support of the United States and other nations, sought a debate in the UN General Assembly, which probably would have resulted in sanctions against Zimbabwe over slum demolition, after other perceived aberrations of the Mugabe regime. China derailed this effort.

Indeed, China has realized as well the potential of a strategic alliance with Africa in an international context, where it was, like Africa but in different ways and degrees, in danger of being marginalized. The hegemonic use of power by the United States manifested in its policy intents and exercises (spread of democracy, promotion of human rights, political and economical liberalism, interference in internal affairs of independent nations, the use of sanctions and embargoes to force the decision of foreign so-called rogue nations, etc.) has always been cause for concern and sorrow to China. Pei Yuanging (2004, para. 14), referring to that concern and to the United States, saw it: "attempting to build a unitary world and impose its own social system, mode of development and values on others, threatening at every turn with isolation, sanction, and even force are mindset and act of hegemony, which goes against the rule of historical development".

The end result of such an attempt was domination, China believed, within a context of liberal institutionalism. Within such a context, China has no other role but subservience. China, however, has an inherently substantive disagreement with such a declared worldview, and therefore it potentially stood on a collision course with the United States. The Tiananmen Square incident and the attempt by the West to isolate China has been a constant reminder since then. Taylor (2006, 8) saw in that incident the impetus for China's Africa redeployment and rebuilding of political linkage:

> However, after Tiananmen and the subsequent (temporary) isolation of Beijing, close political linkages were rebuilt and antihegemonism was redeployed as a rhetorical device to prevent Western interference in state (primarily China's) sovereignty. This was a reaction to what Beijing perceived as a hostile international system, and Washington's growing power".

Hence it was necessary to counterbalance such a hegemonic worldview from the United States. The five principles of peaceful coexistence issued by China, and referred to in earlier chapters, are ontologically designed to do just that. They emphasize the good old principles of international relations to contrast what China considers a bullying behavior on behalf of the hegemonic United States. China's strategy in the international political sphere of action consisted of demarcating itself from the West by proposing a contrasting alternative to Western policies and principles. Noninterference, noneconomic and political conditionality (good governance, human rights, etc.) have become in the postindependence era the norms of Chinese foreign policy in Africa. They stroke a nerve in many African capitals, which are sensitive to such issues, with Angola, Sudan, and Zimbabwe being the most prominent.

China portrays itself as a friend and ally, not an exploiter, because, like Africa, it has suffered the pain of imperialism and colonization. Also like Africa, China is non-Western, which seems to resonate in a subtle way, like background music in China-Africa gatherings. To the enchantment of Africa, China has also articulated in various documents the need for democratic international relations wherein all nations enjoy equal-partner status. In the policy paper, part IV, China vowed to cooperate with Africa in international affairs and seek a more equitable international political economy, justice, rationality, equality, respect of the rule of law, a greater UN role and so on. Taylor (2006, 34) stated that China "has attempted to construct linkages with the developing world as a means to bolster its own position in the international system". According to Eisenman and Kurlantzick (2006, para 6), Beijing's motive in Africa is clear:

> China's growing industries demand new energy and raw material suppliers; its exporters want markets; its diplomats require support in international organizations; and its propaganda still seeks support from allies to advance Chinese interests and, when necessary, to counter the United States.

De facto, China's endeavor in Africa is seen in a greater context, namely to win African states into an anti-US/Western hegemonic world order, with whose core political principles and intentions China does not necessarily agree. In China's quest to derail a Western-centric power politics, Africa is then seen beyond its natural resources as an historical and cultural congenital ally to China. China has accepted capitalism as an instrumental venue to its wealth but has not accepted its world-view. The communist government of China wants the wealth that the capitalist system generates but does not embrace its underlying sociocultural ideology. As China masters the capitalist system of production and becomes comfortable and successful within the paradigm of globalization, it must still win allies to its vision of the world.

With increasing influential capacity globally, to assert a possible leadership role, China needs global allies. There have been tectonic shifts occurring in international relations as a result of the globalization process, which China can both opportunistically and structurally use to gain more influence. Indeed, the globalization process has allowed an increasingly ostensible, ubiquitous distribution of wealth. Some nations have been able to adjust more successfully than others, increasing in the process their economic might, which may be translated into political influence and even into other factors of power such as increased military capacity. These changes will probably force a reevaluation of the world powers' hierarchy, and many[15] believe it is already in progress.

China is not the only rising power. Next to China, India, Brazil, and Russia have been making great leaps with steady yearly economic growth rates averaging 9 percent in the case of China and more than 5 percent for the others. The rise of these nations, referred to by the Goldman Sachs (2003) report as BRIC (i.e., Brazil, Russia, India, and China), justifies this probable hierarchy reevaluation by the world powers. Being the best positioned among the BRIC nations, China, provided it maintains its economic growth momentum and sound policy and creates adequate supporting institutional infrastructure (Goldman Sachs 2003), will around 2025, become the largest economy on the planet. That will buy China more influence. China has acknowledged that fact, the responsibility it induced, and consequently has adjusted by increasing the sophistication level of its foreign policy articulation. Eliot (2007) recently alluded to a poll taken jointly in 2006 by the Chicago Council on Global Affairs and the Asian Society, which found that 87 percent of Chinese respondents thought that China should take a greater role in world affairs.

It is clear vis-à-vis Russia, Japan, Southeast Asia, and elsewhere, as mentioned earlier, that China has been taking the necessary security precautions to safeguard its interests, for example, with naval buildup. China, after all, may reclaim its mythological Middle Kingdom status. This status has never been understood in hegemonic sense; it is not the equivalent of Manifest Destiny of the United States. And China does not intend to go there, based on official policy formulation.

China will, however, continue to articulate a foreign policy and a world vision essentially self-centered. From this perspective, China's strategic alliance with Africa is indeed strategic and therefore anchored in a long-term vision of where China wants to be in the future. Grant (2006, para.23) conclusively put it best: "China has a strategic approach to Africa, in which the market, the energy security and the political relationships are all very much of a piece. They are looking not at the next two or three years but at the next 15 to 20 years"

To reach that goal, China is currently capitalizing on the limits of a Manichean Western approach and its deficiencies and contradictions. China has made great strides, thus offering an alternative to Africa. Adeola (2004, 4) stated, "African countries admire China's success and find its approach to cooperation with them practical, pragmatic, result oriented").

Proceeding with Diligence

Policy intents must be operationalized to reach the expected objectives. Such operationalization takes place through the exercise of diplomacy. The practice and style of diplomacy are exercised by individual states based principally on these following different factors: the individual state's own political culture and underlying ideology or worldview or ideals as well as its practical interests. States therefore must harmonize their ideals, norms, and values with the realism of pursuing concrete interests. Like any other state, China has a certain set of interests that are strategic, political, or economic in nature. China also has a specific political culture and underlying ideology and worldview. These differences of political culture and strategic and economic interests explain not only the differences in foreign policy objectives among states but also the specific strategies and approaches applied by them in the exercise of their diplomacy. This realization suggests that China may have a specific Africa foreign policy strategy, which will have to reflect its own normative references as well as its identified interests.

Therefore, the question of how specific is China's Africa strategy becomes significant, and much more so as China incorporates a set of characteristics that render its behavior potentially unprecedented. Those characteristics are the fact that China is a developing country but with growing influencing capacity. China is a communist country with a free-market-oriented state economy that intend to trade. China also wants to aid Africa, knowing that in the past, trade and aid rather than boosting Africa's quest for economic development, have rather managed to maintain the status quo. Moreover, China has been claiming and proclaiming not to do business in Africa, as others have done in the past. These are sufficient reasons to merit close scrutiny of China's Africa strategy.

China so far has proceeded with diligence, using pragmatic ways of contact, using less and less ideological arguments and more and more empirically efficient cultural, political, economic, and developmental propositions and projects. China has argued strategically that African interests are better served by China, which seems to have found a synthetic approach that merges the old anti-imperialist approach with legitimately utilitarian ends in an effort to extract specific benefits from the continent.

The following chapters consider how these policy intents and China's applied strategy have translated concretely in all of the areas that are spelled out in the policy paper and address the following question: Has the implementation of these policies gotten both China and Africa to what China has called a win-win outcome? This question must be answered to have some measure of reassurance by which to evaluate or judge China's Africa policy. Why do we judge China's Africa policy? It is simply because a growing body of articles published in the recent years includes many that are skeptical of China's activity in Africa.

CHAPTER 6

THE CHINESE WAY

This chapter considers trade, foreign investment and markets, their significance in the changing nature of China-Africa relations, and China's unique approach. The significance of these aspects is in and by itself revealing of principally two different realities. The growing significance of these areas reveals a consensus about the premise of liberal economics, which speaks of them as the tools of economic growth and prosperity and therefore considers them the best engines of cooperation among nations, better than simple aid. The second insight they reveal in China-Africa relations is that China has finally aligned itself with the idea of free trade, foreign investment, and free-market economy, and their implied open nature, which is not a small demarcation for a communist nation. Finally, the significance of trade, foreign investment, and free market for China-Africa relations reveals that China has moved away from cooperation with African nations on ideological grounds to cooperation on a free-enterprise basis in the nature of China's foreign policy. Indeed reforms have transformed China and positioned it to take advantage of all of the tools at its disposal in a globalized economy so successfully that China has been called China Inc., the world factory, and so on. By any usable measure and all accounts, whatever China has been doing since its reform policy called for a new approach to economic cooperation with

Africa in mid-1984 and since it called for Chinese enterprises to dare go out in 2001, it has been successful.

As a result, trade with China, FDI from China, and access to African markets both as a seller and buyers of products its produces and those it needs have steadily increased, making China the second largest economic partner to Africa.

TRADE

China-Africa trade has indeed come a long way from the historical Zheng. He commercial expeditions around 1400, in which products exchanged could have been counted on a few digits. Such trades carried a higher symbolic value than industry-driving value. In the former communist China, formal exchanges remained rather modest as both partners struggled with imperatives of their respective economies and politics.

Postcolonial African trade in general has not been dynamic enough to generate revenues and savings and therefore has not allowed investment in production to induce higher productivity and allow capital formation. African nations have dealt with the problem by using direct involvement of the state, which allowed the situation to endure until the 1980s, the decade of the implementation of structural adjustment programs of the World Bank and the IMF. These programs were designed to circumvent the enduring problem described above, also known as the vicious cycle, and partially have been the cause of the stalled economic development of the entire continent. The importance of trade, since Adam Smith central to economic processes, soon became the pillar of a global economy.

The lack of trade dynamism was a symptom of a larger condition of African economies. Martia Gattamorta (2004, 77-78) echoed this sentiment:

> If it were to be said that commerce is synonymous with well being, which allows a market to recognize an open and dynamic economy, then it is inevitable to detect a sign of an asphyxiating structural weakness with the Africa economic systems; a signal of dysfunction and at the same time a confirmation of

unresolved internal problems that makes it difficult
for an economy to take off.

Gattamorta certainly reflected one of the principled beliefs
of liberal economics, which tends to see in trade the life force
of free-market economies. Trade is the tool that mirrors the
vibrancy and dynamism of one national' economic activity in
that output, investment, and productivity can be translated into
growth, employment, purchasing power, and ultimately into
prosperity. The feeble trade activity on the African continent
suggests therefore the absence of a vibrant, dynamic economy
that is capable of taking advantage of today's global market. The
causes of that deficiency have been debated by development
economists, the dependency school, and the work of Emmanuel
Wallerstein (1974).

The debate has already taken place, and we need not repeat
it here but only recall its main arguments. The then international division of labor provided African economies with a
niche as supplier of raw materials. The continent still holds this
place despite slightly burgeoning food-processing and labor-
intensive manufacturing sectors. These economies have been
structurally induced to export raw materials because of the
colonial powers' neglect to promote the processing industry on
the continent and because of lack of initiatives by subsequent,
postindependence, African regimes. African economies have
never gotten rid of that status simply because of their undiversi-
fied export products. "For 27 out of 49 African countries, fewer
than five products (mostly commodities) account for more than
75 percent of exports. Considering Africa as a whole, crude oil
makes up to 35 percent of the continent's total exports" (Goldstein et al. 2006, 113).

As a consequence, African nations have suffered from the
deterioration of terms of trade (Singer 1950), price fluctuation,
and so on, and have not been able to form and accumulate the
necessary capital, despite the efforts of a big push to invest in
manufacturing and processing sectors. These countries have,
at the same time, remained importers of manufactured goods
(machines and transport equipment, chemicals, and miscella-

neous manufacturing products; Goldstein et al. 2006) favored by the flip side of the same terms of trade.

Colonization, which had introduced Africa to modernity, has not, however, brought about the industrialization of the continent (Mazrui 1985). Knowing that historically no modernization process truly occurs without industrialization, African modernity has as well suffered a malaise we observe today. Away from colonization, postcolonial African regimes and governments caught up in the logic of the Cold War, various forms of nationalism on one hand and on the other the constraints of international world trade, have not been the bastion of inventive, daring, and reforming economic approaches. Nations of East and Southeast Asia that have courageously attempted new ways to improve their economic conditions throughout the 1980s have been successful. They have been much more rewarded by the shifting paradigm of international economics and the advent of globalization as they took advantage of what it offered. In addition, China finally has been rewarded by the same principle.

The ascending economy of China, its growth, and industrialization have resulted in a increased need and demand for raw materials and in 2003 prompted China to become a net importer of commodities (fuels and crude materials; Goldstein et al. 2006). China has seen its annual energy consumption rise from an average of 1.2 percent between 1996 and 1999 to 14.5 percent in 2003. China's crude steel consumption rate likewise rose from 1.7 percent in 2000 to 25.2 percent in 2003 (Goldstein et al. 2006).

This development has been to the advantage of Africa in two ways: first, it has allowed a renewed interest in raw materials and commodities and second, it has allowed the recovery of raw materials prices, as China's demand improved the supply side and, in the process, raw materials achieved higher export unit prices (Goldstein et al. 2006). The price of oil, for instance, has been in constant rise since 2000, averaging an annual rate of 18.7 percent between 2000 and 2004. Likewise the price of copper, though with swing phases, reached 58 percent (Goldstein et al. 2006) and is still increasing.

Describing the Dutch disease,[16] Corden and Neary (1982, as cited by Goldstein et al. 2006) pointed to one of the causes of the resource boom being exogenous when increased demand from a country (e.g., China, which has contributed roughly 50 percent of the global demand growth for major commodities in the past two years; Goldstein et al. 2006) induces the rise in the world price of a natural resource exported by another country (e.g., Africa's abundant raw materials). Although the overall extent of the Dutch disease cannot be verified in the context of African economies, this cause factor is at least given. It has certainly contributed to the highest economic growth in the last thirty years, which in Africa was expected to reach 5.8 percent in 2007.

In addition to raw materials, the service sector has been positively affected by China's spectacular growth. Tourism and the food industry have been affected more directly but also indirectly by the downward pressure exerted by China and India in the manufacturing sector because of their capacity to export menial skills for labor-intensive manufacturing products. Both urban consumers and investors in Africa can only appreciate such a state as they respectively profit from cheaper consumer goods and cheaper capital goods (Goldstein et al. 2006).

In conclusion, China, both as a supplier to African markets and consumer of African products, has provided the continent's economic agents (governments, businesses, and consumers) with a number of unprecedented advantages, which, as elucidated in the following chapters, the continent has not yet experienced.

African trade with China addresses what respective parties have to offer and need from each other. Africa traditionally and predominantly has offered to the rest of the world's economies raw materials and soft commodities (Goldstein et al. 2006). These commodities are: oil (from Nigeria, Algeria, Gabon, Angola, Sudan, Congo), tropical wood (from Gabon), cotton (from Burkina Faso), iron ore and diamonds (from South Africa), bauxite (from Morocco), aluminum (from Guinea), ferrous metal (from Mauritania, South Africa, Zimbabwe), uranium (from the Democratic Republic of Congo), cobalt (from South Africa, the Democratic Republic of Congo), copper (from the Democratic Republic of Congo, Zambia), feed (from

Burkina Faso, Ethiopia, Nigeria, and Sudan), and chemicals (from Niger). Africa also has increased its capacity to export light manufactured goods in the areas of household consumer goods and foods, as well as in the service sector, with tourism. These are in turn what China needs from the continent.

On the Chinese side, trade involves what it can offer and what Africa needs, namely: low-cost consumer goods, industry infrastructure (telecommunications, construction, and power plants), arms and weapons, military hardware, finances, electronics, appliances, and so on.

Because of the China's increased needs for African resources, its share of the African market has become 6.8 percent, surpassing that of the United States (5.8 percent; Fisher-Thomson 2006). This development has been in the making since China's modernization successes and the readjustment of its Africa policy in the mid-1980s, when it started to look at the continent in market terms. In 1978, the year that began the Chinese reform, China-Africa trade volume was $760 million (Morin-Allory 2005). Their bilateral trade, though it represented only 2 percent of China's foreign trade and 5 percent of Africa's, increased 700% between 1991 and 2002 (Collette and Yabi 2004).

By 1999, the annual volume of trade between Africa and China reached $5.6 billion (IMF 2004). Between 2002 and 2004, China-Africa trade jumped from $10 to $28.5 billion (Morin-Allory 2005). By the end of 2004, the annual volume of trade between the two partners rose to $29.5 billion (Guixuan 2005), and by October 2005, the trade volume reached $32.2 billion. The same year, China became the third largest trade partner to Africa, only to outdo itself two years later. Since 2002, China-Africa trade has been averaging a growth rate of more than 5 percent annually (IMF 2004). With initiatives such as the Special Preferential Tariff Treatment (SPTT) implemented in 2005, which removed tariffs from 190 items exported from twenty-five of Africa's least developed countries, trade between Africa and China experienced yearly volume increases.

In 2006, the trade volume reached the $50 billion mark, a fivefold increase from 2000 or tenfold since 1995 (BBC, China defends its African relations 26 June 2006). The same year sub-

Saharan Africa supplied almost 30 percent of China's oil needs. In 2006, , Chinese Premier, Wen Jiabao, expressed the wish to see trade between Africa and China surpass $100 billion by 2010. The overall picture of China-Africa import and export activity is illustrated in Figure 1.

INVESTMENT

FDI inflow in Africa has been decreasing since 2001. The continent attracted $19 billion in 2001 and $11 billion in 2002 (a fallout of 0.6% less than 2001) and just 1.7 percent of world FDI flow (Gattamorta 2004). Africa remains the region of the globe with the lowest share of FDI (1.8%) and the only region that has not increased its share of non-oil exports (Broadman 2007). This statement still is valid but some changes have occurred because of the quasi-simultaneous emergence of China and India. Their respective quests for raw materials underlie the increases in Asia-Africa trade. Whereas Asia received only 14 percent of Africa's exports in 2000, in 2007 it received 27 percent (Broadman 2007). This surge has contributed to a recovery of FDI, with an increase of 39.7% in 2003, reaching $12.8 billion in 2004, and remaining stable since then. China has contributed massively to that recovery as its FDI in Africa steadily grew between 2000 and 2006, reaching $6.6 billion (Chinese Ministry of Commerce 2007). J.Y. Wang (2007,11) among others, warned that

> Chinese official statistics may not fully capture the true magnitude of direct investment by Chinese enti-ties in African countries. The dividing line between trade and project financing by China's financial institutions and direct investment by Chinese enter-prises is often unclear.

The history of Chinese investments in the continent paral-lels that of China's economic success (see Figure 2). A successful economy led China once again into Africa, this time not to lend support to the struggle against imperial powers but in quest for raw materials, commodities, and access to less competitive markets. Since then, China's presence on the African continent

has been practically ubiquitous. Trade, investment, development aid, intense diplomatic activity by Chinese officials,
intense bidding by Chinese enterprises, increasing numbers of
Chinese retailers (which Tanzanians call *Machingas* in Swahili)
and blue-collar workers have covered the geographic surface of
the continent. As China's trade with Africa has increased, so
have the investments of the former in the opportunities that
offer the latter. Chinese investments, like any other, have been
utilitarian in nature. They target resources of a specific country
that are of interest to China. Such investments from China
depend on the resources available, the attraction of a country's
market, and its political status and significance in the landscape
of African politics. Chinese investments are made by Chinese
state-owned, provincial, and city enterprises. Private businesses
are subject to the state-owned Assets Supervision and Administrative Commission (SASAC). This bottleneck structure,
which allows a certain degree of competition among Chinese
enterprises that are willing to go out to Africa, allows China
to execute its investment model. This model combines China's
willingness to invest, to trade, to provide foreign aid, and seeks
alliance in what has been referred to as a package deal.

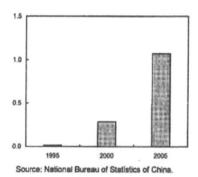

Source: National Bureau of Statistics of China.

FIGURE 2. HISTORY OF CHINESE INVESTMENT IN AFRICA

For African states, the strategy is a fresh approach in the
area of cooperation because it is not accompanied by conditional contractual terms of a political or moral nature that have

complicated the past history of cooperation between African states and Western lenders and donors (both nations and institutions). This strategy has been for China an efficient way to infiltrate the structure of economic activity. The next chapter elucidates the functioning mechanisms of this strategy.

Chinese companies have been successfully entering the African market as the stock of China's investments in the continent has continued to rise. China's FDI in Africa between 1991 and 2003 reached $847 million, or 19.5 percent of the total outgoing investment, or 107.4 million (in 2003, according to Chinese Ministry of Commerce). China's FDI reached $900 million in 2004 (Council on Foreign Relations 2005). By the end of the same year, it reached $135 million (Guixian 2005) and was estimated at $1.18 billion in 2006 (Broadman 2007). In addition to China, India and Brazil have contributed, prompting Broadman (2007) to state that the recovery has been essentially performed by foreign companies of the South. This statement is in itself a novelty in the history of African trade. This is a consequence of the decreasing export activity of the African economy with, let us say, the European Union, considering that Africa's exports between 2000 and 2007 were reduced by half (Broadman 2007).

The FDI recovery has been driven by natural resources, which as a sector retained the most FDI inflows (between 50 and 80% depending on the country). Resource-rich countries (e.g., Angola, Chad, Equatorial Guinea, Nigeria, and South Africa) are as a matter of consequence those that have enjoyed this FDI recovery (Goldstein 2006).

Increased trade activity between Africa and Asia has provided additional opportunities for FDI. Energy and mining sectors are the leading investment destinations, followed by physical infrastructure, industry, and agriculture. The Council on Foreign Relations (2005, 47) stated, "China is also investing in areas that Western aid agencies and private investors have long neglected: physical infrastructure, industry, and agriculture."

Both China and India have been investing in other sectors such as apparel, foodprocessing, retail ventures, fisheries, seafood farming, commercial real estate, transport construction, tourism, power plants, telecommunications, and so on.

However, the need for energy consumption, the need to access African diverse raw materials and commodities as well as its less competitive markets for the growing Chinese manufacturing sector remain the more pressing imperatives that have dictated Chinese investments on the continent, more than strategic needs, for instance, to win the Central African Republic to China's global strategic vision. These economic imperatives ultimately explain the ranking of Africa as China's most important FDI destination. Broadman (2007), using a Chinese source for FDI statistics, noted Sudan with almost $150 million in 2004; followed by Nigeria with less than $50 million; South Africa with less than half of what flows into Nigeria; followed by Guinea, Benin, Madagascar, and others. The Chinese Export and Import Bankt loans, however, pour 80 percent of China's FDI into five African nations (Angola, Mozambique, Nigeria, Sudan, and Zimbabwe). China has signed agreements to set up special economic zones in Zambia, Mauritius, Nigeria, and Egypt. Tanzania may be next.

Despite the increasing significance of the Exim Bank and other Chinese investment-supporting institutions, the West-the United States, the United Kingdom, and France- remains the most important with 70 percent of total FDI in Africa.

Countries that participate are those with resources that are most needed by China's economy, and those with attractive markets are also well countries that are the primary recipients of China's investments and aid. China's investments are expected to increase as cooperation between China and Africa increases, as desired by Beijing.

So far, China's investments have been characterized, among others, by the fact that they have not yet sought equity or stakes in factors of production, as has the West. Because of that, the West holds an advantage in that regard. That has been changing as China has moved evermore toward acquisition and purchase of shares in many production sites and businesses in Africa. So far, however, off-take agreements by China have not resulted in ownership. This is simply the case, as clarified by Jim Fisher-Thompson (2006 para 15): "Unlike foreign direct investment, off-take agreements allow the purchase of raw materials without having direct ownership in the extractive industries that produce them."

Investments will likely grow because of the growing trade surplus in China's treasury, which has allowed China to amass foreign currency reserves reaching $1.07 trillion and for which China needs to find a use. To that end, China announced on 9 March 2007 its intent to create a new government investment agency to manage that accumulated capital. Just as Japan in the 1980s - after robust, trade-oriented, economic growth enjoyed a surplus with its partners- used its funds to buy shares of equity and acquire ownership, China has begun doing just that with some of the global public assets. This will result in an even more ubiquitous Chinese presence on the African continent and elsewhere.

CHINA'S IMPORT-EXPORT FINANCING

The amount of financing funneled into the developing world in the form of grants and loans, concessional or commercial, to recipient nations with the need to promote FDI and export as well as sell credit, international guarantee, official line of credit, and so on, necessitates operations that rely on banking infrastructure. China has established a number of institutional banking structures to respond to that need. These institutions are fully state owned,as such, their lending practices, contrary to international export credit and lending institutions in the West -which even though aligned with conditions stipulated by the IMF still have operational autonomy otherwise- reflect foreign policy goals of the Chinese government.

The Exim Bank and the China Development Bank both founded in 1994, as well as others such as the Agriculture Development Bank and more recently, in 2001, the China Export and Credit Insurance Corporation, and even the four policy banks (Bank of China, Agricultural Bank of China in 1949, China Construction Bank in 1954, and the Commerce Bank of China), which are neither commercial nor for profit were "originally designed to support growth initiatives of the state but now support government's long term development projects" (Davies et al. 2008, 20). They have been incorporated in China's overall holistic approach to overseas projects that are, at the same time from both the Chinese and the African perspective, part of the packaged aid practice.

The Exim Bank, sustained by the bond market, supporting Chinese export with export buyer's credit[17] as well as export sellers' credit,[18] disburses credits, both commercial and concessional, that focus on building infrastructure as well as investment loans to support the most crucial sectors of manufacturing, energy, and mining industries. Managed by the States Council, the Exim Bank is the third largest export credit agency (Davies et al. 2008). By 2005 the Exim Bank had a portfolio worth $15 billion and by the end of 2006; it was financing 256 projects in 36 African countries (Ellis 2007). Most of these projects, 79 percent, were, as one may expect, related to building infrastructure: dams, railways, roads, mining, oil facilities, and power plants (Ellis 2007).

The China Development Bank is a commercial bank that supports Chinese FDI and manages the $5 billion of the China-Africa Development Fund, of which $3 billion are reserved for preferential loans and $2 billion for preferential export buyers' credit. Very active in Africa by virtue of their governmental link (China Ministry of Commerce) and preferential governmental loans and commercial and concessional lending activities, the significance of these banks, and much more so the Exim Bank have gradually increased over the years since their creation. The growing central role of the Exim Bank is justified by its official status. In a communist and unitarist China, that status is both authoritative and inescapable as it functions as the guarantor, administrator, and lending policymaker in all things related to foreign aid.

The China Development Bank had loans worth $1 billion outstanding in Africa and was monitoring more than thirty developments projects across Africa, valued at $3 billion by the end of March 2007 (J.Y.Wang 2007).

Chinese financing that has poured into Africa as grants and commercial and concessional loans for Chinese and foreign investors has become a dynamic factor in the African economic landscape, as indicated in Figure 3. The activities of the Exim Bank and other export and investment banks have not yet reached the importance and significance of traditional, international lending institutions. These are generally Western, though non-Western sources of international lending have been growing. Their approach, with China's overall strategic thinking, has allowed them to strive and walk with giant steps. Indeed, they operate with a certain flexibility that does away with aspiring borrowers' public and private, in-built, intricate mechanisms of eligibility: lengthy calendar and decision-making processes, feasibility, compliance studies, risk thresholds, and so on.

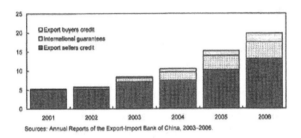

Sources: Annual Reports of the Export-Import Bank of China, 2003–2006.

FIGURE 3. CHINESE GRANTS AND COMMERCIAL/CONCESSIONAL LOANS IN AFRICA

The reduced criteria of these institutions and conditions such as their lack of political and normative conditionalities contribute to that flexibility. Chinese counterparts in Africa delight in this new approach, which does not scrutinize them as they seek help but focuses on practical terms of feasibility rather than on risks or on whether the borrower fits the mold or responds as planners do to the criteria conceived by the lender. The attitude in Africa, therefore, is as expressed by Alden (2007, 25): "Finally, in contrast to multilateral and bilateral Western lending agencies, the Chinese Exim Bank's lending is more flexible, less risk adverse and responsive to African governing elite needs".

The Chinese Exim Bank has quickly developed into an agent of weight in Africa by playing the role that until then was reserved for multilateral and bilateral Western lending bodies and agencies. With rising sources of venture capital and other institutional bilateral financing, the landscape of the international lending system has been changing. Some of these newcomers, such as Islamic, Indian, and Russian finances, as is the case with China Exim Bank, are not Organization for Economic Cooperation and Development (OECD) members as they operate outside of the export credit market rules. In the traditional, international lenders' community, a new vocabulary has emerged, namely that of so-called rogue lending. The legitimacy of the Exim Bank is indeed self-evident and did not derive from the anointing by Western lenders. The term *rogue lending* itself is a problem as these lenders are products of their prosperous free-market participation, of liberalization of the finance market, of the very deregulation preached by liberal economics. This contributes to a competitive financial market, reflecting thereby the spirit of the reigning economic liberalism. They are *rogue* not based on the principles, as they are the offspring of those principles, but based on their nonalignment with references and definitions enacted by specific member nations of specific organizations such as the OECD.

There is, however, a need for some degree of coherence in the lending market and some degree of regulation, to use the term very much despised by advocates of a laissez-faire brand of free-market system, but it ought not to happen to the detriment of diversity of donors or autonomy of operations, terms, and practices. Borrowers are the beneficiaries of such diversity, as they have been so far subjected to conditionalities that they rather would not have endured if they had access to alternative lenders. Just as it is common sense to ensure that the lenders are worthy and are not depleting or embezzling funds, it is equally important that lenders do not use their positions and status to perpetuate a system whose efficacy is doubtful and therefore must be questioned.

Based on that concept, new players in the international lending market present a good development as competition is essential to any market system. As a matter of fact, based on their different criteria and approaches, they end up making different decisions. Exim Bank finances projects in Africa that would otherwise have been rejected by other export credit agencies (Ellis 2007). Underlying that assertion, Michel (2008) provided the example of the dam built at Imboulou in the Republic of the Congo. For ten years, the World Bank rejected financing for that project on the grounds of too much debt, only to see China agreeing to disburse $280 million for the dam's construction in 2002.

MARKET-ENTRY STRATEGY

The intensity of China's market infiltration is by now obvious, with more than 800 Chinese enterprises on African soil to date (2007). Equally obvious is that China has an approach that seems to have surprised both the West and Africans. Encouraged by the "going-out" slogan, Chinese nascent and burgeoning free enterprises in need of markets, contracts, global experience, and exposure have targeted Africa. Africa will become a preferred destination, among other reasons, because of both the abundant opportunity offered by the continent and low levels of market-entry barriers. Chinese engineering, construction, and mining companies were soon to be seen around Africa building stadiums, office buildings, shopping centers, power plants, bridges, roads, dams, schools, and so on.

We have mentioned the successes in the areas of trade and investment. Such successes, however, do not come ex nihilo, nor are they a product of hazard and circumstances. They are a product instead of a conceptual structure whose functional mechanisms explain their successes. China combines political will and goals with financial resources and enterprise capacity and the political sphere with financial and corporate spheres.

The result is a synergy that is not explained by the combination of those spheres and the factor endowment but rather by a coordinated, interpenetrating mechanism that allows the mutual support of relevant agents and ultimately optimizes their actions and effects. The Ministry of Commerce (MOC), according to Gill and Reilly (2007) harbors, first, the Department of West-Asia and African Affairs (DWAAA), which advises policymakers; encourages investment; and distributes information on political, social, legal, and economic environment in given African countries. The same MOC also harbors the Department of Foreign Economic Cooperation (DFEC), which regulates all Chinese companies overseas. Chinese companies that are active in investing on the African continent must register with DFEC if their investment is greater than $10,000 (Gill and Reilly 2007). The grip is further explained by the fact that the DFEC can fire or revoke operating licenses should the licensees fail to comply with MOC regulations and thereby Chinese laws. Third, the MOC also harbors the Department of Foreign Aid (DFA), which must sign off on every aid project and bid by any Chinese corporation. Moreover, the DFA manages the bidding, becomes the guarantor of and overseer of the project when it is under way, and is responsible for carrying out China's foreign aid.

Last, the MOC harbors the Office of the Economic and Commercial Counselor (ECC), which is the extended arm of the MOC overseas. The ECC is located outside of China in Chinese embassies. From there, the ECC practically plays the watchdog role for compliance by Chinese firms with Chinese regulations, laws, policies, and labor issues ad hoc.

The whole MOC institutional infrastructure is tied to the rest of the Chinese political hierarchical order by collaboration with the other ministries such the Ministry of Foreign Affairs (MOFA), the national-level State-Owned Assets Supervision and Administration Commission. These ministries and departments all conjointly or individually report to the state council. Within this institutional infrastructure, Chinese companies are encouraged to enter the African market.

In light of such a functional structure of the Chinese market-entry strategy, the concept of China Inc. and that of aid packages becomes much more transparent. The transparency of this formula is possible as governmental economic aid goals symbiotically align with Chinese enterprises that happen to be essentially government-owned, parastatals, or even privately owned. As such, they have the total support of Beijing to count on a number of issues that are susceptible to emergence with respect to financing, information, diplomatic preparation, and so on.

The concept of China Inc. implies interconnectivity between the involvement of Chinese foreign policy, its state-owned enterprises (SOEs), and the finances it makes available for attainment of economic goals that are conceived in a greater political strategic context. The report by the Center for Chinese Studies (2006, para 3) on activity in construction and infrastructure sectors put it best: "China's involvement in Africa's construction and infrastructure sectors has proved most effective in building relations with African governments-increasing influence and expanding access to natural resources on the continent."

Aid packages are made possible by loans to Chinese corporations that are interested in investing in Africa and are extended arms of the Chinese foreign policy objectives in the fields of aid, trade, and investment. As part of a whole strategy, Chinese corporations enjoy access to sources of cheap capital made available by the Chinese government through export-import credit institutions.

The same source of China's investment capital extends to deals with African nations with low interest rates and extended timelines and whose reimbursement is secured by future revenues from, for example, oil production. These deals encompass infrastructure-building and other development aid by China. This practice has been put to use in instances such as in Angola, which in 2005 received a $2 billion soft loan and a $1 billion loan in addition in March 2006 from Exim Bank with an interest rate of 1.5 percent over seventeen years. This loan was linked to an agreement to supply China with 10,000 barrels of crude oil per day initially and increasing to 40,000 barrels per day, and to an agreement by China to build infrastructure (e.g., transportation, electricity) so needed in Angola after thirty years of civil war. How China further translates its market-entry strategy concretely in the case of Angola is discussed in Chapter 7, section on Angola. In Nigeria, the China National Petroleum Corporation (CNPC) agreed to invest $4 billion in infrastructure (railroad, power stations) and was given the option to explore in four oil exploration blocks. CNPC bought a controlling stake in the Kaduna refinery, which produces 110,000 barrels per day (Taylor 2006). Here again, additional concrete application of China's market-entry strategy with respect to Nigeria is further explored in Chapter 7, section on Nigeria.

Chinese Enterprises in Africa

The political system and organization described above justifies the nature of enterprises we encounter in China, which are the offspring of political will. These enterprises are,therefore, property of the political system that created them. Free-market economies, which presuppose private ownership of property and other factors of production, also rely on free enterprise. In this case, enterprises run on privately owned capital or publicly sought funds from investors who are eager to acquire shares of equity when companies make their initial product offerings (IPOs). Whereas some countries have let companies with private funds coexist with those state-owned companies, in China they were all until recently national-, provincial-, or city-government-owned. They were the only ones allowed to trade and had exclusive rights to export, import, and foreign exchange (H.Wang 2008)

The state has its hand in these companies either totally or with a controlling share. Mirroring the communist economic ideology, they were rather production units (China Facts and Figures 2002) wherein the operations of the enterprise from production quotas and output, price, sales, profit, allocation of revenues, and so on were controlled by the central, regional, or local governments. As such, they suffered the fate of so many other collectively run units of production in statist economies, namely, absence of the individual incentive factor (reward of economic nature over adhesion to ideology), corporate incentive (profit), and a systemic incentive (context of competition among economic agents) leading to low productivity. Adam Smith's argument on self-interest and ownership as a primary source of motivation and therefore efficiency has been successfully vindicated in this particular instance. The reform policy as conceived by Deng Xiaoping, recognizing the inherent deficiency of collectivist enterprises, sought a reform model designed to remedy the situation and built in the profit incentives. Chinese enterprises were allowed and expected to turn a profit. They consequently had to be as competitive as any other companies, as required by the laws of the market.

When China recognized the degree of maladjustment of the architecture and operational structure of its enterprises, the country sought to reform and to enable them to become players in the free-market system. In 1978, the Third Plenary Session of the 11th National Congress of the Communist Party initiated a market-oriented reform that affected Chinese enterprises among other items on the agenda. The main outcome of the congress was the idea of delegation of power, shared responsibility, and shared profits. Chinese enterprise management was to learn to delegate power to provinces or collectives and share responsibility with the enterprises, which opened the door to a certain autonomy. Private investors and entrepreneurship were introduced as was profit-sharing with participants. The most important of the Chinese companies remained overwhelmingly under the control of the Chinese government, but a growing non-state-owned private sector has mushroomed since 1984.

Private and state-owned enterprises are now the new armada of China's modern quest for economic ascent. They are registered either at the national, provincial, or city level, thus mirroring the existing structure of command. In 2006 there were Eight hundred Chinese companies in Africa. Of those, only one hundred were SOEs or parastatals, of which the government has either a controlling share or total ownership. Of Chinese registered SOEs, 88 percent are at the provincial level, and the majority of those are abroad. The rest are private enterprises (joint ventures and collectively owned businesses), profiting in many ways, as described here, by Chinese government support. They all use DWAAA for economic intelligence. These companies are under the local control of the DFEC and use financial resources provided by the Exim Bank.

Because of that, China can allow itself to take financial risks that might be otherwise unacceptable. For instance, Chinese enterprises receive cheap capital from Exim Bank, which allows them to bid below cost. To illustrate the phenomenon, Gill and Reilly (2007) provided the example of Huawei Technology Ltd., a Chinese communications technology company, which in December 2004 received from the China Development Bank a low-cost $10 billion loan to promote its international operations. Huawei used these funds to make successful bids on contracts in Kenya, Nigeria, and Zambia and won a contract worth $400 million to provide cellular phone service.

These companies can afford not to live under the pressure of breaking even sooner or that of shareholders' anticipation of higher dividends. As a matter of fact, they bid even when the profit margin is expected to be low or even to result in a loss. The construction and infrastructure sector is largely state-owned and has been allowed to work internationally since 1979. Its presence was expanded with globalization strategies. A study by the Center for Chinese Studies (2006, 4) reported, "While local and foreign construction companies operate on profit margins of 15–25 percent, Chinese companies usually operate on margins of > 5%, making them extremely competitive." They have outbid the competition: "Where Chinese companies are properly established, the only serious competition they face is from one another, a phenomenon observed both within and without China" (p. 4), which caused Chinese companies to become locked in what Steinfeld (2002, 6) called a "mutually destructive price competition." Chinese competitiveness is explained by a number of factors. In addition to their willingness to operate with expectations of low profit margins, Chinese construction enterprises use cheap and productive labor, enjoy low capital costs, have a lesser cost supply chain, and enjoy lower cost engineering inputs than other traditional multinational corporations (MNCs) (Center for Chinese Studies 2006).

Furthermore, China does not feel bound by the OECD's legal texts on transparency in investment and does not disclose the terms of its bidding (Goldstein et al. 2006). More than economical, China has been taking political and security risks because of the pressing needs of its economy and because of its utilitarian, undiscriminating, and low thresholds of standards, conditions, and what we call intangibles (explored further later in Chapter 9). China, as a result, has been taking advantage of dormant or active gold mines, both literary and figuratively, that are scattered all over the African continent. Fifteen African countries are considered oil rich, which alone constitutes sufficient reason for Chinese involvement on the continent.

Since 2003, Chinese enterprises involved in Africa are registered either with MOC or SASAC. This ministry-level bureaucracy answers solely to the State Council and has ownership and exercises control of at least forty percent of outstanding stocks. Chinese enterprises are therefore under the jurisdiction and authority of both the central government and local (province or city) governments as a result of the reform.

These reform measures did not stop there. A second stage ensued from 1984 to 1991 (China Facts and Figures 2002). I refer to this period as that of the liberalization of the Chinese business sector. Indeed, the 12th National Congress of the CPC passed a resolution on the reform of the economic system that essentially urged all Chinese economic actors and agents to join forces (i.e., join the stock system) in joint-venture and so-called go-out strategies. Respective responsibilities and status were enacted into law, such as the role of the government and that of the enterprise, rights to own and run a company, and so on. In 1984, China established the China Shenyang International Economic and Technological Cooperation Corporation (CSYIC) to allow and encourage companies to venture outside in the quest for international contracted projects, joint ventures, labor exports, services, and acquisition of proprietorship. China decentralized its trade mechanisms and "private and joint ventures firms [became] the dominant forces in export and import" (J. Y. Wang 2007, 17).

China was poised to make a big splash with its entrance into the waters of international trade. China's reform initiatives came at a propitious juncture of the international economic processes. Indeed, a liberalized global economy has allowed a globalized supply chain, outsourcing, and a networked production phenomenon, enabled by new production processes (using digitization to facilitate codification and modularization). Once production steps are codified, they can be disaggregated into separate, manageable, component pieces with the use of modules and standardized to ensure connectivity (Steinfeld 2002). This production process allowed substitutability of standardized pieces of manufactured products by competitors and allowed proliferation of counterfeit items, but most important, it allowed outsourcing (i.e., of partial production operations) and relocation (i.e., total production operation) of big-name, multinational corporations. Since the 1980s, China became the preferred destination and the leading recipient of FDI.

Finally, the last stage of the reforms that affected Chinese enterprise began in 1992 and has continued until today (China Facts and Figures 2002). These efforts have been essentially about the marketization of Chinese enterprise and reinforcement of the status of the non-state-owned sector. As a result, Chinese companies and businesspeople have now become common names in and integral parts of the global commerce.With the help of the institutional infrastructure, China made spectacular progress infiltrating African economic opportunities.

Chapter 7 highlights select African countries—Nigeria, Sudan, Angola, South Africa, and Zimbabwe—to illustrate the Chinese modus operandi and its implications. The reason for choosing those specific countries is also revealed. Here, however, we will illustrate the breadth of activities of some key Chinese corporations on the African continent. Both the African countries and Chinese commercial activities are not exhaustive. Commercial activities are dynamic and always in flux. Further, we have limited our attention to the trends and strategies of China's market entry on the continent rather than attempting to detail China's activity in designated African countries.

Consider the case of CSYIC, which in 2003 implanted itself in more than twenty African countries: construction in Burkina Faso (Dolly Hospital); in Cameroon (Douala University extension); in Togo (Kara Hospital); and in Niger and Seychelles (office building, swimming pools). The company provided light technology in Niger (workshops on the production of agricultural materials); in Seychelles (building water and electricity supply lines); in Benin (medical equipment for Losca Hospital); in Tanzania (equipment and raw materials transportation); in joint ventures in Zambia (shoe andbiscuit factories); and in the supply of professional manpower in Mauritania, Rwanda, Ghana, the Democratic Republic of Congo, Cape Verde, and Guinea (China Facts and Figures 2002). Chinese construction and infrastructure companies seem exceptionally competitive for reasons we have mentioned above and in addition because the sector has long been neglected by local and Western companies. In often remote sites, these companies undertake large-scale projects that have been particularly interesting to African leaders. These companies target construction efforts in African countries that are recovering from years of civil wars (e.g., Angola, Sierra Leone, Ethiopia, Eritrea) and pursue projects in traditionally friendly countries (e.g., Tanzania, Zambia), and in general everywhere, given the overall poor state of the continent's infrastructure. The Chinese firms are bound to dominate the market in Angola where the recent loan of $2 billion stipulates the building by Chinese companies of railway lines, schools, roads, hospitals, bridges, fiber-optic networks, and offices. In Eritrea, CSYIC successfully bid on the construction of Asmara's Oratta Hospital, and in Ethiopia on a $300 million construction of a hydroelectric dam and power plant on the Tekeze River (Eisenman and Kurtlantzick 2006).

In addition to CSYIC, Chinese oil companies (e.g. Sinopec, China National Petroleum Corporation (CNPC), China National Offshore Oil Corporation (CNOOC), Petro-China, Zhongyan Petroleum Company) are becoming powers to be reckoned with in the industry, and Africa is one of the reasons. Sinopec's coup was the purchase of 40 percent of Sonongol, the Angola national oil company. This transaction was accompanied by a $1.1 billion signing bonus to the government. The move was a coup considering the importance of Angola's oil supply to China today, particularly given Angola's high quality (low sulfur) petroleum. Sinopec also gained exploitation rights for Ivory Coast resources (manganese, gold, oil). Sinopec signed a contract with Total Gabon in 2004 to sell Gabonese crude oil to China. Along with CNPC, in 2006 Sinopec acquired drilling rights to Sudanese oil fields worth $600 million. Petro-China has a crude oil deal with the Nigerian National Petroleum Corporation to supply 30,000 barrels per day, worth $800 million (in 2006). Since 2006, CNOOC has a $2.3 billion stake in a Nigerian oil and gas field in Kaduna. CNOOC signed a deal to explore the coast of Kenya for oil. Petro-China signed an exploration agreement with Algeria's Hydrogen Carbide to develop oil fields and improve technology for refinery construction.

Zhongyan Petroleum Company has been drilling since 2006 in the Gambella Basin in Ethiopia. In Madagascar, China has a lockdown on newly discovered reserves.

In mining, various Chinese companies, such as the China Nonferrous Mining and Construction Corporation, Ltd., have invested $800 million to exploit the copper mining in a special economic zone in the Chambezi area in Zambia (*BBC News*, 9 September 2007). In the Democratic Republic of Congo, the Feza Mining Company located in Likasi now imports 85 percent of China's cobalt from that country.

In the agricultural sector, the China State Farm and Agribusiness Corporation (CSFAC) has been active in the Zambian farming sector with a joint venture called the China-Zambian Friendship Farm. The company grows wheat and vegetables, and farms table chickens, cattle, and fish. CSFAC is active in Togo, South Africa, Mauritania, Ghana, Guinea, and Tanzania. In Guinea, the company cofounded the Sino-Guinea Agricultural Cooperation and Development Company and Koba Farm. The joint venture produces high-yield hybrid rice. These projects have been, according to official Chinese sources, successful in stimulating local economy and producing revenues to local farmers. In Tanzania since 2000, CSFAC has been, according to official Chinese media outlets, successfully producing sisal-based processed products (China Facts and Figures 2002). In Mozambique, the Sun and Sea Co., Ltd, farms prawns.

As in many other sectors that are crucial for African development, agriculture has not developed nor kept up with the pace of population growth, leading Africa since the early 1990s to become the beneficiary of 45 percent of the UN's Food and Agriculture Organization (FAO) investments. In addition to factors such as civil wars, drought, and lack of technological capacity and managerial know-how, the result has been that food security is still a problem in Africa. Here, like elsewhere, investment and aid have not been pouring in to allay the danger of food insecurity. The task force of the Council on Foreign Relations (2005, 115) stated, "Between USAid and the World Bank, overall assistance to African agriculture dropped by 90% in the 1990s." USAid reduced the number of its mission in Africa. USAid funding for agricultural development assistance was stagnant if not receding between 2000 and 2004. The European Union has echoed such a trend.

China saw here once again a neglected niche or sector that it could infiltrate. China has plenty of expertise in this sector, a traditional area of communism's labor mythology in which a number of advantages are provided. Indeed, most African nations have favorable provisions in the agricultural sector (e.g., tax exemptions on machinery, factors of production, import of production materials). Africa's agricultural land is fertile, and with the help of technology and management, according to Han Xiangshan, the vice president of CSFAC (China Facts and Figures 2002), China was on a mission to meet African demand.

In construction and infrastructure-building, the China Road and Bridge Corporation has a quasi-monopoly of the market, with one-half of the thousand projects on the continent (Servant 2005). In Egypt, China has secured a bid to build the Merowe Dam on the Nile River worth $6,500 million. The following infrastructure-building projects have been or currently are under way: airport terminal in Algiers, office building in Kigali, presidential palace in Windhuk, recreation park in Freetown, stadium in Lomé, and more (Bartholomaeus Grill, Die Zeit 14/09/2006). The China Civil Engineering Construction Corporation has projects in progress Mombasa, Nairobi/ Kenya, Lagos, and Kano/Nigeria.

In the service sector, in telecommunications, the Chinese giant Huawei has projects in Kenya, Zimbabwe, and Nigeria worth $400 million (Eisenman and Kurlantzkick 2006). The Hisense Group, based in South Africa, manufactures televisions, kitchen appliances, washing machines, microwave ovens, and music systems. Shanghai Bell, a giant in telecommunications in Asia, is now implanted in Angola.

In the utility sector, Chinese investors have invested $600 million to build the Kafue Gorge Hydroelectric Plant in Zambia (Eisenman and Kurlantzick 2006). In 2005, the China Hydropower Company and the China Conservancy and Power Engineering Company jointly built the Takazze Hydropower Station in Ethiopia. In Nigeria, the Cangshi Company produces equipment, mining machinery, mail-producing machines, and so on.

In tourism, contractors built hotels in South Africa, Botswana, and, what has always been a trademark of Chinese cooperation in Africa, namely the construction of prestige buildings called white elephants. Soon, Chinese tourists in Africa will start to enjoy the accomplishments of their home companies abroad, as more and more Chinese have been visiting the continent: 110,000 in 2005, a 100 percent increase over 2004 (Gill and Reilly 2007).

In the manufacturing sector, China has rounded up the panoply of its interests in Africa and taken steps to invest in the sector. There are no reasons that the manufacturing sector would not want to take advantage of the numerous incentives and facilitations extended to Chinese investors on the African continent. The last incentive was the announced $5 billion fund to promote investment. Chinese private businesses in manufacturing are present in Mozambique (batteries), Nigeria (shoes), Benin (ethyl alcohol), and others. China has succeeded in getting some African nations to let it create industrial districts in Liberia, Sierra Leone, Mozambique, and Zambia; some, as in Zambia, include land and export tax exemptions. Other manufacturing companies have inspected locations in Mauritius, South-Africa, and so on (Brautigam 2007)

Considering the significance of the manufacturing sector in the economic development process, it is self-evident that the revitalization of this particular sector is one of the significant features of China's investing efforts in Africa. Indeed, there have been funds injected, debates discussed, approaches attempted, and projects executed on the subject of African economic development. They have all had one thing in common: namely, that they seem not to have imposed any fundamental change on the economic realities on the continent. Investigations that have attempted to determine the causes of stalled economic development have pointed to both domestic and foreign causes. In the meantime, world economic processes continue to unravel, and more and more nations have succeeded in pulling themselves out of poverty and underdevelopment. They have been doing what economic historians have known all along: namely, that economic development is about structural transformation, which allows the movement of the bulk of economic activity, and therefore the GDP sector shares, from sectors of low economic return into those with higher returns; that is, away from the agricultural sector and into the manufacturing sector, better yet, into service. This simply implies that any economic progress throughout modern history passes through manufacturing and mass consumption. It is exactly this particular sector that has not been at the center and has not galvanized the attentions of all those who have been dealing with the issues.

Of course, issues such as technology transfer, capital, infrastructure, and supporting institutions come to mind. These have not been profusely available on the continent. This realization, however, does not justify the lack of concentration on manufacturing. This situation should influence policy- and decisionmakers to focus their efforts on that situation. Instead, we have had an exhortation to liberal economic practices of the structural adjustment era, which have forced a premature liberalization and proceeded without providing incentives to small- and medium-sized enterprises. This realization was taken into account only in 2003 by the World Bank and addressed in its recent policy paper.[19] This is crucial. China, it seems, dared to take on tasks neglected by Western colonialism. Any success at this level would constitute a major landmark. However, we are without any illusion that China by itself will achieve all that needs to be done to stir Africa onto the industrialization path. The history of economics shows that no country has achieved the economic surge necessary for development induced solely from the outside. Africa will require a driven, concerted development agenda, similar to that of South Korea, or an Africa-driven reform initiative, such as that of Japan after the Meiji restoration or China after Xiaoping. Figure 4 describes the key organizations at work in this process.

OFF-TAKE AGREEMENTS

The entire process of cooperation with a third country is driven by the need to secure an agreement in contractual terms

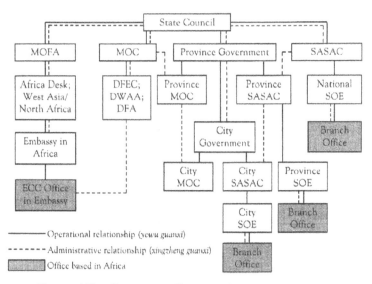

FIGURE 4. KEY PLAYERS IN CHINESE-AFRICAN ECONOMIC
DEVELOPMENT

Source: Africa in China's Global Strategy from: "The Tenuous Hold of China
Inc. in Africa" by Bates Gill and James Reilly, *The Washington Quarterly*, 30,
no.30

that will lead to the satisfaction of mutual interest of parties
involved in a specific area. These areas of common interest
have been: trade, finance, culture, tourism, education, science,
technology, health, military and legal matters, and political and
institutional concerns. However, some areas of cooperation are
more significant than others. A focus on trade and investment
agreements in the case of China, in the area of energy, is most
crucial, followed by investment in construction (infrastructure, plants, buildings, etc.), mining, and finally by all kinds of
low-end products and commodity trade for which China has
sought the establishment of free-trade agreements.

China has been sealing its deals with African countries with
numerous bilateral and multilateral agreements whose exact
number has been constantly in flux. At the 5 November 2006
China-Africa Forum summit alone, the second China-Africa
Business Council produced fourteen agreements between

eleven Chinese enterprise and African governments and firms worth $1.9 billion (Xinhua 2006).

To date, in 2007, China has signed 245 bilateral agreements on economic cooperation with thirty-four different African nations, encompassing specific issue areas such as protection of mutual investments (with South Africa, Sudan, Nigeria, agreeing against double taxation and dodging and evasion on civil, commercial, and criminal judicial assistance) to name just a few. China has even been generous, agreeing to opening its market with zero tariff to 440 export items from the least developed African countries.

China's bilateral and multilateral trade agreements with African countries and the continent's organizations, however, proceed under the macrolevel regulatory mechanisms of the WTO. These agreements are part of the international trade regime for free-trade agreements (FTAs). They must, as a matter of consequence, comply with the FTA guidelines. The agreements also are affected by some of those signed at that macrolevel. One of them is the Multi-Fiber Arrangement, which has been in effect since 1974. This agreement governs world trade in textiles and garments by way of quotas on the amount developing nations are permitted export to developed countries. This arrangement expired in January 2005. The evocation of this agreement here is justified by the fact that its expiration resulted in a liberalization of the textile industry, a sector in which in Africa is competitive but China even more so. The end result has been that it has pinned China's export against Africa's and negatively affected the latter.

Like many other partners with whom China has various trade agreements, Africa has become overwhelmed by the influx of goods from China rather than the other way around. The same can be said about investment, with South Africa's investment in China being the exception.

This leads us to the issue of vulnerability. China's vulnerability in trade with Africa lies in the area of energy. China has taken measures to reduce as much as possible that vulnerability.

Unlike the United States, for instance, in a crisis situation, China has only about ten days' worth of reserves (Navarro

2007)[20] to protect itself in a crisis situation. It is imperative to secure energy to sustain economic growth. The situation can easily become an emergency in the event of disruption. The same situation presents a strategic hazard in the context of security. China therefore needs to secure access and even an ownership stake in some of the production sites around the world. Given this vulnerability, China seeks to achieve a favorable position by enacting agreements. China's agreements have had so far a number of characteristics that merit close examination. In sectors where economic needs are most pressing (i.e., oil and mining), China has sought off-take agreements, which aim to secure contractually a determined number of barrels per year to be sold to China. One immediate effect of such off-take agreements is that they take the product in question off the market and in the process deprive other participants of the possibility even to compete as buyers. The exclusion of the product exacerbates even further the scarcity of the product, making it pricier. China's take-off agreements have the second characteristic of being framed for the long term, effectively locking down the product.

China has been accused of cutting deals to sweeten its lockdown agreements. In the case of Africa, the practice of packaging deals with externalities such as economic aid, building of prestige monuments or palaces, or other incentives has been criticized by many in the West, where it is claimed that these agreements undermine WTO regulations. The subject warrants more discussion, which is provided here in latter chapters.

INSTITUTIONAL INFRASTRUCTURE SUPPORT

Institutional frame-building to cement China-Africa cooperation is in itself a sign and a confirmation of both a real need and a long-run vision on behalf of these partners. In their very essence, institutions are created and exist to serve identified concrete and recurrent social needs. In the case of China and Africa, the increasingly complex need to cooperate has brought about in addition the need to coordinate, to consult, and to identify issue areas of concern. Their raison d'être is met when they efficiently carry out and organize the need for which they

have been created. As such, they are subject to the requirement for efficiency and therefore need a rationally functioning
structure, resources, and competent personnel. Needs that
justify the establishment of institutions are usually entrenched
in recurrent societal interactions and processes. Over time,
institutions, therefore, become entrenched in societal interactions and processes. These enterprises exist as long as the need
that has justified their creation persists and while their ability
to service that need continues. Therefore, such institutions are
generally a long-term reality, which confers upon them referential status. In this capacity, they establish expectations, norms,
common cultures, familiarity, and a history among institutional
partners and clients. China-Africa relations justified the creation of institutions to service emerging needs, and these enterprises have the potential to become entrenched. China-Africa
cooperation would therefore profit from the overall capacity of
institutions to cement relations for years to come and enjoy all
of the other advantages that institutions bring with them.

The so-called Chinese offensive in Africa, due to the
increasingly complex need to cooperate, has dictated the need
to coordinate, monitor, and evaluate activities, to consult and
discuss issues of concern for both partners. Since the year 2000,
this has justified the creation of an institutional infrastructure, the Forum on China-Africa Cooperation. The forum has
an underorganization called the China-Africa Joint Business
Forum (CAJBF), whose purpose is to bring together Chinese
entrepreneurs and businesses with Africans. The CAJBF facilitates investment endeavors, on China's side, through governmental support (from information sharing to taxation, from
cheap capital to labor forces that are unbeatable in their fervor,
efficiency, and cost).

The forum has met every three years since October 2000.
The first meeting was held in Beijing, the second in Addis-
Ababa, Ethiopia (December 2003), and the last to date (November 2006) in Beijing once again. In November 2004, China also
established the China-Africa Business Council in conjunction
with the UN Development Program (UNDP). The purpose
was and still is to encourage and support the private sector in

China to invest primarily in sub-Saharan Africa. These meetings quickly evolved into important international summits. They have been remarkable in the personal interest of African heads of state and high-ranking officials (Eighty from forty four African nations in 2000, more than fourty participating nations in 2003, and equally impressive numbers in 2006). These meetings provided China with the opportunity to unveil concrete objectives and gestures.

During the 2000 forum meeting, China reduced or cancelled $2.3 billion from thirty-one African indebted countries. In 2003, new programs and institutional mechanisms were unveiled, including tax reductions on some products from thirty-four poor African nations. China also announced its intent to participate in peacekeeping missions on the continent and vowed to assist in training of African technicians in health, humanitarian, tourism, and so on.

In 2006, China provided $3 billion in preferential loans and $2 billion in export credit to Africa over three years, and created a special fund of $5 billion for the same purpose. The same year, the China-Africa Joint Chamber of Commerce and Industry was established.

Unlike other trade-related multilateral fora, those initiated by China have the particular distinction of being indeed driven by the government in a way that warrants effective outcome. On 5 November 2006, the institutionalized China-Africa Forum summit built on the successes of previous commitments and provided a forum where Chinese officials and businessman and their African counterparts could sign agreements as mentioned earlier.

In addition to these China-created, Africa-related institutions, there was already one that has been in existence since 1955 and was revived in April 2005. This is the Asia-Africa Summit. With the economic ascent of India and its quest for natural resources (increasingly similar to that of China), these institutions will help establish and support South-South cooperation, which may turn out to be one of the most important features of the expressions of the globalization process.

Appendix B provides the full text the summit's communiqué, which provides the raisons d'être for its establishment.

CHAPTER 7

CASE STUDIES:
NIGERIA, SUDAN,
ANGOLA, ZIMBABWE,
AND SOUTH AFRICA

Previous chapters addressed China's involvement in the African continent and articulated and contextualized its policy on the continent. This chapter focuses on five key Africa states. Although China has established diplomatic and economic relations with all but five[21] African states, and a strategic partnership with some (e.g., South Africa and Nigeria), the significant importance and symbolism of its relations with some African states is more telling than with others. Each of the states with which China has a telling relation--Nigeria, Sudan, Angola, Zimbabwe, and South Africa-- illustrates best the nature, motivation, and implications of China's strategy on the continent. Except for Zimbabwe, they all have oil, which speaks to China's lockdown strategy for African oil that ties Africa to China in a crucial relationship. With Sudan and Zimbabwe, China's Africa policy has been entangled with international political issues. With Angola and Zimbabwe, China's history of involvement with the continent has come to bear. With Angola, China has proven how important a role African states still play in an age in which nations of the continent were relegated to the *Greek Calends.*[22] With South Africa, China has the most complex, the most significant, and the most promising relations in Africa.

Along with Nigeria and a few other selected African nations, South Africa is truly a key partner. These selected nations are Ethiopia and Kenya, countries with a special interest to China for their geostrategic significance, and the Island of Mauritius, which has a particularly hospitable set of policy measures that are attractive to Chinese investment. With these selected nations, those we address here and those we will not explore further, China has a history that is today the most important of China's trading partners in terms of volume of trade.

NIGERIA

Nigeria established formal diplomatic relations with the Peoples Republic of China in February 1971. Three years later, in September 1974, General Yakubu Gowon visited China and Chinese Vice-Premier Geng Biao reciprocated in October 1978. These dates point to the early history of political involvement of these nations with one another. Given the limited historical perspective of the Sino-Nigerian bilateral relations, and given the embeddedness of Nigeria in the commonwealth camp subsequent to the country's independence, this section focuses rather on the significance of Nigerian bilateral relations with China in today's context, addressing first the basis for the strategic partnership sought by China with Nigeria and second, the nature of cooperation now under-way.

STRATEGIC PARTNERSHIP

A number of factors determine the basis for such a strategic partnership. Nigeria is currently the largest producer of crude oil in Africa with approximately 2.6 million barrels per day and 35.2 billion barrels of proven reserves of finest oil, called *bony light*. Nigeria would like to increase its output to 40 billion barrels by 2010.

With a population 130.5 million (UN, 2005), Nigeria is the most populous country on the continent, which may potentially be a factor of power and constitutes a large market.

Nigeria is China's second largest export market and fourth largest trade partner in Africa (China, Nigeria Agree to Expand Economic Cooperation, *Peoples Daily*, 18 April 2005, para. 3).

Nigeria has both the ambition and the vocation of playing the hegemonic role in Africa as posited by Huntington (1996), precisely because of its population, the size of its economy in the African context, and its political will.

Nigeria has demonstrated its political will by being instrumental in establishing both the African Union in 2001 and the New Partnership for Africa's Development (NEPAD), by being the pivotal force in the functioning of the Economic Community of West African States (ECOWAS) and the operations of its military suborganization, the Economic Commission of West African States Monitoring Group (ECOMOG).

This hegemonic role is that of providing leadership and stability as a positive hegemon as described by Keohane and Nye (1973) in their theory of hegemonic stability.

For China, therefore, dealing with Nigeria involves the forging of a relationship with a potential leader. These nations may need one another as China seeks to assert its understanding of international relations processes and Nigeria seeks to establish international status, having expressed already the need to acquire a seat on the UN Security Council, for instance. President Olesengun Obasanjo, hosting Jiang Zeming in April 2002, found it only natural for the largest nation of the world to have relationships with the largest nation of Africa (*People's Daily*, 19 July 2002). This relationship has indeed benefited China and Nigeria as Figure 5 illustrates.

In the brief history of their relationship, Nigeria has proven a reliable partner to China in the latter's most crucial international relations issues. Nigeria supported China's UN membership, the one-China policy, China's adoption of antisecession law, and in 2002, established in Lagos the Nigerian Council for the Promotion of Peaceful Reunification.

This context was enough to prompt Hu Jintao, hosting President Obasanjo in April 2005, to suggest a strategic partnership. What Hu Jintao had in mind is nothing more than:

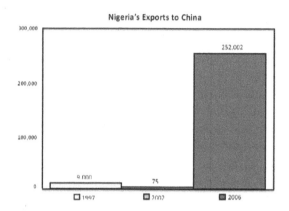

Nigeria's Exports to China

FIGURE 5. NIGERIA'S EXPORT TO CHINA

1. Enhancing political trust through high-level visits and personnel exchange
2. Improving consultation and coordination in international affairs
3. oining hands to maintain the interest of developing countries
4. Boosting South-South cooperation
5. Promoting the establishment of a fair and reasonable new international political and economic order.

COOPERATION AGREEMENTS

Since the late 1970s until the elevation of Olesegun Obasanjo to the Nigerian presidency in May 1999 and since then, constant contact in form of reciprocal visits by Nigerian and Chinese officials. In August 2001, Obasanjo's visit to Beijing, initiated a flurry of signed cooperation agreements. The first agreements were on trade and investment protection. In April 2002, agreements were signed in Nigeria, during the visit of Jiang Zeming, on economic and technical cooperation, avoidance of double taxation, medical and health services, consular matters, and prevention of fiscal evasion with respect to taxes on income. In July 2002, both governments agreed to cooperate to strengthen management of narcotic drugs, psychotropic substances, diversion of precursor chemicals, and tourism. Nigeria has become in the meantime one of China's tourist destinations. In March 2003, the Nigerian government, in collaboration with the Food and Agricultural Organization, succeeded in associating China with a food security initiative worth $22.7 million that was designed to allow the sharing of knowledge and experience in food production. The rationale is to bring together countries of the South with relevant expertise, such as China, to provide crucial insight into food production in the context of a bilateral cooperation between Nigeria and the FAO. China agreed, according to the FAO, in March 2003, to provide twenty experts and five hundreds field technicians to collaborate with their Nigerian colleagues over a period of four years in an effort to secure food production, improve crops, and diversify production and ultimately food security.

In April 2005, during Obasanjo's third[23] visit to China, additional agreements were signed on investment, telecommunication service, and technical and scientific cooperation. President Hu Jintao then suggested an upgrade to the strategic level of Sino-Nigerian cooperation.

In April 2006, Hu Jintao visited Africa for the third time, including a stop in Nigeria. A $4 billion investment deal was announced as China tried to lock down Nigerian oil production. China bought the controlling share in the Kaduna, a 110,000-barrel-a-day refinery, as mentioned in the previous chapter.. The same year, CNOOC bought 45 percent of Nigeria's underdeveloped Akpo field, covering almost 500 square miles, for $2.27 billion. Later the same year, the company bought a 35% stake in a license to explore oil in shallow water in the Niger Delta for $60 million (OPEC-China-Nigeria Mating Dance Could Benefit All Sides, Dow Jones Newswire, 11 April 2006). Sinopec received the first right of refusal for an exploration of four blocks, should licensing be offered: two in the Niger Delta (onshore and in shallow water) and two in the inland Chad basin (BBC, April 2006).[24]

All of these agreements and the strategic meaning of Nigeria to China have produced one of the most important of China's relations in the continent. China has not ceased to climb the ladder of most important trade partners to Nigeria, as China has increased its level of investments and other involvements in the country. In the area of trade, Nigeria exports petroleum, timber, and cotton to China and imports light industrial, mechanical, and electrical products. Just as China needs to increase its import from Nigeria, Nigerians have developed a taste for Chinese low-cost products and other joint-venture opportunities. This growing appetite for low-cost Chinese products in Africa has occurred to the detriment of high-priced western manufactured products. The limited opportunities for joint-ventures with Europeans and to the European continent due to restrictive visa practices have only contributed to the amplification of the phenomenon. Chinese companies and retail merchants have been taking advantage of this overture. There are now more than thirty-eight companies and counting, dispersed all over Nigeria, operating either wholly owned by the government of China or as joint ventures. These companies are involved in the rehabilitation of the Nigerian infrastructure and some have been involved in package deals such as the one in Kaduna, wherein oil deals are tied to infrastructure building. This explains, next to Sinopec and CNOOC, the massive presence of Chinese giant companies such as the China Geological Engineering Company, the China Harbor Engineering Company, and the China Civil Engineering Construction Company.

As for the presence of Chinese retailers, with the overall Chinese population in Nigeria estimated to be more than 20,000, the best illustration is the emerging Chinatowns in Lagos and elsewhere. As a consequence, the trade volume between these two countries has been steadily increasing and reached $2.18 billion in 2005.

Nigeria, however, showcases both the boldness of Chinese policy in Africa and its potential limits. Indeed, the overt reign of corruption and poverty in a country that derives 65 percent of its revenues from the oil sector has made Nigeria one of the potentially explosive countries even before we consider the country's cultural conflicts between Muslims and Christians. Issues of redistribution of oil revenues have become the cause of grievances mostly from local Niger Delta populations that continue to live in abject poverty while witnessing the exploitation of their land resources despite the government's claim that it redistributes 13 percent of proceeds back to producing states. The region is 100,000 square kilometers of swamps and creeks that feed the Niger River as it runs into the Atlantic Ocean and is a gold mine of black gold of the best kind.

The exploitation of that region has caused environmental degradation manifest in polluted river waters that sicken babies and adults alike. Fishermen catch dead fish and miss their harvest because theyir fish suffocate under oil-infested waters. The country is poorly equipped to respond to environmental concerns and air pollution continues unabated. Many abandoned facilities remain neglected and are transformed into hazards in the otherwise green local environment.

The schools are precarious or nonexistent and there is no infrastructure. The disenchanted and disenfranchised population has resorted to sabotaging the oil production infrastructure, the destruction of pipelines and pumping stations, and the kidnapping of expatriates who work for the oil companies. The largest oil companies are represented, from ExxonMobil to Royal Dutch Shell, which is the biggest foreign oil operator in Nigeria. Chevron, Total, and the Italian Eni SpA all have subsidiaries in the region. Their employees have no contact with local populations and live in secluded compounds separated from local villagers by barbed wire, buffer zones, and thirty-foot walls, guarded by retired military personnel from either the French or the U.S. Army. In 2007 alone, two hundred expatriates were kidnapped. Ransom demands to U.S. citizens cost more than those to the British and French with those to Asians next. China has seen some of its citizens captured, which suggests that the country has accepted this cost of doing business in a politically and economically restless context. China is not the only oil-needy country, and the imperative of this energy source has forced nations to tolerate a situation that is becoming irresponsible and exploitative. The response of these oil companies has been that they are not alone to blame for the situation in the Niger Delta region. Part of the reason is that they must turn over to the Nigerian government, which split revenues with operating companies after they have recovered development costs. Current contracts require that the companies fund 100 percent of revenues as the local manager of the French oil company Total recently revealed ("Local Manager in the Delta," *Envoyé Special*, 22 January 2008). The tendency of the Nigerian government has been to augment continuously their share of the profit. Oil companies, according to the *International Herald Tribune* (22 April 2007), have typically kept 7 percent of the profit from oil sales, leaving the balance to the government.

The newly elected president Umaru Yar' Adua announced a plan in October 2007 to revise contracts with foreign oil companies operating in Nigeria in part to promote greater efficiency in that sector and to address corruption that has become systemic due to loopholes, lack of accountability, and lack of government will to enforce transparency in its own efforts to fight corruption. Indeed, Nigeria continues to appear prominently on the Transparency International and Human Rights Reports as one of the most corrupt nations on the planet. China, as part of the oil exploitation scene in Nigeria, also is associated with these issues.

SUDAN

Sudan is in many respects an interesting African country and equally interesting with respect to its relations with China. Sudan is the largest African country and, with Egypt, one of the birthplaces of early African Nubian civilizations. Sudan exhibits traces of the Islamic and Arabic presence since the seventh century C.E. To this heritage, the relics of the British colonization are added. Sudan has been governed, like many African countries, dictatorially since its independence. Two reigns have been particularly long and have determined its fate: Jafaar al Nimeiri, who governed the country between 1969 and 1985, and the subsequent reign of Omar Hassan al-Bashir since June of 1989 until 2007 and counting. Their dictatorial styles, their claim to Arab descent as well as their Islamic faith, and their roots in the northern part of the country have been cited as factors that have led to policies that have excluded from power and economic resources the southern populations of black Sudanic origin and those of the Christian faith. These leaders have therefore entertained and created grievances and have justified and caused, as do all dictatorial regimes, their own opposition and conflict.

The result has been years of civil war since 1983. Twenty years later, the same dynamic that explains the North-South conflict in Sudan likewise explains another conflict between the government in Khartoum and the population of Darfur. Many African nations have been trapped in postindependence internal conflicts due to the ascent to power by liberation movement parties. Those left behind have essentially been at the origin of the internal conflicts given that openly democratic opposition parties are not tolerated. This state of latent civil war has been permanent in many African countries, which has prompted the parties in power to spend most of their energy to keep themselves there. Occasionally these nonaddressed and nonmediated conflicts broke up or produced coups d'état. In the case of Sudan, and elsewhere in Africa, the conflict between the North and the South has endured only to be fueled in the aftermath of Cold War as African dictatorial regimes lose their respective support from either the Western or Eastern superpower and thereby become vulnerable to internal opposition. That aftermath resulted in pressure for democratization reforms. The difficulty of negotiating a transition to democracy has produced many of African nations' internal conflicts. Sudan is no exception. A long civil war between the North and the South reached stalemate, as it did in Angola, in which the party in power was not strong enough to eradicate the rebellion and the rebellion was not strong enough to evict the government. In The meantime, both in Sudan and Angola, the situation has since evolved. Sudan has split into a North and a South and in Angola the former MPLA has cimented its grip to power.

Under these circumstances, China articulated its presence and policy in Sudan. Although Sudan and China have conducted official diplomatic relations since 4 February 1959, China's presence in Sudan became significant and relevant since the mid-1980s as China attempted to tie its economic aid in Africa to its own changing economic needs induced by the reforms of modernization. With its interests in turning a profit, entering the African market, and accessing its raw materials, China's presence in Sudan has been, since the early 1990s, essentially articulated around oil. In the late 1990s, Sudan became an important exporter for China. Although not a member of OPEC because of its feeble output and reserves (only 0.4% of world's total oil production), and thus having just an observer status, Sudan had between 630 and 700 barrels of proven reserves (in 2004). Its estimated total reserves, however, are 5 billion barrels, which could last as much as fifty-seven years. China's long-term view, given the doubts surrounding the longevity of Saudi oil, is clairvoyant.

In this regard, Sudan is an ideal case study of China's Africa relations. In Sudan, the expressions of China's Africa policy will be brought to light. Sudan was under siege by Western capital attacks and victim of U.S. sanctions, which banned investment by U.S. firms in 1997. Chevron abandoned its investments in 1992 and Occidental Petroleum Corporation was prohibited by Congress to do business in Sudan. Other European companies, such as the Austrian OMV and the Swedish Lundin, as well as the Canadian Talisman, were unwilling to expose themselves to criticism or feared the instability of the civil war and backed away. Sudan needed foreign investors to revitalize its oil industry and could not have gotten a new friend at a better time. In light of such circumstances, China developed into the Sudan's most important trade partner. On the other hand, the soon-to-be new friend, China, important enough not to align ipso facto with the embargo reflex of the West, braced for a global market-entry strategy just as the energy need was becoming strategically even more imperative than ever.

Unable to carve out a sizable market share in the Middle East, where the United States has locked down roughly 45 percent of the market share, the opportunity for China to tap into the Sudanese oil market also could not have come at a better time; China would gladly fill the void left by Western companies. Sudan welcomed China's interest. Soon, China was accessing and securing Sudanese market by way of production-sharing agreements.

A systematic and aggressive infiltration strategy and moves ensued. In 1996, the China National Petroleum Company (CNPC), investing in the Greater Nile Petroleum Operation Company (GNPOC), paid $441 million to acquire 40 percent of the majority share, surpassing Sudan's 35 percent share and that of Malaysia, India, and the rest. In May 1997, CNPC outbid the competition to win a large-scale project for the production and transportation of oil in western Kordofan. This twenty-year project encompasses three blocks: Unity, Heglig, and Kaikang in the Mughlad Basin. In January 2005, these blocks produced 325,000 barrels per day (Shichor 2005).

The pipeline built by Sinopec to transport oil from the Heglig oil field in Kordofan province to Port Sudan on the Red Sea was worth $1 billion. The pipelines' length is more than 1,500 kilometers, and it became operational on 23 June 1999. It is the largest pipeline built by China abroad. A refinery, part of the project worth $540 million, was built and inaugurated on the tenth anniversary of the Islamic party of al-Bashir. By June 2004, the refinery's processing capacity was 70,000 barrels per day; the CNCP offered $340 million to expand this capacity to 100,000 (Shichor 2005). With such an outburst of successful projects, Sudan became a net exporter, exporting 600,000 barrels a day from the Bashir regime. On 1 October 2001, CNPC, with a holding of 41 percent of stocks and Sinopec with 6 percent, created the Petrodar Operating Company (PDOC), which took control of blocks 3 and 7, covering 72,000 square kilometers in the Melut Basin. Subsequently, the China Petroleum Engineering and Construction Group (CPECG), CNPC's construction arm, won the bid to build a $215 million oil terminal to service blocks 3 and under PDOC control. CNPC has 96 percent control of block 6 in western Kordofan and southern Darfur, with a potential production rate of 170,000 barrels per day (Jamestown Foundation 2005). China continues to connect the dots, which consist of exploration, production, refinement, and transport. In August 2003, CNPC was authorized as a result of a deal to build a 730 kilometer oil pipeline from Fula oilfields in western Kordofan to the oil refinery in Khartoum.

As a result, China consumes 64 percent of Sudanese oil (Shichor 2005). Half of China's overseas oil was imported from Sudan in 2005, which justified the tenfold increase of China's imports from Sudan between 1999 and 2005, which soared from $1.47 million to $1.71 billion (Shichor 2005).

Other sectors of the Sudanese economy have been of interest to China. Such is the case of the power, gas, agriculture, infrastructure building, armaments, petrochemicals, and so on. In the case of the gas sector, China became active in 2002 and already controls 100 percent of Sudan's Petroleum Trade Project, 50 percent of the holdings of the Khartoum chemical industry, and CPECG supervises the operations of Sudan's polypropylene project (Shichor 2005). In the power sector, the construction of Qarre I and II stations by Harbin Power Company in 2002, financed by China's central bank, allowed Sudan to produce 330 megawatts about 50 kilometers north of Khartoum. The construction of the Kabar Dam by Chinese investment ($470 million or 85 percent of the total investment) produced a hydropower plant with a capacity of 300 megawatts. An agreement was signed on 8 June 2003 for construction of the Merowe (Hambad) dam, worth $555 million and financed for the most part by the Chinese government loan. Shichor (2005) projected that when this plant became operational in 2008, it would double or triple Sudan's electricity-generating capacity and therefore turn Sudan into an electric-power-exporting country.

The successes of China's economic presence in Sudan did not evolve without some measure of concern of both internal and external natures. These concerns are justified by the implications of the Chinese actions in the exercise of power by the regime in Khartoum. The fragile political stability that was maintained as a result of the stalemate shifted in favor of the regime in power as a result of Chinese involvement in Sudan. The government in Khartoum became increasingly bold as oil cooperation with China started to yield revenues. This income has filled the Khartoum military budgets and allowed the government to conduct incursions in the South where most of Sudan's oil fields are located. Since 1995, Beijing has provided fighter craft (6-7 F-7M and Mig-21), antipersonnel and antitank mines, Chinese T-59 tanks, anti-aircraft (Human Rights Watch 1998), Chinese military trucks, Mi-8 helicopters, rocket-propelled grenades, T-59 tanks, and Chinese 37mm antiaircraft guns to the government of Sudan as part of its economic cooperation package. This package deal involved oil and economic and military aid between Beijing and the government in Khartoum.

Pressure was exerted on the populations of Dinka and Nuer, with many expropriated and displaced (4 million) or killed (2 million) since the civil war began (IMF 2004). The effort under way since early 2000 produced in 2005 a comprehensive peace accord between the warring factions in the South, principally the Sudan People's Liberation Army (SPLA) and the government in Khartoum. Tensions have remained between them, justifying the presence of the military to protect Chinese workers in various fields. This tension also explains the need for Khartoum to take advantage of military cooperation with China to build a weapons factory near Khartoum. China, with different foreign policy stipulations than those of the predominant actors of international politics, saw no reason to constrain its cooperating with regimes involved in internal conflicts. Indeed, China's principles that govern the sale of arms state that arms exports should: (1) boost the legitimate self-defense capability of the recipient country; (2) not prejudice regional and international peace, security, and stability; (3) not interfere in the internal affairs of recipient countries.

These clauses have been problematic in two ways. First, noninterference in internal conflict risks being seen as complicity with the regime in place when Chinese arms are used to silence internal opposition. This has been the case both in southern Sudan and in the western region of Darfur. The potential consequence is for China to lose its privileges in the event that the opposing faction prevails and to arouse the antipathy of local warring factions, as demonstrated in the case the Niger Delta region where Chinese workers have been kidnapped.

The second problem caused by such an attitude is that internationally, some of these regimes with which China associates, as in the cases of Sudan and Zimbabwe, are not acceptable to the international community. The atrocities committed by the Khartoum-backed Janjaweed militia in Darfur are associated with China's support of the regime in place.

China has therefore been pressured to adhere to the way dominant members of the international institutions deal with such issues. This consists of either providing incentives or articulating threats to particular nations that are deemed in dissent with the rest of the international community. China therefore has been urged to align itself with that modus operandi, which in the case of Sudan means articulating threat, or applying sanctions or embargos.

China, however, is not a proponent of these practices, which are very dear to Western leading powers. As a matter of fact, China considers those practices counterproductive. China argues from a non-Western perspective that this approach presents two alternatives: either do that which the embargo seeker considers right or suffer embargo. China is not a proponent of what the West considers right or wrong and argues in favor of dialogue as the best means by which to solve differences. With respect to Sudan, China has been pressured to intervene. China forcefully advocates a number of principles of the UN Charter that address noninterference, respect of sovereignty, respect of territorial integrity, and so on. China's dilemma with respect to Sudan consists of either remaining faithful to its principles of noninterference and risking a diplomatic black eye or reacting to international pressure and attaching conditions to its aid to Sudan as a means to express threat. This approach runs the risk, therefore, that China must abandon a core principle of its foreign policy and diplomatic practice. In that case, China will become just like any other foreign power. This may result in China losing the edge that it has so skillfully acquired. For all practical purposes, China so far has walked that difficult path.

The undiscriminating policy attitude and principles of China's foreign policy allows that country to set aside her reservations with respect to the host country under the stipulation of noninterference, which is more designed to exclude other nations' interference in its internal affairs. The notion of political conditionalities (good governance and democratization, human rights, etc.) is defined in China's own terms. China has that prerogative as a sovereign nation and these matters therefore are not on China's foreign policy agenda. Sudan's harsh, undemocratic, and unlawful treatment of its population has not been, until recently, an issue to China. An estimated 200,000 people killed and 2.5 million displaced have been the headlines from Sudan, competing with China's increasing economic ties to that country. Whereas the economic partnership with Khartoum is not per se in question, the sale of weapons worth over $100 million between 1996 and 2003 (Sriram 2007) to the government is, as it is linked to these killings and other atrocities committed by the proxy Janjaweed militia in Darfur, even though China has provided less than 10 percent of the Sudanese arsenal.

The UN Security Council resolution 1564 passed in September 2004 that sought to impose an embargo on Sudan was rendered meaningless as a result of China's veto threat. China continues to sell arms after the second resolution, 1591, passed in 2005. However, resolution 1706, accepted by China, passed, urging Sudan to accept the UN peacekeeping mission, thus illustrating Chinese navigation through its delicate position. Chinese officials have been discretely, since the visit of Hu Jintao to Khartoum on 2 February 2007, signaling its willingness to address the issue with the government in Khartoum, urging Khartoum to use caution and more flexibility.

All things considered, Sudan has become very important to China, which receives 7 percent of its oil from that African country. CNPC alone has invested $15.5 billion in Sudan. On the other hand, because of this cooperation, China has become the most important Sudanese foreign partner, and Sudan has, as a result, been displaying an economic growth rate averaging 6 percent since 2000. The marriage between these partners so far has been mutually beneficial as constantly claimed by Chinese foreign policy papers as illustrated in Figure 7.

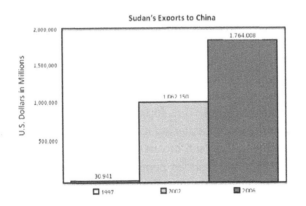

FIGURE 6. SUDAN'S EXPORTS TO CHINA

ANGOLA

Angola, like other oil-producing African nations, has been on the radar of China's offensive in trading with the continent since the successes of its open-door policy. This interest in Angola, however, is not recent. We have already, in chapter 3 on China's history of involvement in the continent, alluded to China's active involvement in Angola's political affairs during the struggle for independence from the 1950s to the 1970s. Angola was one also of the countries where the limits of China's independent foreign policy vis-à-vis, in China' eyes, the imperialist United States and the Soviet Union have been exposed. Indeed, China has had to concede the superiority of Russia and its appeal to more African revolutionary movements than it did at that particular time. As the elite movement of the Front National de Liberciao de Angola (FNLA) aligned with the Soviets and subsequently took the reins of power after independence in 1975, China had to sever its political ties with Angola, which had entered into a civil war that lasted twenty-seven years. During this time, the FNLA opposed União Nacional para a Independência Total de Angola (National Union for the Total Independence of Angola; UNITA), which became a pro-Western movement, leaving China with no horse in the race. Since the events prior and subsequent to Angolan independence, China has been a distant observer and a marginal player in Angolan political affairs. That changed in 1983, when China finally established diplomatic ties to Angola. This renewed interest could not have come at a better time; better yet, this renewed interest cannot be dissociated from China's overall strategic readjustment in the 1980s. In the middle of that decade, China began to develop a new approach to its development aid policy, reconsidering its attitude toward international trade and its institutional infrastructure, as mentioned.

When Chinese Premier Zeng Peiyang visited Angola on 25 February 2005, nine cooperation agreements were signed: (1) development of Angola's oil and gas riches; (2) general infrastructure construction; (3) technical aid and material assistance worth $6 million a year to the Angolan ministries of petroleum and geology and mining; (4) financial aid (interest-free loans); (5–8) three oil agreements wherein Sinangol (Angolan oil company) and Sinopec agreed on a long-term supply of oil to China; and (9) the building of the Lobito refinery, 400 km south of Luanda, to process a capacity of 240,000 barrels a day and to be completed in 2010, whose negotiations have failed so far to materialize. Indeed Angola possessed only one refinery near Luanda with an insufficient capacity of 40,000 barrels a day. The Angolan government approved the building of a second refinery in 1997, announced by Sonangol, which has the monopoly. The South Korean company Samsung obtained the contract for construction and engineering in 2000, and the construction began in 2001. The deal, however, ran into some difficulties with contractual terms.

Among additional deals between China's Sinopec and Angolan Sonangol was the agreement to evaluate conjointly the offshore blocks 3 and 5, to the detriment of Total. China's oil companies have been striving since 2005 as Shell, British Petroleum, Total, and Chevron were losing their foothold in the country. Chevron fell out of grace due to political considerations, and Shell has divested its oil interests, 50 percent equity share in the deep-water block 18 operated by British Petroleum (BP), which prompted Sonangol to exercise its right of refusal and ultimately give its equity share to Sinopec (Hare 2006). Sinopec finally acquired part of offshore oil block 3, to the detriment of Total, whose concessions were renewed by Sonangol. In March 2006, a joint venture between Sonangol and Sinopec created a consortium, SSI, which dominates the oil sector in Angola. SSI acquired a 40 percent equity share of deep-water blocks 17 and 18 on a bid of $2.2 billion. These two blocks are operated by the technologically say Brazilian Petrobras. The consortium failed, however, to acquire block 15 as the Italian company ENI outbid the Chinese by $900,000, leaving SSI with a 20 percent share.

When China established diplomatic ties with Angola, the latter was still in a civil war, which formally ended in 2002. At that time, Angola's cities and infrastructures, once Africa's jewels and a legacy of Portuguese colonialism, were destroyed, leaving a massive need for infrastructure-building. The country, however, has a major asset: oil. Indeed, Angola is the second largest African oil producer behind Nigeria, pumping 1.3 million barrels a day in 2007. Angola may soon overtake Nigeria as expectations and projections for 2008 were 2 million barrels a day. Angola has a proven reserve of 10 billion barrels of high-quality crude oil with low sulfur that is less difficult to process, easier to refine, and yields high quantity of gasoline.

Angola is currently China's second largest trading partner (after South Africa), with one-fourth of China's trade with Africa. Sustained economic growth in China means increased need for energy. The situation brought together two nations whose respective needs and their capacity to alleviate them is complementary. Indeed, Angola's exports to China have steadily increased since 2002 (see Figure 7).

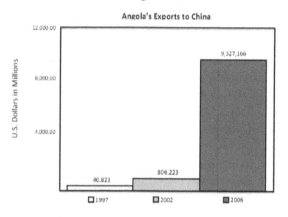

FIGURE 7. ANGOLA'S EXPORTS TO CHINA

China's nascent manufacturing industry will be instrumentalized alongside its increasing massive foreign reserve to outbid the competition and propose an attractive development aid package to Angola. With oil as the exchange currency, China obtained access to its prized resource. As a result, the cooperation between these two nations continues to increase and has yearly and gradually reached new heights. Trade between these countries has increased from $190 million in 1998 to $372 million a year later; from $1,876 million in 2000 to $4.9 billion in 2004, and reached $6.95 billion in 2005 (Economic Trade Cooperation Between Angola, China Bodes Promising,

People's Daily, 5 April 2001, para 2). These increases, though initially modest, have grown exponentially since March 2004 when EximBank, the Chinese export bank, agreed to offer a $2 billion oil-backed loan to Angola (with one more to follow). This signaled the beginning of close cooperation with enormous significance for both partners and repercussions beyond their respective borders.

This cooperation will materialize essentially as loans with soft conditions, including the low interest rate of 1.5 percent, a seventeen-year reimbursement plan, with a five-year grace period (Angola-China 2004). Another condition stipulates that 70 percent of subcontracted reconstruction firms will be Chinese, leaving 30 percent of this work to Angolan firms. With these terms --a quid pro quo arrangement that seems to sell oil for infrastructure--, the reconstruction of the infrastructure in Angola will be carried out by Chinese firms. This includes the construction of railroads, of which three are in progress, among them one that links the capital, Luanda, to the interior town of Malanje 180 km away. Another is the Benguela railroad that links the port of Lobito on the Atlantic coast to the Democratic Republic of Congo and Zambia. Additional efforts include the construction of low-cost housing, hospitals, bridges, and roads by the private Chinese Roads and Bridges Corporation; airports at Viana in the outskirts of Luanda; the rebuilding of telecommunications by Mundo Startel; a military and commercial telephone network by ZTE corporation; a mobile phone factory; a training institute for Angolan employees; the electronics sector; and the household electric appliance sector, as stipulated by the terms of the loans.

Because of their overpowering bids and offerings, Chinese firms have obtained the lion's share of these construction contracts, taking on infrastructure development projects worth up to $1.9 billion. These firms have become the controlling shareholders in individual projects, such as the construction of the airport at Viana, of which two-thirds is financed by China. This situation has contributed greatly to the frustration and worries of local entrepreneurs. When it comes to the oil sector, since 2004 China's companies have simply outmaneuvered their competitors. The fact that Chinese investment is state-driven or state-sponsored and monitored, it has by nature, in addition to the private sector's self-interest focus, a public sector dimension that compels Chinese companies to align with China's *raison d'état* as trade and economic cooperation are under the same jurisdiction in China.

With respect to external actors, namely international finance institutions such as the IMF, whose role has been central in the determination of the structure and processes of political economic choices in developing nations such as Angola, this new involvement of China will not be without repercussions. These institutions have done their best to provide finance and guidance to developing nations, and their efforts have been received and judged at best with mixed sentiments. These institutions have been resented in Africa since the era of the Structural Adjustment Programs (SAP), which have been described as medicine that caused more damage than the illness, as they intransigently persisted to act on liberal economic principles (necessitating liberalization, deregulation, and harmonization as bedrock) and gained a foothold in the economic structures of African nations. SAPs have been seen as attempting to remedy chronic balance-of-payment deficits and mounting debt crises. As such, SAPs were deemed imperative and were implemented by these institutions, which used the need for finances from developing nations as a pawn in the quid pro quo agreements. Principles of liberal economics have become a condition for access to loans. By 1989, thirty-six African nations had been subjected to SAPs.

In those African nations where economic growth has been positive (e.g., Uganda, Ghana, Tunisia, Mozambique, Mauritius), the population at large has not felt the positive effects. In many other African nations, the risk of marginalization has been increasing. At the continental level, Africa's contribution to the volume of world trade has decreased and has neared insignificance. Cries from African nations and from concerned organizations of international civil society and their attempts either to dissociate or to propose alternatives of their own have been met with rigorous refusal or with other alternative schemes designed to bring temporary ease to the levels of lamentation.

Numerous studies have been conducted to document the impact of SAPs in Africa. Mustafa H. M. Mkulo (1994), in a document titled "The Impact of Structural Adjustment Programs on Social Security in Eastern and Southern African Countries," documented the hardship caused by these programs.

With nowhere else to go and no other viable alternatives, these lamenting African nations, despite their frustrations, resorted to dealing with the imposing World Bank and IMF. The bargaining power of developing nations in general and African nations in particular decreased even more with the collapse of the Soviet Union. Africa lost what has been to some extent an alternative and African nations have become even more vulnerable.

Two decades after these policies were implemented *ad absurdum* in Africa, and after many of these African nations learned to deal with their exigencies, China re-entered the continent. Under the above-described circumstances, China's new approach to investment, to development aid, and its mere presence on the continent have been a refreshing development. China soon became the alternative to the West and its international finance institutions. China became the possible exit by which to escape the pressures of conditional engagement of international finance institutions that have for so long frustrated many African nations. China indeed came with an all-around capacity to deal realistically with African political and economic realities. In the case of Angola, it accepted in April 2000 the IMF-monitored program, which, however, collapsed in June 2001 because of lack of progress resulting from disagreement over issues of budget control.

A huge credit with China providing development funds to the war-stricken country became a reality in August 2005, which weakened IMF leverage. The increasingly intrusive prescribed program of management of African economies had become too much for Angolan authorities. Indeed, the IMF had, since 2005, two types of policy instruments and programs designed to assist national economic policy decision-makers to manage their funds and various programs in their most valuable sectors (e.g., oil): the Policy Support Instrument (PSI) and the Staff-Monitored Program (SMP).

By accepting the most intrusive of these policy instruments (i.e., SMP), Angola would have shown goodwill and motivation and as a result benefited from IMF funds and from Western donations from the Paris Club, whose operations have been closely aligned with those of the IMF. The program is intrusive in that it does not only have influence over economic policy choices but also the right to monitor on an annual basis how governments use and account for those revenues. The assumptions and better yet, allegations of a corrupt political class and embezzlement by the authorities in Luanda constitute the background of this intrusive policy instrument. Indeed, the Human Rights Watch Report of January 2004 stated that $4 billion in oil revenues simply disappeared from the Angolan treasury between 1997 and 2002.

Angola has moved away from IMF-prescribed recovery programs in favor of a homegrown policy such as that detailed in the Poverty Reduction Strategy Paper. In March 2005, the government in Luanda decided to create a development bank wherein 5 percent of the Angolan oil revenues will flow, against the will of the IMF, which cited fear of mismanagement. The bank's purpose is to move the Angolan economy away from oil dependency and finance projects that induce diversification. Angola cited as reasons for its change of heart the focus on a clientele other than the Angolan people, as well as the IMF's intent to control the country's use of its revenues. Indeed these new tools of the IMF have been seen by advocates as tools to help bring about good management, transparency, and efficient allocation of oil revenues, whereas critics[25] see in them new "tricks in the bag" of these multilateral institutions to perpetuate their control and the interest of the largest contributors in the economies of developing nations, as these programs always come with contingencies.

The Angolan Minster of Tourism, Dinho Chingunji, justifying the Angolan change of heart vis-à-vis the IMF in favor of China, wrote:

> Each time Angola meets some conditions, the goalposts are always shifting. People are dying. We need hospitals. People want schools. Farmers want roads so they can sell their produce. We want solutions.

> The Chinese say they will give us money, build the infrastructure, and then they will get out. When they say this road is going to be built in six months they usually meet it. (Bloomfield 2007, 86)

Needless to say, reactions to such a distancing from IMF collaboration have been multiple and various outside of Angola. Many organizations in international civil society and the IMF itself lamented that this was a sign that the authority in Luanda wanted to perpetuate the culture of corruption for which they were already known. Angola indeed has been rated by Transparency International the 151st country out of 158 in its 2005 annual corruption index. In the capital city, Luanda, 70 percent of the population lives on less than a dollar per day according to the United Nations. In that city, signs of mismanagement are manifest, public infrastructure and plumbing still absent, stagnant waters harbor decomposing debris that has been responsible for an outbreak of cholera, and electricity is unavailable most of the day.

Voices also have been directed toward China's so-called unorthodox methods of dealing with African partners.

The attitude of Angolan authority presages a predicament increasingly faced by the IMF and other international donors in Africa as sources of international finance become more ubiquitous and the West gradually loses its grip on the international financial market. This potential IMF predicament is part of the world's dynamic of shifting paradigms of international politics and economics in process as a result of different levels of success as nations seek to cope with new imperatives of globalization. In March 2007, Angola announced its lack of interest in formally structured IMF programs but was still interested in participating in the yearly or regularly scheduled procedure that all funds clients undergo as stipulated by Article IV of the IMF's Articles of Agreements.

With a boom in natural resources and most particularly fossil energy, Angola is more than ever on solid ground concerning prospects for increased revenues as evident from the number of active exploration and production companies onshore, offshore, in shallow waters, and in deep waters in

Angola (e.g., Total, Chevron, BP, ROC oil, Maersk, Exxon, Eni, Devon, Occidental, Sonangol, and Sinopec). Some of them (e.g., BP, Total, and Chevron) have been announcing new discoveries in their respective operational blocks in the last five years.

In April 2006, Angola surpassed Saudi Arabia as China's largest crude oil supplier (Petromatrix GmbH Report, 2006) to account for 15 percent of China's oil imports, making China the second-largest consumer of Angolan oil (after the United States). China's cooperation with Angola has justified the doubling of the budget of the latter, from $13 billion to $25 billion between 2005 and 2006. Fifty-four percent of this GDP is generated by the oil sector. As increased demand of rising world economies for natural resources contributes to the price boom, Angola has taken advantage of the situation and has been seen its economy grow by 16.7 percent in 2006 and by 20.8 percent in 2007 (China-African Adventure 2006) and its real GDP by 31.4 percent in 2007 according to the IMF.

ZIMBABWE

Zimbabwe is one of the African nations, despite its lack of a petroleum-driven economy, for which it is worth exploring the features of Chinese involvement in the continent. Zimbabwe is, however, not the only African nation to have enjoyed the interest of China despite not being an oil exporter; China's special relationships in Africa are not solely driven by oil. Other resources, of which Zimbabwe possesses a few (e.g., platinum, of which Zimbabwe is the second largest producer, gold, coal, diamonds, chrome, tobacco, copper, and silver); and other strategic considerations and historic affinity come into play). Zimbabwe itself recognizes its limited strategic significance to China. China's interest in Zimbabwe therefore is dictated by the need to access natural resources to meet market-entry needs by China's own manufacturing companies and by the historic affinity that China has with Zimbabwe since the creation of the Zimbabwe African National Union (ZANU) on 8 August 1963. The reasons that underlie China's interests in Zimbabwe are the focus of this sectionr.

An historic perspective on China-Zimbabwe relations reveals a tight collaboration since day one of the aftermath of split of ZANU from the Zimbabwe African People's Union (ZAPU), which was founded in 1961 under the leadership of Joshua Nkomo. As a pro-Soviet organization, the party had to deal with radicalization toward the extreme right of white Zimbabweans, then called Rhodesians, to counter a possible fall into communism, producing a win by white supremacists in the December 1962 election (Taylor 2006). The election resulted in the banning of ZAPU. In addition, internal divisions within ZAPU a year later produced a branching out of ZANU, led by Ndabaningi Sithole (president), Leopold Takawira (vice president), and Robert Mugabe (secretary general).

From that point on in the 1970s, both ZAPU and ZANU fought a guerrilla war against the white settlers who by then considered themselves as belonging to the land. ZAPU was backed by the Soviets and ZANU was backed by China and North Korea. In Zimbabwe, contrary to occurrences in Angola, China sided with the winning party with respect to the struggle for independence and was able to reverse the winning streak of the Soviets in Africa. This was a random outcome, however, as Beijing courted ZAPU before the split in March 1963 (Taylor 2006) just as ZANU sought the support of the Soviets and were rejected twice in October 1978 and May 1979 (Eisenman 2005).

Assistance in form of training of ZANU militia in guerrilla warfare, logistical and financial support, as well as advice were provided. In the meantime, Zimbabwe became independent in May 1979. Assistance continued practically until ZANU-PF (Patriotic Front) won the majority in the House of Assembly in 1980. The same year, Zimbabwe established diplomatic relations with China. Concentrating first on the liberation struggle and then on the political ideals of Marxism-Leninism with a dose of Maoism, this collaboration evolved over time to encompass and address Zimbabwe's economic concerns. Chinese officials have therefore repeatedly referred to the relations between these two countries as an all-weather friendship. This friendship has been supported by such acts as the five-year, interest free loan worth

$26.6 million made to Zimbabwe by China in the aftermath of independence.

A year after the independence of the country where he won the elections against ZAPU, in May of 1981, president Robert Mugabe visited China. From that point on, China's relations with Zimbabwe, just like its relations with other African countries, evolved according to oscillations of policy changes and other practical issues that determine the pace and path of the internal political landscape in China. Mugabe visited China after Mao's death and Deng was established as the new leader of the Communist Party and of the entire communist China. This was at the same time an era of great policy changes, from the open-door policy of modernization to its implications in the issues of trade, economic profitability, and the need to deal with China's own internal economic needs. These imperatives of China's internal political landscape had repercussions in its rapport with African nations with respect to development aid. China started to demand some type of trade-off for its economic aid. Even though the visit by Mugabe to China yielded two agreements in the areas of culture and trade, the quid pro quo in the trade agreement was that China needed sugar and tobacco and would provide economic aid as Zimbabwe sought to import commodities from China (Taylor 2006). This principle, already in use by the West, has found its way in the newly declared pro–free-market China.

Back and forth, goodwill visits occurred on both sides, beginning in January 1983 when Premier Zhao Ziyang visited Zimbabwe and then Mugabe's second visit to China in August 1985. By the mid-1980s, China's economic aid largess was constrained by the pressures of modernization. This situation lasted until 1989 (Taylor 2006) as a result of worldwide repercussions of the Tiananmen Square massacre. Zimbabwe, like many other African nations, officially rebuked the attacks against China's human rights record. As isolation loomed large, China counted Zimbabwe among its friends. At the beginning of the 1990s, China's reform policy started to show signs of success. Confident of its economic takeoff phase, in need of a consolidation of its ties with the rest of world, and in need of economic support derived by tapping into other nations' natural resources, China had a change of heart such that aid started flowing anew to those nations that fit the picture. In the case of Zimbabwe, the decreasing rate and volume of aid witnessed throughout the 1980s changed directions and started to increase. In May 1993, President Mugabe again visited China. The terms and foundation of the renewed relations aligned with China's new credo of mutual gain.

In 2000, Mugabe implemented the long-awaited and expected land reform, seeking a fairer redistribution of land that had long favored white Zimbabwean farmers. Indeed the Lancaster House Agreement of 21 December 1979, signed in Great Britain, resulted in ten years of protection of white Zimbabwean farmers in the aftermath of independence and rearticulation of the terms of redistribution. The transition proceeded peacefully. A sum of 44 million pounds was promised to Zimbabwe to help absorb the cost of the reform from the perspective of white Zimbabwean farmers who stood to sustain losses. The United States under Jimmy Carter sponsored the agreement. President Carter lost the election two years after the agreement. The conservative administration of Ronald Reagan came to power and did not feel compelled to honor the promises of the predecessor. In Great Britain as well, a change of heart occurred and the promised funds never reached Zimbabwe. As time passed, the government in Harare became impatient. To avoid a rebellion by black Zimbabweans and the pressure the ZANU party, which fought and promised a better future to their fellow citizens, Mugabe decided to enforce the terms of the agreement but without its compensation clause. The result was a mess by all accounts.

Although the intent of the reform was historically and morally justified, its implementation, however, since the year 2000, was brutal, forcing thousands of white farmers to evacuate their land. Those who did not were forced out without compensation. Their land was seized. The Mugabe regime blamed the lack of support and the backpedaling by the British from their promise to provide compensation to farmers. The brutality, however, cannot be anyone else's responsibility but Mugabe's. Since the land reform, the British have also spearheaded the sanction effort against Zimbabwe since 2002, along with the European Union and the

United States as Mugabe refused to back off from Mugabe's reforms and the way they were implemented.

The sanctions prohibited foreign investment from Western businesses, aid and cooperation, loans and finance programs from the IMF and the World Bank. These measures handicapped trade and induced a lack of foreign exchange on one hand and the absence of the farming output from experienced and highly productive farmers on the other. This put the country in economic jeopardy.

To remedy this situation and to keep the economy from imploding any further, the regime in Harare developed a Look-East Policy designed to attract economic partners in the form of investors from Asia to replace those from the West. In an interview with Xinhua in October 2006, while visiting China, Mugabe said, "In most recent times, as the West stated being hostile to us, we deliberately declared a Look-East Policy" (Interview: President Mugabe Hails Zimbabwe-China Ties, Xinhua, 28 October 2006, para. 8).

China, an old and reliable friend, heeded the call. Just as in Angola, such an acute need for cooperation could not have come at a better time for both partners. China's industry was in need of expansion. Eager to invest, China seized the opportunity in a country it had historically known and whose political and economic problems were familiar. China officially backed the land reform via Premier Wen Jiabao in December 2003. Mugabe was present at the China-Africa summit in Addis Ababa the same year and did not waste the opportunity to court Chinese investment in Zimbabwe.

The tie between the two countries found other venues of expression. An example is the forum of the UN Commission on Human Rights, where both China and Zimbabwe cooperated in 2004 to fend off resolutions aimed at condemning their mutual records on human rights. For the most part, however, these economic external expressions are of secondary significance. The economic and military expressions of cooperation characterized this friendship.

Mugabe's speech, celebrating the twenty-fifth anniversary of independence in May 2005, declared, "we have turned East, where the sun rises, and given our back to the West, where the sun sets" (Hilsum 2005). Mugabe definitely sealed Zimbabwe's commitment to the East, and in 2005, Mugabe went on the offensive in courting China. Chinese assistance to Zimbabwe principally encompassed agriculture, minerals, and hydroelectric resources as well as the military. A fund of $12 billion was reserved in 2005 to support Zimbabwean Small and Medium-sized Enterprises (SMEs), among them the textile, soap, tile, and fiberglass industries and the Zimbabwean Iron and Steel Company (Eisenman 2005); a $200 million loan of agricultural farming and fertilizer from the EximBank; a $1.3 billion loan to use in the energy sector against energy and electricity shortage as Zimbabwe Electric Supply Authority no longer could satisfy demand, which prompted Zimbabwe to import electricity, among other things, from South Africa and Mozambique. In 2006 China signed a contract to build three coal-powered thermal power stations on the Zambezi River, on the Zambian border to be paid for by chrome, whose exploitation is under comanagement of Chinese and Zimbabwean firms (BBC, Zimbabwe Signs China Energy Deal, 12 June 2006). A $2 billion loan was offered to boost the imploding economy. The Chinese supply chain, equipment, and companies such as China's National Aero-Technology Import and Export Corporation, China North Industries Corporation, China Machine-Building International Corporation (CMEC), Huawei, and so on, were the contracted beneficiaries with stakes in key sectors such as electricity generation, where China has a 70 percent stake (Taylor 2006). Infrastructure building included railroads, hospitals, stadiums, roads, bridges, airports, telecommunications, and the border post with South Africa at Beit Bridge

The regime in Harare accommodated Chinese guests in some instances to the detriment of Zimbabweans. Zimbabweans who settled farming properties left behind by white farmers in the Mashona area were removed to make room for the Chinese, who were ready to exploit the land for agricultural and tobacco needs (Taylor 2006). In 2003, the Chinese-owned firm China International Water and Electric was the beneficiary of 250,000 acres of farming land in southern Zimbabwe. The engineering expertise of the firm was needed as irrigation is necessary to achieve the goal of 2.1 million tons of maize production per annum (Eisenman 2005).

In the meantime, China imported 12.4 million kilograms of tobacco in 2007 from Zimbabwe (Zim-China Trade to Go Up $500 Million, *The [Harare] Herald*, 5 March 2007, para. 7). China in this respect was a worthy replacement for Britain, France, and Belgium, the former Western tobacco buyers.

In the military area, China's assistance to Zimbabwe has been both significant and a source of concern. The following purchases were made between June 2004 and April 2005: 6 MA-60 passenger planes, 12 FC-1 fighter jets, 100 military trucks, radio-jamming devices, military equipment, 6 K8 jet aircraft, and Chinese radar systems. This military cooperation has been source of concern because of the stalling democratization process in the country. The Harare regime was considered as dictatorial by many because of un-free elections (e.g., on 31 March 2005), maltreatment and imprisonment of members of opposition parties, the harsh treatment of populations in slums and farm lands, and so on. In light of such a political landscape, the arming of authoritarian regimes is seen as intimidating, empowering, and deterring the dissenting population and the opposing parties. Often China's critics associate the images of beaten Morgan Tsvangirai, the leader of the opposition party (i.e., the Movement for Democratic Change formed in 1999), and the use of Chinese equipment to crack down on the opposition.

In the case of Zimbabwe, the regime in Harare did not hesitate to put its arsenal to use on many occasions. Those who arm dictators are considered their accomplices. In Zimbabwe, as in Sudan, China endured this criticism, which is the collateral damage of China's own policy of noninterference in the internal affairs of independent nations. However, the criticism against China, even given the argument of the consequences of noninterference, has been without any moral clout, considering the fact that many other nations with or without an interference clause in their arms sale policies, have armed dictators. Other nations that depend on their strategic and economic interests have made choices that have not always had an idealist purpose, such as human rights, as their ultimate, political goal.

As a result of its involvement, however, China became the single largest investor in Zimbabwe. Trade between Zimbabwe and China was projected to reach $500 million in 2008, according to Yuan Nansheng, the Chinese ambassador to Zimbabwe (Zim-China Trade to Go Up $ 500 Million, *The [Harare] Herald*, 5 March 2007, para. 1). Despite this presence, China has not been able to stop the downward spiral of Zimbabwe's national economy since the withdrawal of the West and its implications. Zimbabwe became a net importer of food. After being known as the crop basket of the continent, the country became unable to feed its population. In addition to unstable security conditions, many Zimbabweans must fend off both oppression and hunger. As a result, many Zimbabweans, including 30 million who have been displaced, have left their country to seek a better future. In the process, they have created other forms of insecurities in host nations. As of 2007, the country had a per annum inflation rate of 1,700 percent, considered to be the highest in the world (BBC *Q&A Zimbabwe Meltdown*, 12 March 2007).

To make matters worse, a crackdown against informal or parallel economic activities has been proactively enforced (operation Murambatsvina in mid-May 2005), resulting in the dismantling and banning of flea market locations by demanding commercial licenses, levying of fines on others, and considering as a subversive political act the selling of food crops such as maize meal, sugar, and bread (Roger Bate, *The Weekly Standard*, 25 May 2005, para. 7). With an unemployment rate of about 70 percent (BBC *China Raises Stakes in Zimbabwe*, 12 November 2004), a population that is left out of the formal economic circuit has only the parallel economy as refuge. The informal sector has played a major role in African economies that often are partially penetrated by free-market structures on one hand and by traditional reflexes or subsistence economy on the other. Social networks facilitate the inclusion of every one. Many find in this informal structure the bedrock of survival that usually answers the question arising[26] from official statistics that a family of six survives on an income of $50 dollars a month.

Such a phenomenon may simply come down to exacerbating the lives of people who are already in dire straits. In addition, it does address the root cause of the problem by attacking its manifestations. This line of argument was expressed by Innocent Makwiramiti, the Chief Executive Officer of the Zimbabwe National Chamber of Commerce (ZNCC), who deplored the lack of foreign exchange when even their important trade partner, China (when not expecting raw materials in return for its investment) demanded international commercial rates for its service (Zimbabwe "Look East" to Avoid Economic Collapse, *Afrol News*, 29 July 2006, para. 10).

In the midst of this economic conundrum, Zimbabweans were beneficiaries of the policies of the regime in Harare as it accommodated Chinese investors' needs in the country (e.g., by cracking down on the informal sector that profited Chinese peddlers, by freeing land for tobacco plantations, or by discouraging the use of the term *zhing zhong* to refer to Chinese cheap goods with a short life span, and as lifesavers when the very cheap goods come handy to populations with a weak purchasing power and nowhere else to go but to Chinese peddlers and small business owners).

China must be aware of both its privileged status in Zimbabwe but also potential consequences as this status is closely identified with the regime in power. The current unsettled situation may spin out of control in the aftermath of the presidency of Robert Mugabe. China must recognize the need to keep any potential resentment under a certain tipping point. Historically, however, China has proven on many occasions that it knows how to be pragmatic.

SOUTH AFRICA

Illustrating China's relations with Africa using a few specific nations as points in case dictates the inclusion of South Africa for many reasons. The first is that South Africa is the largest of China's trading partner in Africa, with a bilateral trade volume accounting for 20.8 percent of total China-Africa trade. Second, South Africa has shown how China-Africa cooperation can become a two-way street and how Africa stands to profit from China's market. Third, China has a strategic need for South Africa and would like to engage African giants such as

Nigeria and South Africa for its vision of South-South cooperation, which constitutes a pillar of China's standing vision of the international order. Fourth, China capitalized on its historical ties with South Africa, going back to the struggle against the apartheid regime.

Although China-South Africa relations have been officially established only since 1998, concrete steps have been taken to punctuate what both China and South Africa seem to see as the beginning of a great story. The recent history starts after a change of allegiance from Taipei to Beijing. This followed the creation, in December 2001, of a China-South Africa Bi-National Commission by Thabo Mbeki and Jiang Zeming, who upgraded and redefined their relations as a *strategic partnership* that encompasses both political and economic relations when Wen Jiabiao visited South Africa in June 2006.

This strategic partnership did not constitute an isolated concept but rather a cornerstone of an edifice from which China hopes to build a vision of the international system that can be effectively brought to bear. The context of the transformation of the economic world with emerging nations that are adapting better than others and therefore building wealth affects the hierarchy of economic power and the ensuing political power. With a vision of "the universality of particular norms of behavior" (Le Pere and Shelton 2007), China aims to galvanize the South. China spearheaded this effort and therefore needed allies of weight such as Mexico, India, Brazil, and South Africa in the global South. In this scenario, South Africa deserves strategic partnership status. With the qualitatively significant increase of influential capacity from the global South as it came to the center of the engine that propels global trade, China's vision may be anything but utopian.

Indeed this global South no longer struggles against colonialism and imperialism but against marginalization by increasing trade with each other, which further affirms its identity and therefore makes it a bearer of a different agenda on the international scene. China is very much aware of this shifting process, which, if it is strategically negotiated by the global South, may very well produce better positioning and may counter the political and economic marginalization process from which it has suffered. After attempting and failing to fend off its vulnerabilities and sensitivities by a calling for a new world economic order in the 1970s, the global South is positioned better than ever before. After learning to adapt by implementing needed reforms that allow them to capitalize on favorable aspects of globalization, emerging markets of the global South are increasing their shares of both global trade and politics and as a result may very well become successful in the quest to revise some of the aspects of the current international order that they claim are to their overall disadvantage. It is exactly for the purpose of actively pleading for consideration of new norms in the international behavioral codex, grounded in principles that are both truly universal and acknowledge the particulars, that we should examine China's strategic interest in South Africa.

That said, China-South African relations, however, have come a long way since as far back as 1905, when South Africa and China under the Qing Dynasty first established diplomatic relations (Taylor 2006). This long precommunist dynasty (A.D. 1644–1911) has seen the dawn of China as a modern republic from the opening of the twentieth century and until the rise of Chinese nationalism. With China under the foreign reign of the Manchu dynasty and later under Japanese siege and subsequently in a civil war in which the Kuomintang (Taiwan's pro-Western political party, or KMT) fight for supremacy against the Chinese Communist Party (CCP). After 1949 and the triumph of the communists in China, South Africa was under apartheid. Pretoria aligned with Taipei, then in the hands of KMT. The ensuing context of the Cold War allowed the amalgamation of the white race and apartheid and designated the West as the enemy of the dominated majority of South Africa.

In the struggle against white rule and domination, the anti-apartheid movement impregnated by the anti-imperialism discourse that was already spreading in the early twentieth century found support from anti-imperialist forces. China and the Soviet Union, active elsewhere in Africa, competed for anti-apartheid clientele in South Africa. Here again, the Soviet Union had the upper hand. The African National Congress (ANC), founded in

1912, progressively became a Soviet client, whereas the most radical anti-apartheid party, the Pan-Africanist Congress, created in 1959, enjoyed China's support.

China, in direct contact with the African National Congress, since the Bandung Conference, witnessed the emergence of that party and yielding to the privileged position of the Soviets. China scaled back its activism in South Africa but continued to keep its eye on South Africa and resorted to a known rationale of continued denunciation of anti-imperialism and anti-hegemonism of both the Soviet Union and the United States in South Africa. This rationale persisted until a new era of China-South Africa relations became possible, induced by the release of Nelson Mandela in February of 1990.

One problem, however, impeded the normalization of China-South Africa diplomatic relations: China enacted a one-China policy while South Africa still maintained official diplomatic ties with Taipei. The final obstacle was removed with Pik Botta's visit in October 1991, Nelson Mandela's visit a year later, high-ranking Chinese visits to Pretoria, and a loosening of Mandela's position vis-à-vis South Africa's commitment to Taipei. Indeed, on 27 November 1996, South Africa did as many other African nations and switched allegiance from Taipei to Beijing. With nothing in the way of their relations, South Africa and China have since developed a full-fledged relationship with MFN status. South Africa acquired an Approved Destination Status, with the establishment of Confucian colleges at Stellenbosch University, the recognition of China's market economy status (which potentially allowed China access to the free-trade zone of the Southern African Customs Union (SACU), and so on.

Today, China-South Africa relations have become a two-way street supported by the South Africa-China Business Association. With the most advanced economy in the continent, and a population long kept out of reach of purchasing power and therefore a potential consumer of Chinese cheap goods, South Africa is an ideal launching board for Chinese commercial activity. China and South Africa are each other's recipients of FDI and access each other's markets. South Africa has a number of sizable, high-end companies (e.g., SAB Miller, Naspers,

Anglo-American PLC, Anglo Coal, Anglo Platinum, Sasol, the MIH Group, Landpac, Nedcor, Iscor, Anglo Gold) with experience investing abroad that combine to produce a total of investment that exceeds the total Chinese investment in South Africa (Timberg 2007). For the most part, they have used jointventures to carve out a piece of the market. A complementarity that suits these two commercial partners seems to be in place. High-tech industry, modern services and agriculture, environmental friendly industries and infrastructure, as well as additional investment have helped develop China's western region and revitalize old industrial bases in the northeast. South Africa still hopes that multinational companies will establish R&D centers there (Guijin 2005). China-South Africa bilateral trade presents multiple venues and possibilities, more than in the case of any other African nation, which explains the high volume of trade between these two partners on the continent. China, according to Ambassador Liu Guijin, prepares for the next phase of its developmental process, aiming to acquire high-tech industrial and service know-how to compete effectively and join the league of the advanced economies, leaving behind, as others have done, the natural resources concentration of economic activity. Such structural transformation is possible with joint ventures and investment from advanced economies to which, in many cases, South Africa is a representative. By 2006, bilateral trade reached $9.8 billion from $2 billion in 2000.

This China-South Africa partnership, however, has not been without conflicts. China has undoubtedly used its comparative advantage of low-cost labor, high labor productivity, and economies of scale in every market it has accessed. This also has been the case with South Africa. China's comparative advantage has been expressed painfully in the case of South Africa in the textile sector. Imports of textiles and clothing have been growing steadily since the establishment of trade relations, from f40 to 80 percent of clothing imported by the end of 2004 (Lyman 2005). This has translated into a steady increase of layoffs in that sector in South Africa, prompting the leadership of the Congress of South African Trade Unions (COSATU) to use forceful anti-China rhetoric to force change. The end of the Multi Fiber Agreement in January 2005, which allowed application of quotas to clothing and textile imports from some specific countries, allowed China's comparative advantage to play out into other markets and thereby suffocate African exports. Lyman (2005, para. 14) stated, "More than ten clothing factories in Lesotho closed in 2005. South Africa clothing export to the United States dropped from $26 million in the first quarter of 2004 to $12 million in the first quarter in 2005."

The conflict over textiles and South African complaints have not fallen on deaf Chinese ears. A mutual understanding in the form of an accord was reached whereby, among other things, China agreed to restrict its textile exports into South Africa.

CHAPTER 8

CHINESE APPROACH TO FOREIGN AID (CONTRAST TO THE WEST)

As early as the 1960s, aid became an issue area in China's Africa involvement. Seventeen African nations became independent in 1960, and all of them were in need of all kinds of assistance (technical, financial, logistical, personnel training) to invigorate their quest for economic development and truly have the taste of independence. The 1960s also were the era of reckoning for a need for a systematic program of aid that would favor the developing world. In the pool of potential sources for help were the industrialized and wealthy nations, both former colonial powers that wished to keep, in altered forms, their grip on former colonies, and the United States that was eager to expand its sphere of influence in the raging time of the Cold War. The Soviet Union, for the very same reason—spread of sphere of influence—resolved to assist the developing nations.

China also stepped in with an autonomous identity and intentions. China could not desist and understood the logical necessity to provide aid to nascent African states and economies, but a number of factors were to play a role in China's attitude vis-à-vis foreign aid. One of them was the fact that China preferred to offer its aid without conditions. To expect something in return for helping actual or potential ideological comrades was incompatible with the very notion of communism. The other factor was the fact that China itself had limited resources and therefore would be careful about their use. Alaba Ogunsanwo (1974, 89) wrote: "With the Chinese economy dislocated by the Great Leap Forward and by natural disasters, China's ability to enter the aid race was severely limited." This circumstance explains, in the case of China, the overwhelming use of assistance in kind, in the form of personnel, technicians, apparatus, equipment, logistic, and so on, which is illustriously exemplified by the construction of the Tanzania-Zambia railway, a legendary symbol of China's early Africa cooperation. The agreement for this project was signed in 1967.

Conscious of its limitation vis-à-vis both the West and the Soviets, China had avoided entering the aid race. The third factor that influenced China's attitude about foreign aid was that it considered aid a venue and instrument of imperialism used by both the West and the Soviets, both of whom considered by China as hegemonic. China, therefore, sought early on an authentic understanding of the concept of aid that avoids the traditional structural channels that end up creating a *rapport de force* that recreates in turn a structure of subordination that is very much disdained by all revolutionaries.

Two documents serve as reference to this history of the Chinese notion of foreign aid. They are the Eight Principles Governing Chinese Foreign Aid articulated by Zhou En lai during his Africa visit (December 1963–February 1964 (see Appendix C). In January 1983, Zhao Ziyang reduced the principles to four. These principles present, with the usual simplicity and clarity of typical Chinese policy papers, the intentions, goals, and practical purposes of Chinese official development assistance.

China remained faithful to this understanding through the years even as they pragmatically adjusted to reflect the current state of affairs, as demonstrated by the four principles by Ziyang, which improved on the objectives articulated by Zhou twenty years prior. As a result, it quickly become apparent that

China's presence and involvement in Africa deviated from the typical structures and processes that were already established by Western involvement on the continent. China moved in ways that were sometimes new or defied Western customary practices since 2002, when China accelerated its offensive to access international markets. As a result, China's approach in Africa differed from that of the West in both principle and practice.

In principle, China offers free grants and gives preferential loans that are specifically lenient in their reimbursement principles and modalities with respect to maturity and interest rate. China also provides commercial or concessional loans to projects with real prospects that they will be both lucrative and profitable. China's grants-loans ratio has been around 50:50. This is not a particularity of the Chinese approach.

Where China's principle varies is in the nonrefusal to tie aid to paradevelopmental purposes. China's approach has been deliberately dissociated from the Western approach.The commonly accepted, quid pro quo principle of instrumentalizing aid to serve political and strategic foreign policy goals, or normative goals such as human rights, good governance, and such was rejected by China on the grounds that this approach would interfere in the receiving entity's internal affairs.

In practice, although China uses traditional ways and tools to provide foreign aid (grants, loans) and occasionally targets specific projects in areas (investment, trade, aid), China's foreign aid has been characterized by the package-deal model, which reflects what Kenneth King (2007) referred to as an holistic approach. This corporatist approach amalgamates the interests of involved principals – the state, businesses, labor, and resources – to the service of goals and objectives defined by the government.

As a consequence, according to J.Y. Wang (2007, 23), "For Africa, China has been a market, a donor, a financier and investor, and a contractor and builder." In addition to this holistic perspective are the flexibility and complementarity of both China and Africa. Summarizing his paper, Wang agued that

> Though in the past official development aid predomi-
> nated . . . government policies, markets for each other's
> export, Africa's demand for infrastructure, and China's
> differential approach to financing have together
> moved commercial activities-trade and investment-to
> the center of China-Africa economic relations.

Note the use of the adverb *together* as it translates the holistic argument made by King (2006).

An argument can be made that the ever-growing effects of globalization that lead to ubiquitous distribution of wealth, the increased significance of economic processes, and the intensified quest for resources with strategic importance have blended the interests of the fields of international trade with those of international politics. This development justifies this Chinese functional amalgamation of trade, investment, foreign aid, and foreign policy. In this context, the role of the Chinese Exim Bank is revealing. The trend, which had been noticed since the collapse of the Soviet Union, was only temporarily reversed, out of attention from international processes in favor of the discourse on terrorism since 11 September 2001. The Goldman Sachs report (2003) on the BRIC nations sounded an alarm to signal the new trend and its implications both in terms of a new distribution of wealth status among nations and potentially a new distribution of the world power hierarchy.

With the holistic approach, "China uses grants, loans, and debts relief alongside commercial investments and preferential trade access in order to gain access to strategic resources assets or to build stronger political ties" (Davies et al. (2008, 4). With such an end in mind, all agents, businesses, officials, and financing actors involved in a project are expected to work in unison. This approach has caused problems to those in the West whose pre-established definitions and structural models distinguish what aid was and what it was not. The result is that Chinese statistics for official development assistance or aid has not always been reliably understood from a Western perspective. China does not publish country-specific aid statistics.

A feature of Western epistemology has been the need to break down, categorize, classify, describe, and ascribe nomenclature to objects studied. This analytical approach has advanced a number of issues but has been at the same time, in some cases, the very reason that it lacked the practical flexibility occasionally necessary in apprehending and appreciating synthetic approaches. This lack of flexibility has been cited as one of the causes of the inefficiency of Western foreign aid delivery by all relevant studies on the issue, as it has failed to think outside its own box. China, in contrast, favors symbiosis and coordination of various principles. This approach arises from the nature of its culture, which seems to privilege a fusion of agents who act toward the same goal, as noted in the earlier quotation by Michel Jan (2006), which mentioned a propensity by the Chinese to confound convictions and conformity.

China also, as we shall explore shortly, will soon run the risk of being overwhelmed by the different motivations and goals of its agents, as described by the theory of principal multiple agent dilemma. All involved actors who have their hands in the pot as China pursues its interests in Africa have slightly different bottom lines. Multiple government agents from the Ministry of Commerce to the Ministry of Foreign Affairs, the state council, and their respective employers and so on, serve official political, diplomatic, and strategic goals that may not necessarily be the same and also may not always harmonize with those of Chinese (primarily) private enterprises, which may very well be driven by economic rational choices.

We believe that the holistic approach, however, encompasses, translates, and projects an awareness of the complexity of the concept of development as we shall discuss in the upcoming section: Deliberate Dissociation. The concept is not justified by picking an area, an issue, and one aspect of it and developing a project to service. We cannot expect to affect the grand project of development without taking into account at least the entire sector, how it connects, and how it is affected by other sectors that are interconnected within a social or political system. All systems function viably if and when individual elements interact, each performing its own function in the expected fashion. The pattern of expected behavior produces social or political structure. The scheme implies interconnectivity, which warrants the holistic approach favored by the Chinese.

This model, we think, reflects a cultural trait of the Chinese, just as a certain material rationality, as defined by Max Weber; analytical judgment, as defined by Immanuel Kant; and positivist leanings, as defined by Francis Bacon[27] can easily be retraced and reflected in many of the pronouncements in Western foreign policy papers and approaches.

In retracing such cultural imbrications into today's political minds, we should invoke the planners' attitudes from the West, as described by William Easterly (2006) and point to their need to operate within a certain frame or rational mind-set that establishes a goal such as poverty reduction or millennium development goals, and determine a time frame, a means, and so on. Indeed, Easterly defined planners as those experts or thinkers who design development plans with goals and signposts from a rationally logical perspective, accepting vindication in implementation. They usually design a different plan in case of failure and many such plans have come and gone without any consequence. Kenneth King (2005, 11) seems to have grasped just that when he wrote with respect to Western foreign aid as the reflection of its culture:

> The Western donor's preoccupation is with poverty reduction and with meeting the millennium development goals (MDGs). The whole UN apparatus of target-setting at the world level, and then measuring all countries against these time-bound goals, namely 2015, is a deficit model in which Africa in particular comes out as a current and also likely future failure.

This illustrates such a Western operative mind, which has indeed been successful throughout history but also, throughout history, it has demonstrated from time to time its shortcomings.

DELIBERATE DISSOCIATION

The deliberate dissociation from the Western approach is manifest in a certain conception of aid. China views this as an instrument and a relic expression of global hegemonic intentions as it has created a context of quid pro quo that consists of dictating what the donor perceives to be the kind of help needed by the recipient and whereby the recipient abides by the donor's demands. These demands have addressed the recipient nations' economic policies, namely liberalization measures and other objects of interest to the donor, such as participation in the war against terrorism with contributions to intelligence-gathering or by permitting the buildup of US military bases, as we have described, while exploring the terms of the African Growth and Opportunity Act (AGOA). More generally, foreign aid's terms of the quid pro quo, which also are known as conditionalities, have formulated demands such as political transparency, democratization, organization of elections, respect for human rights, fight against corruption, and so on. This context has allowed the emergence of an international aid regime whose conditionalities have furthered the grip of the West on the African continent as articulated by Noam Chomsky,[28] who described this process as a way to keep these nations in chains.

China has not historically been part of the aid regime as understood in the West and has remained true to its tradition of independent foreign policy. The consequences of such principles are expressed in the foreign aid approach in a typically Chinese, pragmatic fashion captured best by Large (2008, 160): "The official Chinese approach works through and within existing political contours in Africa, rather than seeking to change these according to its own prescription and models". In practice, therefore, China's foreign aid is typically Chinese. By *typically Chinese* we mean pragmatic, humble, and to the point, with a transparent scheme that African leaders have come to appreciate a great deal.

China's foreign policy formulation, and by extension its foreign aid, have always reflected three factors: (1) China's own internal transformation, (2) Africa's practical realities, and (3) the overall dynamics of international politics. China's foreign aid reflects the pragmatism implied in the attempt to adapt and adjust to accommodate the changing dynamics of those domains. After being ideologically grounded in the

1950s, 1960s, and 1970s, Chinese foreign policy vis-à-vis Africa became less unconditional and more nuanced in the 1980s in reaction to Chinese internal economic constraints and fully focused on a win-win cooperation ground when China went global in the quest for sustained economic growth. China's foreign aid, therefore, is by definition nonnormative. The consequence of such vision is a non-Utopian and non-social-engineering approach that articulates ideals such as the eradication of poverty and a design plan by which to obtain that finality. Instead, China privileges practical, concrete, and definite projects whose results are palpable and tangible, support mass appeal, and therefore have a political effect. Such mass appeal and political effects are manifest in African capitals and villages where Chinese projects have been undertaken. To that effect, Fola Adeola (2004, para.13) wrote,

> There is much [African countries] can learn from China's inspiring approach to development which acknowledges difficulties, appreciates the complexities, and offers an empowering menu of approaches to tackle otherwise overwhelming challenges.

As for the humility of the Chinese foreign aid approach and practices, it is revealing to read documents signed to launch the China-Africa Forum in Beijing in 2000 and subsequent other documents. The forum adopted two documents: the Beijing Declaration and the Program for China-Africa Cooperation in Economic and Social Development. The forum also established follow-up committees that represented twenty-one government departments. A close reading reveals the simplicity of the goals formulated, the language used to describe them, the time frame for reaching them, and the consultative mechanism for monitoring progress. Subsequent fora have and will follow that scheme.

These documents contrast with any documents published by the IMF and World Bank with respect to their activity, work, and programs in Africa. This difference points to a significant schism that Easterly (2006) characterized as that of planners and searchers. China's approach is clearly that of searchers that avoids a top-down dictation of the nature of the development, and therefore avoids the patronizing, paternalistic, and so-called white-man's-burden attitude toward the beneficiary of their foreign aid. Echoing this attitude and welcoming China's interest, Congolese member of parliament Barnabé Kikaya stated, "China's growing presence might encourage Western governments to drop their patronizing attitude, that we know what's good for you" ("Congo Has Something" 2008, 14).

This somewhat generalized sentiment among Africans has led many to advance the argument of a Beijing Consensus. This consensus describes a Chinese vision that contrasts with that developed by the West in 1982, which was called the Washington Consensus. The contrast is more than ideological (i.e., communism versus liberal economics). The contrast is in many ways East versus West, a philosophical contrast about how to deal with less powerful partners, how to address the right thing to do, or the right policy to adopt. The Washington Consensus is a typical example of how the rapport de force, or balance of power, is used in the international arena. China's divergent approach, which claimed and delivered on its consensual focus and stripped of all kinds of strings, ultimately gave to developing nations a breath of fresh air after they endured suffocating conditionalities that emanated from the Washington Consensus.

China's approach to foreign targets, by way of economic aid packages to key sectors of individual African nations, entails essentially the physical infrastructure that China endeavors to construct with its financial aid. Companies are the first leg of the quid pro quo, and where African nations allow exploitation of specific natural resources used by China, likewise they constitute the second leg of the quid pro quo. In September 2007, the Democratic Republic of the Congo revealed an agreement with China wherein $12 billion, possibly more depending on need, will be loaned to Congo for infrastructure-building, railroads, roads, and mines in exchange for China's rights to mine copper ore of the equivalent value ("Congo Has Something" 2008). This constitutes a victory of sorts for China, which failed, some forty years ago, to secure an enviable position among Congolese political groups that are sympathetic to communism or socialism, such as those led by Antoine Gizenga and later Pierre Mulele or Gaston Soumialot during the struggle for independence and in the aftermath of the Congolese independence (most precisely in the aftermath of the assassination of Patrice Emery Lumumba). China had to lay low during the President Mobutu years only to emerge en force under the current President Joseph Kabila.

The transparency of this formula for package deals, and above all the possibility it offers Africa to utilize what it already has in natural resources, is attractive for the following reasons. The natural resources of Africa are collateral of this new deal. With this arrangement, Africa need not contract loans and credit to exploit its natural resources and does not need the economy to generate revenues to pay in a contest that has not allowed African economies to accumulate capital. This situation justified the debt crisis because of the fluctuation of raw materials prices in the international market. Furthermore, the very interest in raw materials has occasioned a booming raw materials price hike that in addition helps Africa increase its export revenues. African economies have thus grown not as a result of a developmental scheme concocted by the consultative IMF groups but by benefiting from the rise of Asian economies. The developmental stage of the West alone has structurally ceased to be the lung through which African economies breathe.

In this context, the Chinese government and Chinese firms are able to target sector-wide projects (piecemeal) in specific areas that are not too big to recall the Utopian social-engineering approach of the planners but not too small to replicate the *projectitis* of Western *assistantialism*(Nuschelr 1994), which consists of building a school here and a sanitary station there, for example, as opposed to the building of physical infrastructure, all of which are necessary but whose impact reminds us of the German expression, *Tropchen auf dem heissen Brett.*[29]

A sector-wide approach, known as SWAP, explained John Mbaku (2004, 194), "Rather than provide aid or support to individual projects within a given sector, the donor community would support the entire sector." This approach affirms that any rational measure has the potential to entail a more palpable impact, as suggested by the South Korean economical rise from underdevelopment.

All in all, China remains an atypical donor country. China indeed is still a communist country, still a developing country, and is still learning to trust the international system and therefore exercises all due caution. The success of this Chinese approach can be documented in the simultaneous growth in volume of trade, investment, the spread of Chinese enterprises, increases in Chinese foreign aid, and subsequent influence as important partner to Africa.

CONTRASTING WITH THE WEST

Why contrast China's approach to aid, investment, and trade in Africa with that of the West? The reason is because China is not the only significant international player involved in Africa in those areas. Therefore, China competes with others who also claim to provide foreign aid, trade, and investment in Africa. China also has claimed to do business in Africa differently from the way the West does it. Its action in Africa therefore begs the comparison. Is there any one better approach to the practice of trade, investment, and provision of aid in Africa? For trade and investment, the answer is measured by the margin of return on investment (ROI) and the importance of trade volume and balance extracted from trade with Africa. For aid, the answer to the question is more intricate as explained in the next chapter, as the simple idea of aid has blossomed into a complex reality and endeavor that has rendered it difficult to delineate the responsibilities, costs, and benefits incurred by various individual actors in light of the sincerely recognized inefficiency of its official institutional mechanisms and results.

The idea of aid and the inception of governmental aid in the West were born out of moral, economic, and strategic reasons. The moral reason consists of striving to help those in need. This notion has led individual efforts by Western nations to get involved in "helping" developing nations to emerge from economic underdevelopment. Some of the nations involved have been more dedicated than others. Among them, Scandinavian countries, the Netherlands, Canada, and Australia based on the share they devote to foreign aid compared to their GNPs. These countries have been giving more than the required 0.7 percent share. In general, all advanced nations have been opening ministries, departments, or governmental agencies whose sole purpose is to manage and disburse development aid grants and loans. These countries have been either directly or indirectly involved in finding and financing developmental projects.

After vacillating between protectionism inherited from mercantile practices and the adoption of free-market practices as advocated by Adam Smith in the late eighteenth century, the West finally used the depression of 1929 and World War II to see the emergence of a consensus in favor of free trade. The post–World War II period therefore signaled the change of zeitgeist in favor of international trade and the creation of supporting institutional infrastructure: the IMF, the World Bank, the International Trade Organizaiton, replaced by General Agreement on Tariff and Trade, which turned onto WTO. Other related organizations, such as the World Health Organization (WHO), the International Labor Organization (ILO), UNDP, the United Nations International Children's Emergency Fund (now United Nations Children's Fund; UNICEF), and the Food and Agriculture Organization (FAO; Easterly 2006).

In the midst of imagining the institutional infrastructure to sustain international trade, another institutional infrastructure was in the making to serve as A vehicle to facilitate the flow of resources, namely foreign aid, from economically advanced nations into developing ones. Foreign aid gradually became part of the emerging international order in the aftermath of World War II. Furthermore, one of premises of liberal economics posits that there are more advantages to trade with equally rich neighbors than poor ones. The alleviation of poverty in developing nations ultimately meant creating purchasing power and new market outlets for advanced economies.

In the United States, the idea of aid goes back to 1949, during the Truman administration. A new mind-set was emerging and with it the need to open new chapters away from colonization in favor of self-determination, away from race-based nationalism and militarism to economic cooperation, away from the indifference of rich countries to the need to sympathize with the poverty of underdeveloped nations (Easterly 2006). Both foreign aid and development economics were to become the buzzwords. The Marshall Plan (1948–1951), the aftermath of the Korean War (1952), and the dawn of the Cold War have been respectively the manifestation and the context in which this new foreign policy tool was established.

The zeitgeist in favor of development aid also has resulted, after much jockeying in the attempt to develop an accurate description and competence of the agency since 1953, in the creation, in 1961, of new, specialized development aid agencies such as the United States Agency for International Development (USAID) by the John F. Kennedy administration. The new issue area of international aid justified development economics and produced a number of scholars whose research has influenced the policy. These scholars are Walt Rostow (1990) whose five phases of economic development informed early policy formulation of USAID, Paul Rosenstein-Rodan, Gunnar Myrdal, Alexander Gerschenckron, and others.

The works of these scholars, although different in focus, came to be seen as advocating the idea of a big push, as coined by Rosentein-Rodan (1943) or the notion and need to evade the vicious cycle, in which most economies of developing nations seem to have been trapped, as the remedy for underdevelopment. This remedy often changed over time and become integrated with world trade, to advocate modernization, to implement the principles of liberal economics by using structural adjustment programs until the paradigm of globalization sealed the deal.

USAID's purpose was "to prevent the social injustice and economic chaos upon which subversion and revolt feed" (Bate 2006, para. 8). Foreign aid was congenitally linked to the issue of national security. "By blending development aid and national security interest, the USAID became a 'soft power' weapon in the cold war long before the term itself was invented". This very conceptualization of development aid explains the remoteness of the moral dimension otherwise suggested by the concept, namely that development aid is an instrument of foreign policy rather than of compassion. The proof lies in the fact that indeed talks about abolishing USAID after the Cold War were serious as the agency's purpose and institutional shortcomings were manifest. As European nations recovered from the destruction of World War II, they subscribed to the idea of aid. This became much more imperative as European colonial powers sought to safe guard influence in areas where they still had various forms of interest. They have since each created their own agencies to carry out projects defined as official development assistance.

This good intention of foreign aid was rebaptized by Easterly (2006), borrowing from Kipling, as the burden of the white man. Indeed Easterly tied to the notion of foreign aid a certain arrogance by the West, pretending to know what is good for these other nations compared to the West, an attitude wherein he saw the cause of the failure of foreign aid. Indeed, Western official development assistance has been a matter of bureaucratic formalism, which has undermined its efficiency. Western official development assistance is characterized by innumerable and not necessarily coordinated projects, conceived by the donor/lender nations, and which have produced fragmentation and therefore caused their lack of impact. The combination of the innumerable uncoordinated projects and their planning from above, without the participation of the recipient nations, was noted by Celia Dugger (2008, para.7): "American foreign aid often takes the form of modest, short-term projects that are planned in Washington and carried out by American contractors and charities".

This approach to foreign aid explains for instance the fact that the agency picked and chose its projects to favor or neglect certain sectors. A case in point is the neglect of the agriculture sector. Quoting Easterly (2006) on Western foreign aid choices, and most precisely the World Bank, Dugger (2007, para. 10) wrote, "Here's your most important client, Africa, with its most important sector, agriculture, relevant to the most important goal—people feeding their families—and the Bank has been caught with two decades of neglect". Changing times have caused the need to adapt mechanisms of trade with developing nations after the Reagan years in the United States have the privileged trade over aid, and have considered trade as a form of aid.

The Trade Development Act of 2000, which produced AGOA, sought to remedy some of the shortcomings in previous official development assistance from the United States. AGOA included provisions for free-trade agreement for certain articles from countries that: (1) make progress toward establishing a market based economy, (2) do not engage in activities that undermine U.S. security, and (3) do not grossly violate internationally recognized human rights. Despite some eligible African nations that have profited somewhat from the agreement, the major obstacle was eligibility of most protectionist measures on products for which Africa has some degree of competitiveness. In the end, the agreement has not done much to reverse the marginalization of the continent. One of the reasons for this shortcoming is the fact that products that are subject to this agreement are determined by the United States, which in turn picks and chooses them based on their potential to interfere and compete with local American products. These products, categorized as import-sensitive, now number 6,485 items that are essentially agricultural in nature and subject to a generalized system-of-preference program. The most competitive African sector, textiles and cotton, is subject to a different regime that aims to control trade with African nations. In the end, although the United States under Reagan preferred to trade rather than give aid that nation and the West in general dictated what products were allowed but also, although advocating for liberal free trade, subsidized the agricultural sector. The OECD released the figure of $349 billion in production and export subsidies to farmers in industrialized nations.

In 2003 a new agency, the Millennium Challenge Corporation, was created in an effort to reinvent U.S. foreign aid. The model and objectives fell short of addressing Africa as a full economic partner. In 2005 the Council on Foreign Relations released a task force document that urged the United States to think of Africa not in humanitarian terms and recommended a strategic shift in its approach toward Africa, as China seemed to have done.

The European Union (EU), in its previous shape, has had a long history, since 1963, of engaging both bilaterally and multilaterally with the continent of Africa and some nations of the Caribbean. Multilaterally, Europe has provided aid to Africa via preferential trade agreements, thus facilitating Africa's commodities exports. Europe offered unrestricted, nonreciprocal access to its markets as well as duty-free or dutyreductions and quantitative access for agricultural products (sugar, beef, bananas, veal, and rum). The EU had established to that effect a mechanism aimed at stabilizing export earnings (STABEX) and minerals (SYSMIN). Two Youndé accords (1963 and 1974) and four Lomé accords between 1975 and 2000 have targeted two complementary goals: facilitation of Africa's integration in the world economy and provision of development aid via trade cooperation. These acts, however, according to Khadiagala and Lyons (2001), were not altruistic. The North faced resistance from the South as the latter denounced the distribution imbalance on the grounds of unfavorable terms of trade, using the argument of dependency theory and emboldened by the successes of OPEC's dissociation from the grip of the North. The North still needed raw materials from the South and therefore was willing to make concessions.

Africa's integration into the world economy has not improved and the continent was at the verge of marginalization as a result of its shrinking share in global trade. The nature of trade between the EU and the African, Caribbean, and Pacific (ACP) nations was based on the very division of labor whose terms of trade and distribution effects did not work in favor of African nations as they continued to export primary products and import capital-intensive products. The result was that socioeconomic conditions have not improved many decades after such agreements the EU signed with ACP in search of exactly the opposite effect.

In the meantime, 60 percent of aid for Africa comes from the twenty-five member nations of the EU. Bilateral official development aid continued to flow toward sub-Saharan Africa, reaching $23.8 billion in 2003, which amounts to 34 percent of total, worldwide, official development assistance, according to OECD. Yet the success and the result of foreign aid have not been what planners have expected. Sub-Saharan Africa's social and economic welfare indicators remain alarming many decades of later.

Life expectancy averages forty-six years and roughly half of the population lives in absolute poverty, to name just two indicators.

The EU's official development assistance suffered the fate of the planners' approach, just as others so far. The planner mentality, however, has not subsided and has informed even current attempts to remedy old weaknesses of official development assistance.

The limitations of the EU's official development assistance were not to be argued away. Of course, the realization of the failure to reach the development goal has prompted new thinking in that area, examination of the reasons for the failure, and consideration of possible remedies. Regarding reasons for failure, the poverty trap (German Development Institute, 2005) was mentioned, principally by Jeffrey Sachs et al. (2004). Other reasons identified were those known since the 1980s, namely: bad governance, corruption, structural deficiencies, lack of technical and administrative capacity, endemic diseases, political instability, and so on. Possible remedies derive consequently from the above-identified causes and therefore are, according to Sachs et. al., an argument in favor of a not-so-new idea of the "big push" and advocate for massive increases in official development assistance. The pledge to use 0.7 percent of the Gross National Income (GNI) of donors' economies for official development assistance remains elusive, as the often-promised amount for foreign aid takes years to be disbursed.

Against this argument, claims have become louder that official development assistance in developing nations such as in Africa have had the effect of suffocating indigenous initiatives and the "need to mobilize national resources" (German Development Institute 2005, p. 1). James Shikwati, a Kenyan economist, argued in the German newspaper, *Frankfurter Rundschau* ("Hilfe laehmt," 1 June 2007) that foreign aid created a climate unpropitious to entrepreneurship as it shifted back to the West the need for Africans to solve African problems. Does this mean that Africa wants to be left alone? No. Does it mean that the stalling economic development of Africa is the responsibility of the West? No. This simply suggests that official development assistance, as conceived and applied by the West, has not delivered. This realization triggers introspection, and some of the possible remedies may lie, as Shikwati suggested, in a model that altogether does not rely essentially on external aid. History seems to suggest that true societal structural transformation from a traditional and agricultural economy to a modern and industrialized economy has been possible only when conceived, initiated, and carried out by concerned subjects.

Speaking of structural transformation, remedies of the 1980s in favor of trade liberalization continue to be favored by the Europeans. New remedies acknowledge the need for flexible, coordinated aid that involves recipient nations and their peoples as partners in the inception and implementation of projects in a sector-wide approach and seek sustainable development. International donors and international finance institutions were part of the debates about the failure of foreign aid and have been therefore in the forefront of framing new objectives and venues to guide and seek more efficient foreign aid.

As an institution, the European Union has been part of and concerned by the debate about the failure of official development assistance. In 2000, the European Union aligned itself with the goal of poverty reduction articulated by the UN Commission for Africa. The European Union has endured many changes since then, and the need to readjust to the new environment both in Europe and in Africa has become imperative. Institutions such as the G8 summit in July 2005 in Gleneagles, Scotland; Tony Blair's initiative for a Commission for Africa and its report in March 2005; a UN Millennium Project report by a team of experts headed by Professor Jeffrey Sachs in January 2005; a gathering of a team of 256 experts aimed at the development of a concrete action plan to achieve the millennium development goals set for 2015; the work of the seventeen members of the Commission for Africa; and others have all contributed to what has been dubbed *the year of Africa*. In the same spirit, the European Union articulated in December 2005 a new strategic partnership with Africa supported by all twenty-five heads of state and a reached a consensus on development. The European Union issued the Paris Declaration, which aimed to guide both bilateral and the collective EU body policy with regard to official development assistance. The document, which revamped the EU-ACP Cotonou agreement, tried to achieve coherence, coordination, and efficiency while recognizing the shortcomings of the EU's conception and practice of official development assistance until the present.

The European Union, which has, in the meantime, subscribed to the millennium development goals, has vowed to rectify the identified sources of the shortcomings of its aid programs. The new context of the reconfiguration of European official development assistance and stimulation deriving from increased successes of China on the continent have justified the intensification of contact between the European Union and Africa. A new EU strategy for Africa was proposed by the president of the European Commission in October 2005 and adopted in December the same year. This proposal addressed EU official development assistance challenges and aligned EU aid to the objectives of the MDGs. The European Parliament Council Commission produced a document in December 2005 titled "The European Consensus" that articulated the EU development policy (European Parliament Council Commission 2006) vis-à-vis foreign aid, with a common vision, objectives, and principles and aimed at countering some of the identified causes of its shortcomings, namely fragmentation and lack of coordination of its aid. The purpose of the policy was to allow the EU to participate effectively in the fight to eradicate poverty. The consensus followed up the concerns articulated in the Maastricht Treaty, which sought coherent coordination and complementarity of policy from the EU's member states.

In October 2006, the European Commission held its meeting in Addis Ababa to review the implementation of the EU Strategy for Africa, among other items on the agenda, as an additional sign of institutionalizing a continent-to-continent partnership and to express the European Union's commitment to Africa.

The EU-Africa Business Forum of Brussels (16–17 November 2006) and EU-Africa summit in Lisbon (8 December 2007) produced additional communiqués, papers, and resolutions that have always been good at identifying the problems and setting new goals but always seem to fall short in addressing practical, technical problems of their implementation. In the end, since the readjustment of the EU official development assistance in 2005, the forum has sought to involve regions and recipient nations in the elaboration and implementation of development projects with the purpose of achieving sustainable development. The plan seeks to avoid dispersion by focusing on key sectors such as infrastructure and agriculture and seems to resemble what China has been doing for some time now. The European Union has developed a new European strategy.

WESTERN FOREIGN AID: A MISNOMER?

There are various ways through which aid is provided: as currency or in kind as grants, as concessional or preferential loans, interest-free or low interest loans. Some of these means are commercial and based on promotion of development and others on profitability.

Proponents of each claim, to varying degrees, the moral and practical right to be called *aid*. With the addition of the political realities within which aid has been delivered, the concept became a little more complicated than it appears at face value. Furthermore, different nations have had different practices and different ways of considering, delivering, counting, and evaluating aid. All these differences have contributed to the imbroglio in the field of development aid regimes. The OECD Development Committee defined *aid* as "grants or loans that are extended to developing countries when they are undertaken by government or governmental bodies, with the promotion of economic development and welfare as their main objectives, at concessional financial terms" (Davies et al.2008).

The idea to associate the rest of the developing nations to the successful effort that has assisted the European recovery after World War II was almost self-evident given the availability of funds, the political will, and newly created institutional infrastructure through which to channel aid. These new nations, recovering from colonization, were having, *mutatis mutandis*, a similar experience to that of Europe in the sense that Europe had recovered from the destruction of war. Both needed to rebuild their economies. If Europe was to be helped by the United States, it was in part because of economic reasoning, which consisted of helping nations in trouble now to become trade partners later. Today, Europe is very much part of the global economic regime in ways that are beneficial to those who funded the restoration effort. The idea of economic assistance was thereby justified and vindicated.

What was appropriate for Europe also was appropriate for the rest of the developing world. With respect to that developing world, the success story of development aid has yet to be written. Indeed, in the case of the developing world, the intent and purpose of development aid entailed both economic and moral dimensions. So in addition to the economic viability of these new nations, which requires that we scrutinize the efficiency of foreign aid, the moral dimension requires as well that we scrutinize it on moral grounds to try to understand what went wrong.

For starters, the terminology of aid does not translate the entire reality and nature of the process. The traditional approach made many in the developing world believe in some kind of compensation, relief, or even reparation for such institutions as slavery and colonialism (Galtung 1998). In the developed nations, on the other hand, populations were still genuinely deceived by the perception that aid is truly just that—a charitable handout to help developing nations. Although some are aware of the conditional aspect that reflects more of the ideals and expectations of donor nations than those of the recipients, many more remain unaware of the many ways such aid ends up creating political leverage for the donors. As early as the 1960s, foreign aid had already been instrumentalized to serve the foreign policy objectives of donors. McKinlay and Little (2006), analyzed Western foreign aid, particularly British aid disbursed by the Ministry of Overseas Development (established in 1964) and suggested two distinct political consequences that illustrated the instrumentalization of aid: namely, that it projects the commitment of the donor to the recipient and results in dependency of the recipient on the donor. With a focus on dependency, McKinlay and Little counted four ways that aid achieves just that. First, such aid shifts the balance of domination in favor of the donor because the recipient stands to lose if the donor withdraws conssessional finance. Second, dependency is achieved as the donor buys a strong bargaining position because of the high demand for financing from nations in need. Third, the donation of aid buys access into the internal affairs of the recipient nation. Fourth, repayment problems that require rescheduling also prolong the advantageous bargaining position of the donor.

As a result, McKinlay and Little (2006) concludes that France uses its aid to maintain influence (political and economic) in former colonies, whereas the United States buys political and security leverage, and the United Kingdom remains a little ambiguous as to the final preferred outcome in terms of leverage.

The various expressions of capitalization on the created dependency have allowed and justified the criticism of neo-imperialism and neocolonialism. The late president of Burkina Faso, Thomas Sankara (Shuffield, 2006), addressing his popula-tion, pointed to whatever his people found on their plate that was imported or donated in the form of rice and other goods as expressions of imperialism. He emphasized the fact that impe-rialism was not an abstract notion but a reality that is expressed in many ways.

As a result, this foreign aid is *stricto senso* not truly aid. The ethical dimension of development or foreign aid has been solely reflected in humanitarian and charity organizations of the third, the nonprofit, sector, if we define aid as an uncondi-tional act destined to relieve pain, regardless of its nature. The nonprofits are the true donors, as opposed to lenders. This level prompted Johan Galtung (1998) to speak of development aid as the offspring of a Christian missionary mother. However, that is not the only acceptable definition. Another definition very much considers aid to be any forthcoming act toward a party in need regardless of the negotiated terms. However, regard-less of the impact of the concession made by the client, or to the potential lender, the credit still qualifies as aid if it devi-ates somewhat from the higher interest rates of the financial market. The deviance of aid terms from real market conditions becomes the criterion that justifies the definition of aid in the context of economic development aid. This simply means that aid is determined by the concession that the lender or creditor is willing to make, namely soft conditions. The lender, however, reserves the right to determine ways by which to capitalize on the investment, also known as *return*. When donors choose to abuse their moral and financial superiority status to the detriment of the borrower, which is often the case, we have a situation that disqualifies this process as aid because it results in a greater benefit to the lender. Indeed, in the case of foreign aid, lenders have succumbed to the temptation to abuse the lender-borrower relation. In many ways, as we will shortly explain, Western foreign aid has borne such results.

Such has been the case since the activity of foreign aid has blurred the differences in the two definitions above. The intense activity in the field of foreign or development aid, forty years later, has blurred the distinction between the fields of development aid, the promotion of global trade, and the promotion of donors' political interests.

This rationale therefore leads donor nations to seek some kind of benefit from taxpayer monies from respective loans to recipient nations. National governments have sought access to the recipient nations' markets, which turns their development aid into a field of promotion for their own national export industry. Client nations are contractually required to purchase and order equipment from their industry for the various projects they envision. The donors likewise seek to benefit their employment markets as they link the hiring of their own experts to loans, to the detriment of locals in the client nations. In the case of Africa there are between 40,000 and 80,000 expatriate experts whose respective salaries equal that of one hundred local laborers. Because governmental development aid has increasingly worked via projects, there has been a proliferation of projects that Franz Nuschler (1994) referred to as an epidemic called *projectitis*. On the African continent, in nations such as Botswana, Burkina Faso, Ghana, Kenya, Tanzania, Senegal, and Zambia, there are between thirty and forty development organizations with more than six hundreds projects.

With the deviation of the initial definition and purpose of aid into a tool of export enforcement, the ambivalence of the work of the development regime reaches new heights. The deviation further indicates the primacy and importance of liberal trade over aid. Governmental aid agencies have thereby started to resemble and to become miniaturized multinationals. According to *West Africa*, in 1991 (and since) 74 percent of the British bilateral development aid was linked to the purchase of goods and services from Great Britain. This practice is commonly the case in France, Canada, Germany, and other nations.

How has this transformation been achieved? Governmental aid agencies accommodate the developmental aid aspect by providing loans with soft conditions, following the International Development Association's (IDA's or World Bank's) guidelines whose funds are accessed by less developed nations with an interest rate up to 0.75 percent extended for forty years with a ten year exemption period. Other developing nations are offered loans at 2 percent interest for thirty years also with a ten-year exemption period. The liberal-trade character of these loans, as opposed to their aid dimension, is shown by the increase of the overall debt due to accumulating interest. The bottom line, therefore, is that this aid becomes, in the long run, profitable to the lender in a very complex way as it ties the lender to the borrower. The lender accomplishes that link by applying a number of provisions to their loans (e.g., World Bank, IMF).

One specific characteristic of projects that are performed in this context usually does not necessarily reflect the concept of development in client nations but that of the lender, which claims a preponderant say in the determination or choice of to whom they make their loans. Donors ask potential clients to participate in the negotiations to determine which projects will be financed. Even when they get to suggest or conceive their developmental projects and submit them to potential lenders, nations in need of funds still must obtain the approval of potential lenders. The dominant criteria are not those elaborated by client nations. Donors claim a right of veto over the recipient's choice of projects should they not agree with it or should the proposed project fail to meet their predefined criteria. This situation can lead to the withholding of funds. Donors enjoy the advantage that results from the shortage of finance in potential beneficiary nations. Few potential beneficiaries (e.g., Botswana) have had the audacity to refuse funding of projects because their own criteria have not suited the vision of the potential lenders. In development cooperation, Botswana privileges its own policies and concepts over that of potential lenders.

In some ways, these restrictions on behalf of donors have been justified by abuses of aid by local governments in client states. As a consequence of this chain of observations and given national mismanagement, aid has not been helping much. In many other cases, it failed to respond to the local historic culture and social imperatives.

As a result, the entire realm of development assistance has not been successful in effecting substantial change in the structure of economic deficiency in developing nations. The assistance has therefore accompanied that deficiency through the years, despite sporadic success here and there. Proponents of development aid have been quick to point out a few successes. They argue that aid has been responsible for doubling the per capita revenues in developing nations since the 1950s. Aid, they say, contributed to the improvement of life expectancy up to fifteen years from 1960 until 1980. Aid has increased the literacy rate from 26 percent in the poorest nations up to 60 percent in 1992 or greater in the rest of the developing nations. Average per capita revenues rose from 49 percent to 79 percent. The work of assisting developing nations has become institutionalized in developed nations. Thus, aid, like humanitarianism, conceived to be conjectural, has become structural. This process of rendering a conjectural situation into a structural one has produced the phenomenon that Nuschler (1994) called "assistantialism". From this angle assitantialism has rendered aid into a quasi permanent charity rather an agent of change.

From the perspective of developed nations, this assistantialism is explained by more than forty years of infusing money, expertise, and technical assistance without really affecting underdevelopment but at the same time providing a venue through which these nations create employment, export markets, and capital returns for their own benefit. Material-ized in projects, this development assistance has the merit of helping to resolve ad hoc a given development-related problem, in a given space, and for a limited time. The projects are run by budgets, screened for efficiency that takes into account the promotion of the donors' industries, and have neither pretext nor intent to change the overall structural causes of economic underdevelopment. After more than thirty years of devel-opment aid conceptualization (Dankwortt 1990, as cited in Nuschler 1994), most concepts still do not accurately describe its complex reality.

In the case of Africa and developing nations elsewhere, despite risks, the index of development resource output exceeds its input by a 1-to-4 margin. What here is true about develop-ment aid is equally true about investment, once we assume the risk factor. Such an index result has recently tended to increase in favor of output, an argument used by Jerry Rawlins, former president of Ghana, to incite American investment in his country.

Regarding ROI in developing nations, private investors have joined the caravan. Despite the risk involved in investing in developing nations (except Latin America with more than 5 percent), in 1997, FDI fell by 4 percent ($166 billion), during the same time that it soared by 39 percent (to $639 billion) elsewhere. Returns have been estimated at four times higher. The FDI of most aggressive oil companies in Africa, despite the risk, constitute proof. These companies do not hesitate to get involved in local political conflicts (e.g., Elf in Congo/Brazza-ville, Shell in Nigeria, mining companies for columbo-tantalite in the eastern Congo-Kinshasa conflict, diamonds in the Sierra Leone conflict) to secure their positions. They have started a new era of multinational corporation interventionism. Their presence in the most lucrative sector justifies the very criticism of the dependency theory, which says that, at the end, corporate benefit deprives locals of the ability to take advantage of their own resources, as illustrated by the dispute over the share of Chad in its oil reserves. Corporate benefit transfers to national headquarters. Development aid has been taken hostage in the context of global economy, reducing even further the prospects of achieving its purpose.

There are, in addition to international or multilateral and governmental development organizations, nongovernment organizations whose work also has a developmental vocation. They are mostly found in third sector (nonprofit) organizations. They are those we have identified as responding to the first definition of aid insofar as they do not seek return for their activities. They are those who, because of their social idealism, are to some extent financed by governments or are exempted from taxation. These organizations are instead nationally located organizations with a transnational purpose and impact. Because they belong to the field of development, their activities are directly or indirectly destined to improve the material standard of living of populations in the areas of basic needs. Basic-need categories have been established in the areas of health, to seek increased life expectancy or lower mortality rates. Nutritional goals aim to increase calorie consumption per day and to improve habitat and hygienic conditions. The fight against endemic diseases, such as cholera and malaria, and epidemic diseases, such as HIV/AIDS, are among these needs, as is the fight against illiteracy, which seeks to increase the numbers who participate in education, now becoming ever more important because of the information age. We finally have the need for clothing as matter of pure protection and decency.

Because economic development can directly improve these areas of basic needs, the whole endeavor of developmental work has been made synonymous with economic process. This has led to the equation of economic growth with development itself. Parameters of economic growth have then been used to determine the stage of development, but this is not unequivocally accurate. The complexity of the problem warrants caution; the following observations provide the reasons. The first is a proven fact that economic growth does not mean social welfare. The second is the fact that material welfare does not mean well-being (or the rise of prosperity would eradicate depressions in most prosperous nations, which in fact seems to have the opposite effect). The last observation is the distinction between material poverty and poverty of the mind. By equating development with economic growth, we simply reduce humanity to materiality.

To react to the imperfect picture often projected by the emphasis on economic parameters of projects with respect to the state of development, and to insure that the economic parameters considered translate into measurable human and social benefits, the United Nations developed and proposed what it calls an Index of Human Development in the mid-1990s. This index considers relative the importance of purely economic indicators that do not necessarily translate into human and social benefit. A growing view that directly links the notion of development to the human element has given way to an interpretive elasticity in the work of development aid. So many works of men and women can be widely interpreted as developmental. Environmentalists can rightly argue that fighting for trees is essential to life because of the oxygen they create, which will help sustain generations to come. Oxygen produced by trees preserves lives and protects humankind and therefore contributes to human development. The distribution of condoms in developing nations can be justified as developmental work given the argument that it helps protect humans from contagious diseases that weaken them to the point that they can no longer contribute productive work as members of society. Human rights activists use this argument. Indeed had it not been for the conscience arising out of the concept of rights in France before 1789, the French Revolution, instrumental for both ideal and material well-being of following generations, this development would not have taken place. These points signal the difficulty encountered when we dissociate physical human well-being from ideal well-being as they go hand in hand.

Some critics of materialism find here causes of modern emotional disequilibrium and psychological pathologies and deficiencies. The extension of the interpretive elasticity of the term *development* to its human factor has hereby its justification. The use of the adjective *material* for standard of life is designed to point out the exclusive material feature and does not give away any information as to the state of the rest of the community under consideration. Without our advocating the primacy of materialism over idealism, the emphasis of transnational developmental work, however, will be mostly of that material nature.

Conclusively, despite the overall minimal impact in the context of the globalization process, developmental aid has been established as another international regime. Other considerations help keep it on the map of international activities: on ethical grounds, the collective conscience in economically advanced nations wants to help calm down and contain the suffering in developing nations; on liberal economic grounds, one consideration stipulates that it is much more beneficial to trade with an equally wealthy partner than with a poor one. Africa has a population of 700, 000,000 million. Only 50 million are considered consumers. The rest is lost market opportunity. What is true about Africa is even more so about China, with a population of 1.3 billion. This number explains the eagerness of nations with strong export capacity to establish commercial interests in China. Another consideration consists of helping developing nations not to compromise the much larger undertaking of globalization, which is very much essential to capitalism. The need for development aid will be irrelevant if global liberalism delivers on the promise articulated in its premises of market participation and its expected gains. The parameter by which to measure such a success remains the disparity between rich and poor nations. All development aid regimes and other international trade regimes recognize the need to reduce such a disparity. The failure to remedy this situation opens the way for alternative approaches down the road, considering the fact that history is a dynamic process.

The consequence of the resulting ambiguity is of significant magnitude for the developing nations and explains why voices have been raised to criticize the entire practice of foreign aid. Galtung (1998), once again, because of that, described foreign aid as the offspring of an imperialist father.

During the Cold War, the poverty of the continent turned African nations into rent-seekers, clients, and satellites whose alliance with ideological donors was rewarded with foreign aid. The West, being more financially potent, has literally capitalized on the vulnerability of rent-seekers, allowing the West to intervene in African affairs as it deems necessary. To that effect, Easterly (2006, 8) stated:

> This poverty in the rest [nations other than the West] justifiably moves many people in the West. The Western effort deploys a variety of interventions besides foreign aid, including technical advice and lending from the international Monetary Fund and the World Bank, the spread of the knowledge of capitalism and democracy, scientific interventions to cure disease, nation-building, neo-imperialism, and military intervention.

Ergo, the terminology of aid has rather been a perfect example of political correctness that tends to beautify descriptive denominations mostly to the detriment of the empirical reality.

A History of Falling Short

Signs of shortcomings of Western foreign aid have been appearing since the 1970s. Dependency theory fairly arguably successfully provided the explanation for that reality. In 1974, a development committee was created to deal exclusively with the transfer of resources into developing nations to counter that effect. Soon, however, the work of the IMF became more and more exclusively solicited by adjustment efforts. With the 1979 creation of an adjustment loan, it deviated from its purely macroeconomic purpose to get involved in development policies. The International Finance Corporation had encouraged investment by private enterprise in high-risk nations, whereas the IDA had persevered as lender of loans without interest. Regional development banks were still dedicated to try to serve the developmental purpose of the World Bank. United Nations Industrial Development Organization (UNIDO) capitalized on the somewhat constant increase in manufacturing production in developing nations to project a goal of a 25 percent share of industrial production to be extracted in those nations. This projection counted on the decreasing rate of industrial production in advanced nations in favor of the service sector. This development in advanced nations opened the way to a transfer of industrial production to nations with cheaper labor. This goal was to reverse the ratio between commodities and manufacture production in developing nations.As far as GATT and later the WTO were concerned, they incorporated and extended the most favored nation (MFN) status to its developing nation members, a favor that certainly will lose most of its potential effects as worldwide trade barriers are reduced or maybe altogether removed. These organizations have further adopted a rule that proscribes developed nations to consecrate 0.7 percent of their GNP to promote development. These kinds of proscriptions in international organizations, however, do not represent an obligation, nor is there any sanction mechanism in place to enforce them.

Still the deterioration of social conditions in Africa kept growing throughout the 1980s and 1990s such that even the IMF and the World Bank themselves have recognized the situation.

More and more in the 1980s, debts increased, debt servicing became suffocating, and international civil society began to voice and address their criticisms toward Western nations. To some extent, this made the West responsible for deteriorating conditions in Africa through the decades. On the issue of debt alone, African nations have been caught in what Cheryl Payer (1975) called *the debt trap*. Africa's economies grew at an annual rate of 2.7 percent in the 1980s and 5 percent in the 1990s. From their budgets, African nations spend 40 percent ($13.5 billion annually) for debt servicing alone. An overall estimated $160 billion have been poured yearly into Western lending institutions for debt financing purposes. The World Bank figure of 1999 states that on average, $128 million is transferred every day from the sixty-two most impoverished countries to the wealthy. With the time it takes to repay, they need to service $13 on old debts for every dollar they borrowed in grant aid!

The logical consequence of such a flow of capital in Western capitals and international finance institutions is the drain of funds away from education, health, and other social programs in those nations. In the southern hemisphere, 1.2 billion people tried to exist on less than $2 a day in 1998, and that figure is said not to have changed since. Half of the 600 million citizens in the forty-one highly indebted, poorest countries (HIPCs; most of them located in Africa) try to get by on less than $1 per day.

The movement for debt relief has been using that argument in juxtaposing such a Westbound flow of capital with 19,000 children that die per day as a direct result. The classic and most logical argument, therefore, has equated that amount with lost opportunities, as they tie up resource allocation in developing nations. The overall picture was painted by Mark Hertsgaard (2000), who pointed out that 4 billion of the population (from indebted nations) on the planet face deprivation inconceivable to the wealthiest 1 billion.

Debts and debts servicing have been inducing the kind of adverse results in these nations they seek to remedy in the first place. It should not then come as a surprise that the antiglobalization movement uses such examples to bolster its case. The criticism of this movement has not been landing on deaf ears. The IMF, the World Bank, and the G7 have reacted by initiating debt-relief programs. These initiatives have worked out eligibility criteria, called debt sustainability, that attempt to move indebted nations out of debt. These criteria are based on export and fiscal policy. The first targeted the debt/export ratio fixed in the range of 200–250 percent. Because many of these nations had difficulties in reaching that ratio, it was lowered by the Cologne Debt Initiative in June 18, 1999, to 15 percent. The second criterion was defined by fiscal policy and applied to nations with following characteristic, according to the HIPC'[30] initiatives: an export/GDP ratio of 40 percent and tax revenue/ GDP ratio of thirty percent. This simply meant for these nations to have a debt sustainability defined by debt/government revenue ratio of 280 percent. The G7 meeting in Cologne once again lowered these figures as follows: the minimum export/ GDP ratio became 20 percent, the minimum tax revenue/GDP ratio was reduced to 15 percent, and debt sustainability was lowered to a debt/government revenue ratio of 250 percent (Morrison Oversea Development Council 1999).

At the G7 meeting in Prague in Septemeber 23, 2000 state members of the group and international lending agencies realized that the goal to forgive the debts of twenty nations by the end of 2000 was going to fall short. They agreed instead to rethink the eligibility criteria and moved to make them more flexible. They chose to grant debt forgiveness if nations just produced a less rigorous strategy to meet the requirements. Out of twenty-four applications, debt relief for ten nations was in progress, and a sum of $17.5 billion was set to be relieved to facilitate the relief of ten other nations. This forgiveness, however, did not relieve the outstanding total debt of a given nation but only a certain percentage that varied from nation to nation.

The hardship caused by debts and debt servicing was used by the debt relief movement to suggest a reverse in the question of who owes whom. Inspired by the biblical concept of writing off debt, the movement for debt relief, led by Jubilee 2000,[31] made international lender institutions and rich nations that sanction their policies responsible for making a bad situation even worse in Africa and elsewhere in developing nations. The movement gained momentum in the 1990s with the involvement of prominent musicians, religious leaders, and Nobel prize winners who argued that debts are illegitimate based on following reasons. The overall indebtedness situation was caused by the international system of commerce whose history has been sustained by international lending institutions and so-called first nations. These have loaned money to developing nations, which became indebted because the inadequacies of the system in question to provide structural and procedural benefit for less competitive nations. Instead, to sustain the overall system, both international lending agencies and first nations have subsidized debts, profited from them by charging interest,[32] and used them as instruments to impose further the functional mechanisms and conditions worldwide in structural adjustment programs (SAPs).

The debt-relief movement pointed to a variety of cases to cement its argument, including arbitrary implementation of recommended measures of liberalization and deregulation that have facilitated the exploitation of resources in developing nations with the free flow of capital, which allows among other things, the repatriation of capital, profit, and tax back into the industrialized nations that gave rise to the MNCs, making them the primary beneficiary of the international trade infrastructure.

The debt-relief movement, therefore, argues that debt has been used to force first-world capital, know-how, banks, and MNCs into developing nations. The movement's proponents further argued that these debts were contracted by dictatorial, corrupt, and plutocratic regimes that privatized the funds, leaving the rest of their population to pay for them. Nowhere in these indebted nations were populations consulted regarding a matter of such magnitude and interest to them. Yet, at the same time, they have been asked to pay. These populations have suffered on both ends, as they were asked to pay back debts and interest that they did not contract but in fact had imposed upon them, on one hand, and suffered the consequence of conditions attached to those very debts and their servicing, on the other hand.

Recommended measures of international lending institutions, the debt servicing, and these corrupt regimes have deprived the populations of necessary resources to devote to fundamental needs such as adequate housing, education, access to medicine and clean water, basic health care, and nourishment. The debt-relief movement has, therefore, further argued that the atrocious consequences of the intrusiveness of measures applied by international lender institutions in these client nations focus on management of debt rather than the alleviation of the human suffering it caused. Indeed, most of the activity of the Western development aid regime, which combines bilateral and multilateral (the work of the World Bank, the IMF, and other Western lender organizations), has been in recent decades almost exclusively predicated on debt management, SAPs, and their unbearable costs.

The criticisms of the international civil society in addressing both the inefficiency of the Western development regime and mismanagement by megalomaniacal, corrupt African regimes, as well as the deteriorating social conditions on the continent, were loud enough to prompt donor nations and institutions to react. Western metropolises have articulated a vision of necessary reforms to counter the criticism of inefficiency and have attempted to undercut the repercussions of the debt crisis. The World Bank and IMF report of 1989, known as the Berg Report, addressed techniques for acceleration of the development process in Africa and, for the first time linked the need for political reform to economic liberalization.

The concept of good governance became part of the new conditionalities applied to their client states. In the early 1990s, governments, using bilateral aid and loans, and international financial institutions, using multilateral aid and loans, coupled their services to political transparency.

Three events indicate such a process: First was the conference of June 1990 at La Baule in France, where heads of francophone states met for their regular meeting with French President François Mitterrand, who expressed the wish to see as much political openness as possible, showing some regard to what he called the particular nature of African politics to access French bilateral aid. This conditionality did not specifically ask for political democratization as such. Instead, it created an atmosphere wherein true democratization would soon become a requirement.

Second, in October of 1991, there was a meeting of states of the Commonwealth in Harare/Zimbabwe, during which the same issue of political reform dominated the agenda.

Third, the European Community organized a meeting of member nations in November 1991, during which a charter was signed that linked community aid and other loans to willingness on behalf of the client state to apply democratic principles. This principle envisioned the recognition of human rights, independence of the press and the justice system, the fight against corruption and embezzlement, and so on.

The most significant reaction however had started a few years earlier. It was the Washington Consensus (Williamson 1989). This consensus was about targeting the true causes of stalling economic growth in developing nations and chronicling their balance-of-payment deficits, mounting debts, and consequent poverty, which were perceived to be of structural nature. The answer given by the Western economies (including Japan), was that the malaise was caused by lack of sufficient participation in trade. Trade was then to be promoted instead of aid. To do so, the structural fundamentals of developing economies were to change and agree with liberal economic principles. These economies had to be helped to rid themselves of elements of subsistence economy, dual economy, Keynesianism, and even statist economies. They were to liberalize, deregulate, and harmonize their economic practices with those of free-market economies.

Deregulation, liberalization, and harmonization have now become the norms. They were recommended and applied in developing nations on a one-size-fits-all basis. In the process, these developing nations lost some prerogative in their self-governance, rendering the West and international finance institutions coresponsible for their economic fates. Liberalization, a pillar of the SAP, encourages the opening of banking systems, which has allowed the infiltration of foreign capital and the influence of foreign banks and other financial institutions to play a role in the internal conduct of economic practices of a participant nation. The SAP has recommended liberalization of the employment market (which simply means less labor protection, less social protection cost, minimum wage), and monetary devaluation, which in turn has induced price hikes even while the purchasing power of local populations has remained the same or even diminished. The SAP has further encouraged investment, privatization of the state-owned industries, austerity in fiscal policies, and reduction of public expenditures. The SAP also was intended to dismantle trade barriers and reduce tariffs to encourage inflows of foreign commerce, which has exposed domestically produced goods to competition from goods produced cheaply abroad, and the infiltration of foreign MNCs, imperiling local industries that depend on import goods. Trade, like any economic calculation, is essentially rational.

Although the premise of liberal classic economics promises some kind of distributive payoff to all market participants based on their absolute or comparative advantage, it also produces casualties. This is the natural consequence of competition, which also is an inherent reality and an essential principle of liberal economics. The orthodoxy of liberal economics as practiced since the 1980s has not taken into account the needs of infant economies, which are more vulnerable and sensitive to trade interdependence incurred as a side effect of liberalization measures. Vulnerability suggests the incapacity of some nations to resist or counter any overwhelming negative effect of open trade with more powerful and more competitive trade partners on their own. Sensitivity refers to the inability to correct, block, or influence international decisions even though their application may have devastating effects on a given African country's economy.

The case of dumping is one expression of vulnerability and sensitivity issues. Some in the West (e.g., European Union and Canada) have used market liberalization to dump their agricultural products in the African markets. Subsidized products were poured into the markets of western African nations (e.g., milk and tomatoes in Senegal, cereals in Kenya, and beef from South Africa in Namibia), depriving local farmers in these countries of the ability to compete. Then, in the early 1990s, local tomatoes cost circa 900 Franc Communauté Financière Africaine (FCFA) per kilo. Tomatoes form the European Union, especially from southern Europe, held at about 550 FCFA.

This dumping constitutes an invasion against which local producers cannot protect themselves. It occurs to the detriment of the local economic infrastructure and activity in Africa. Small and infant processing industries are jeopardized as cheap manufactured goods are dumped into local markets. This has the effect of discouraging local entrepreneurs and investment, which contributes to the erosion of the employment market. Speaking of economic sensitivity, the lack of political power and the weakness of the economic competitiveness of African nations have put them in a position, internationally, such that their influence is minimal in determining the fate and conditions of international trade. Jeff Atkinson (1994) illustrated such a weakness with the case of coffee. Raw, the coffee was sanctioned by a tariff rate of 9 percent; processed, it rated 18 percent. For raw tropical fruits the tariff was 8 percent, but processed they were exported with a tariff rate of 24 percent in

Europe in 1989. Atkinson pointed out that due to liberalization measures and the unitary tariff in the new Europe, the privilege of African nations as determined by the Lomé agreement to export in Europe was losing its advantages.

Furthermore, liberalization measures in the banking system, financial markets, and free circulation of capital are applied based on the argument that they encourage FDI, which is assumed to bring about advantages as a result of the spillover effect. Questions, however, remain as to the sustainability of such advantages as profit is repatriated, technology and know-how are not transferred, and MNCs neglect to invest in the training of local labor for managerial positions.

The 1997 research of Ousmane Badiane, 1999 of the International Food Policy Research Institute in Washington, DC, on the sustainability of foreign firms in Africa found that foreign firms in Africa have no training programs. They leave when resources have been exploited, many times leaving behind environmental conditions that sicken the local population, as in the Niger Delta in Nigeria, and thereby forcing host nations to clean up behind them.

The World Bank report of 1997 stated, "Reducing trade barriers means that consumers can buy from the efficient source and producers can reorient production toward items in which they have a comparative advantage" (p. 291). This implied liberalization of trade. Such liberalization implicates not only production and corporations that may relocate or implant themselves elsewhere to take advantage of economies of scale and scope, but also the means of production, such as finance, which could circulate. These measures have allowed banks, next to corporations, to be the true beneficiaries of such a new development. Their operationalization was enabled by international regimes whose work aims at harmonizing monetary policies (e.g., IMF), obtaining desired balance of payments (e.g., World Bank), and reducing tariffs and trade hurdles (e.g., GATT in 1995, replaced by the WTO).

Deregulation, as part of the overall package of SAP recommendations, consists of encouraging governments to resist market regulation or loosen the grip on their respective trade, custom, tariff, labor, fiscal laws, monetary policy, commodity and service prices, and so on, in exchange for the promise of a payoff from participation in an unrestricted market system. African nations have since deregulated. In many areas of trade, such as in the agricultural sector and in the case of cotton most particularly, African nations have been victim of protectionist measures by nations that have pushed deregulations on them.

The last pillar of the SAP recommendations and a necessary condition for the globalization process is harmonization. Because international trade transactions occur between partners from different countries, with different internal market, political, and monetary policies and diverse and various practices and laws, there is a need to harmonize the rules of the game. *Harmonization* means "getting nations to play by the same rules and not to interfere with free commerce" (Greider 1997, 35). Harmonization has further sought to achieve just global competition and to contain reactionary measures by individual states. This goal has been achieved with the help of various international regimes, which prescribe rules, norms, and procedures to be observed and respected by state members.

The shift in favor of these pillars of liberal economics occurred as the brand of economic teaching of economists such as Friedrich Hayek (1943) and Milton Friedman (1957), in better alignment with conservative ideology, were preferred over the brand advocated John Maynard Keynes (1936) who favored state interventionism in key political-economic issues such as inflation, employment, and price stabilization. Indeed, the brand of economics advocated by Friedman targeted specific changes in macroeconomic policy, encouraged export-led growth, sought reduction of the role of the state in economy, and public sector reform to reduce subsidies.

Export-led growth also means a shift in focus away from aid, which is a form of state interventionism, toward trade, which in turn implied liberalization and deregulation. The result was the transformation of what had been until then a development aid regime into a trade regime. The nominally ethical dimension implied in the notion of aid, wherein rich countries feel the obligation to help poor ones, has been very much overridden by advocates of the new mercantilist approach we have called neoliberalism. Advocates of this approach have succeeded in the transformation of the essence of economic development assistance into an export field.

As a matter of fact, the failure of the SAP to spur equilibrium in balance-of-payment deficits and overall economic growth and to improve social standards of living was documented by the fact that two-thirds of nations where these principles were applied in the 1990s have quit the program. In 1989 Adebayo Adedeji in collaboration with the UN Economic Commission for Africa detailed an alternative SAP intended to spur transformation and economic recovery to revise and remedy some of the negative side effects of SAPs.[33] The alternative program proposed by Africa, which did not reject the initial program but rather supplemented it, as Robert Browne (1996) rightly pointed out, expressed the proposition according to which African the development strategy should be inward-oriented, concentrated, and based on regional trade. Such a strategy should promote collective self-reliance. International financial institutions, however, have always looked unfavorably on all propositions that deviate somewhat from the liberal economic orthodoxy. To document this attitude, Browne pointed to the Lagos Plan of Action for the Economic Development of Africa (OAU 1980), which, according to him, had been subject to sabotage by the World Bank since it had recommended self-reliance instead of trade liberalization as economic strategy. The World Bank published its own report titled "Accelerated Development in Sub-Saharan Africa," known as the Berg Report, which promoted an export-led development strategy. Africans have resisted the tendency of the World Bank to publish apologetic reports about its work on the continent. The report titled "Sub-Saharan Africa from Crisis to Sustainable Growth" is one of them, whose publication (Browne 1996) was delayed for about eight months for that very reason.

By then the amalgamation of developmental regime, trade regime, and foreign policy became reality. The basic principle, however, on which ground the creation of an institutionalized canalization of development aid is founded, differs from the basic principles of liberal trade institutions or regimes. Whereas aid is driven by compassion, trade is driven by profit. The entire development aid regime was subjected to a dichotomy, that is, the navigation between profit and compassion. Conciliation of these two motivational impulses constitutes the source of ambivalence of the development aid regime. Indeed the consensus established in the wake of discriminatory trade practices and favoritism, which induced the climate of World War I and the recession in 1929 in favor of free trade, made liberalism, and therefore trade, the credo by which post–World War II institutions have lived. The concept and regime of aid, once established, coexisted with free trade as a secondary entity. This was the context in which the work of the development regime was to be executed. Within such a context, donors, creditors, and lending institutions operated, as they disbursed their loans, enforcing demand and the requirement of the international finance institutions (i.e., World Bank and the IMF) in a way that made them part of free-trade advocacy and became an additional tools through which the imperatives of the free market supplanted those of aid.

In the meantime, neither structural adjustment measures nor integration into the global trade arena has been particularly favorable to the indebted countries. Developing nations have found themselves struggling to finance debts, restructure their economies to meet the standards of liberalism, and face the effects of the new dynamics of the global market caused by the process of globalization. The effect of that dichotomy was integration of the world economy that produces wealth and disparity on one hand and a foreign aid regime that fights the same disparity. The United Nations statistics of 1990 indicated that the same disparity has grown by 15 percent since the 1960s.

As the industrialized nations advocated and in fact imposed the principles of liberal economics, emphasizing export-led growth, they were at the same time protecting their markets from the competitiveness of African commodities from the agriculture sector in which African economies are competitive and wherein most African economic activity is generated. Indeed,

> Agriculture provides two thirds of Africa's employment, half of its export and over one third of its gross

> national income. But in spite of their free-market
> rhetoric, most western countries provide very sub-
> stantial subsidies for their agriculture sectors. (Wild
> and Mepham 2008, 70).

In the end, it seems that the coexistence of the two principles—aid and profit—has allowed a process in which one band-
ages the casualties incurred by the other. In many instances,
the casualties have grown too large for the bandage to fit and
therefore effect of the bandage has been marginalized.

The rather simple concept of aid to developing nations has
been revealed to be complex enough to explain the effort we
have seen in that field. To sort out and elucidate that complexity, new theories, models, and approaches have been suggested
and even tried. The concept of development will prove to be
even more complex as these theories, models, and approaches
fail, one after the other, to deliver on their promises. Among
these approaches and models are formalism and legalism, which
emphasized the role of the constitution and laws as well as formal
procedures in the conduct of modern state affairs that ultimately
would lead to better management of resources. Others followed,
among them the classic and neoclassic: dualism, imperialism,
and structuralism. Among the theories, we have modernization
(imbedded in the classic and neoclassic paradigms), dependency
theory (imbedded in structuralism), imperiaslism (imbedded in
Marxism), and indigenous theories of development (inspired
by the paradigm of dualism). In the same breath, slogans such
as: dissociate from world trade, trade not aid, self-reliance, and
finally sustainable development and social development have
followed and succeeded one another. They each possess an
appeal that helps revive the debate over development aid.

Each of these concepts and theories, though fraught with
positive intentions, has yet to yield results in resolving complex
problems. Developing a nation is a complex endeavor that
requires formulation of goals and the coordination of inputs
from all elements of a social fabric in a realistic setting using
actual resources at hand and at the same time dealing with
external interference. The many pragmatic elements required
by development efforts have been the source of difficulties for

many theories. It is simply difficult to determine all relevant elements, their values and significance, their possible impact on each other and overall, and formulate a theory that accommodates all of them. The most evasive element certainly is the cultural element, as it is economically not quantifiable despite attempts made to do so. The empirical and casuistic model is recommended. Newly industrialized nations are the best sources of empirical models as general theories have proven inappropriate to specific conditions.

The limited success of theories and concepts has warranted caution for new ones to come. We have used Easterly's (2006) terminology of planner versus searcher approaches, and the latter seem more adequate as they factor in realities. However, all new approaches must take into account the new context of globalization and be designed under the premise of worldwide free-market activity in a generalized liberal mode, at least for now. This new global regime that must be considered in individual development approaches has been forged by global adoption of liberal economic principles by nations, cemented by international trade institutions, and facilitated by new technology. Unlike or more than the two previous industrial and economic revolutions (industrial in the eighteenth century and the wave of inventions in the nineteenth), the benefit of information technology (IT), considered the third revolution, has far greater consequences. IT has potential and it is making good on it in terms of reaching most people (quantity), in little time (speed), and in the same way (quality) all over the globe (space). The paradigm of globalization proposes a complex machine of liberal institutionalism to navigate through the sea of underdevelopment. As far as developing nations are concerned, it has yet to bear fruit.

ENTRENCHED STRUCTURAL WEAKNESSES OF WESTERN AID

Economic underdevelopment was at the beginning of the need for financial capital infusion in developing nations as a result of the big push call by Rosenstein-Rodan (1943). In international trade, the division of labor left Africa in the role of raw material exporter. Africa's export products, with no value added, have not allowed the continent to accumulate and form capital for the reasons advanced by Gunnar Myrdal (1957) and the dependency school. Trade as practiced with Africa today has not allowed African economies to achieve structural transformation from essentially agricultural into manufacturing economies. That has perpetuated Africa's vulnerable position. Therefore, whatever economic goals Africa cannot achieve by itself, it seeks in foreign aid. Foreign aid, however, in and of itself, cannot develop Africa. That aid has been pouring into Africa since the 1960s.

Five decades later, massive poverty and economic under-development are still not eradicated. Furthermore, suffocating debts have added to the list of African hardships, and the difficulties of debt servicing, decreasing per capita income, sustained dependency on foreign aid, and other forms of assistance (e.g., FDI, handouts to the third sector, and the various activities of nongovernmental organizations—NGOs) seem to have become established as features of the African economic landscape. Moreover, African economies have not accomplished a structural transformation from being predominantly agricultural into concentrated activity in the manufacturing sector. In fact, even the agricultural sector has experienced diminishing returns throughout the years, turning Africa into an importer of food. Overall, African economies have stagnated at best despite positive economic growth rates registered since the 1990s. The idea of foreign aid, if not a failure, has shown its limits.

A decade after the big-push call, as early as the late 1960s, the dependency school brought forth an analysis intended to explain why such a failure was to be expected. The limit of the big push was further manifestly exposed in the constant balance-of-payments deficit in the developing nations. Decade after decade, mounting debt and the lingering insolvency of many in the developing nations continued.

As a consequence, the situation cried out for new remedies. The paroxysm of debts was reached in the form of Mexico's insolvency in the early 1980s. It represented a tipping point that coincided with the coming to power of conservative governments in both the United States and Great Britain. As these governments saw that the causes of economic hardship in developing nations were rooted in their interventionist economic policy and antiliberal economic features, they proposed a U-turn away from the big push and its conception of development aid and foreign aid in favor of trade. The push for trade liberalization replaced the big push. We have mentioned the terms of the Washington Consensus, which instrumentalizes the same institutions through which the capital was infused into developing economies by way of loans to induce the very terms of the Washington Consensus and its credo of economic liberalism.

Almost three decades later, after pushing aside state economic interventionism by implementing SAPs, and after elevating the free-market mechanism to be the sole regulator of all things related to prosperity, not much has fundamentally changed for the better in Africa. In African economies, 70-80 percent of the total population is supported by agriculture. Low productivity, which started diminishing almost as soon as most African countries became independent by 1965, since the 1980s, has turned the continent into a food importer. In 2000, food constituted fifteen percent of the continent's total imports, as its food production has not kept up with the population growth rate of 2.9 percent. Forty-five percent of the FAO budget is invested in Africa.

SAPs have not, before China's investment, changed the dynamics of FDI in favor of Africa. With respect to poverty, 44 percent of Africans live on $39 per capita per month. Fifty-one percent of Africa lives below the poverty line according to UNDP (2000) official figures. These figures have not improved but in many instances have worsened, as demonstrated by life expectancy figures. The UNDP Human Development Indicia ranking of 2003 indicates that the lowest performers are African nations. Most HIPCs are still located in Africa, where on top of debt, debt servicing continues to suck in almost 40 percent of the budgets of African countries.

Both Keynesianism, since the 1950s, and the application of Milton Friedman's economics, since the 1980s, have not significantly altered the fundamentals of African economies and in the process the fate of Africans for the better.

Most intriguing, however, is the fact that regions and nations that have not been consumed by the application of policy remedies suggested by the West and their institutions have been the ones where economic development has occurred. Indeed, nations of Southeast Asia, where the state was instrumental in the conception and implementation of development plans designed to achieve economic structural transformational and thereby induce economic development through industrialization, have little to do with remedies from the West (Easterly 2006). Other newly emerging markets have been successfully transforming their economies by using internally induced reform tools and reacting to the current imperatives of globalization.

The precarious economic conditions in Africa, despite faithful application of the principles of economic liberalism, point to the fact that free markets react to the laws of demand, stability, legal rights, property, prospects for high return margins, and so on. When and where these conditions are not met, economic liberalism produces casualties. Africa is, in many instances, a casualty of economic liberalism that has been applied with legalistic rigor. The African situation prompted Tony Blair to commission a "Report for Africa" (March 2005) and to advocate on behalf of Africa at the G8 summit in Scotland (July 2005). With his then chancellor and subsequent British Prime Minister Gordon Brown, Blair called for a second big push to alleviate the intolerable conditions of poverty in Africa. Others in Great Britain, such as Bono and Bob Geldof, have become emblematic figures of the planner mind-set, albeit with good intentions.

Persistent economic hardship in Africa, after five decades of foreign aid and $2.3 trillion spent, begs a much bigger question, namely, why has so little has been achieved?

In an attempt to answer the question, Easterly (2006, 4) started by presenting the following realization:

> This is the tragedy in which the West spent $2.3 trillion on foreign aid over the last five decades and still had not managed to get twelve-cent medicines to children to prevent half of all malaria death. The West spent $2.3 trillion and still had not managed to get four-dollar bed nets to poor families. The

West spent $2.3 trillion and still had not managed to get three dollars to each new mother to prevent five million child deaths. The West spent $2.3 trillion, and Amaretch is still carrying firewood and not going to school. It's a tragedy that so much well-meaning compassion did not bring these results for needy people.

His answer boiled down to two concepts: planners and searchers. His argument was that the Western inception of foreign aid comes from a mind-set of those who think of themselves as experts who are full of good intentions who design plans and models in a technical manner, despite the complexity of the undertaking. They put less emphasis on implementation because they are not accountable, being from the outside, for complexity and effectiveness as are business experts. He differentiated these planners from business experts. Searchers seek definable and concrete projects with piecemeal progress. At the end, concluded Easterly, they achieve more because they base their calculations and goals on concrete realities, demands, and expectations rather concocting social engineering plans, such as ending poverty! Poverty cannot be eradicated by a plan.

The intrusiveness of planners in Africa allows us to induce that whatever successes foreign aid has achieved will have to be claimed by the West, and whatever shortcomings and whatever else went wrong on the continent in that respect will have to be addressed by a revised concept of foreign aid and what exactly should be done about it.

There have been attempts to explain the fact that development economics and foreign aid have not produced the expected result. The vicious cycle, the debt trap, international factors of dependency, the monoproduct-based export economies of the developing nations, the deterioration of terms of trade, and so on have been some of the explanations. With their focus on economic factors, these explanations leave behind some of the internally induced causes of enduring economic underdevelopment in the developing nations, namely, political instability and civil war; mismanagement and lack of legal, institutional, and physical infrastructure.

Sources of additional explanations are multiple. They seem to be adjacent to the very idea of foreign aid and are therefore structural in nature. We have mentioned the notion of the white man's burden evoked by Easterly (2006) in suggesting an attitude by the West to take it upon themselves to decide what is good for the developing nations, an attitude that has shown its limits in that the empirical complexity of issues faced by the developing world do not always fit the conceptual mold that the planners dreamed out in the offices of institutions whose purpose is just that. The result is a patronizing attitude that reminds Africans of the Belgian paternalist colonial policy, which relegated Africans to functions that enabled them just to follow through with whatever they were told. With a yearly shortage of cash of $64 billion, African nations are in constant need of resources, aid, and assistance that has allowed them to take up such a role in the international division of labor in international foreign aid regimes. This vulnerable position is paralyzing.

Political realism explains substantially the reason for such a subordination vis-à- vis those with the capacity to affect the fate of Africans, but African governments have long resented the situation. As they had nowhere to turn, many went along, and now that they are here and there are other possibilities to cut loose from the leech of international finance institutions, some African nations have been voicing the frustrations they long kept inside.

One cause of such frustration was conditionalities imposed as an integral part of the decision-making process for loans from the West and their institutions. These conditionalities have been applied without exception in a one-size-fits-all mentality, which as been referred to as the orthodoxy of the IMF and the World Bank (George and Sabelli 1994), or *imperiale Liberasierung* (i.e., imperial liberalism) by Alvater and Mahnkopf (2007). This has been a structurally embedded cause of weakness as these conditionalities were not driven by the true needs and wishes of local governments though they seem to be the most pressing of their needs. Addressing just that, a Congolese member of the National Assembly and former presidential spokesman Barnabe Kikaya bin Karubi was quoted in *The Economist* (15–21 March

2008, 14) as saying, "If we say to the Europeans that we want a highway, they say 'hold an election first' sort out your finances, crack down on corruption, and in the end the highway never gets built." This is a typical example of planner action, as contrasted with the searcher approach in the vocabulary of Easterly (2006).

Both the patronizing programs dreamed up by planners of the IMF and their externally induced origins bring about the issue of identification and adhesion on the African side. African governments have been led, despite consultation meetings typically pointed to by the IMF, to suggest a harmonious agreement, to sign and agree with its stipulations without substantive accommodation of African inputs and objections. The resulting implementation of these programs therefore is a product of coerced accord. In other words, how many African governments would have signed up for the IMF program voluntarily without the threat of not accessing any funds from any legitimate donors in the West? The anticipation of a positive answer to that question begs another one, namely about the commitment by Africans to IMF programs. The consequence must certainly be a passive or lukewarm identification, which may explain the sense of detachment from IMF programs observed by many. Under such a state of detachment, compliance by African governments with IMF requirements can therefore only be justified by fear of consequences, not necessarily by the conviction of the potency of the remedy they claim, at least with respect to current realities.

A bigger problem caused by such detachment in general is an overall distancing by Africans from the idea of development implemented by the West because they do not recognize that it was a product of a process whose steps cannot be artificially implanted. An attempt to apply social engineering and induce economic development has been by all accounts part of the cause of the limits of development economics. This attempt has discarded key realities of the continent. Observation of this detachment led Axelle Kabou (1991) to wonder whether Africans did not want to develop!

The shift of emphasis from aid to trade has constituted as well another structural element in Western aid regime. In the aftermath of the Washington Consensus, which the alignment of Western donors, creditors under the tutelage and guidelines of the IFM have created a triangulation between creditors, international institutions, and bilateral foreign aid that has further restricted the diversity and chances of the aid regime.

This new element has not necessarily as of yet changed the course of African economies and has in many instances contributed, in SAPs in the 1980s, to further degradation of social conditions in health care, education access, and employment in the public sector as a result of reduction in allocations and expenditure as recommended by the IMF. Such deterioration is cause for additional foreign aid. Two decades at least went by during which Africa suffered the consequence of the IMF orthodoxy and exposed the limits of its approach. Indeed the triangulation between Western donors and creditors, the IMF, and bilateral foreign aid attempted to bridge two principles: on one hand that of aid based on compassion and on the other hand that of trade based on profit. The bridging of these principles has produced at best an ambiguous result in the case of Africa.

The point we are making here is that despite the capacity of the free market to generate prosperity as it has historically demonstrated, some ill-prepared market participants are naturally casualties of its competitive nature. The question is, do the prospects of a comparative advantage suffice to brush off the need to protect infant economies from competing in the same league as advanced economies?

Of course, many other factors come into play with respect to Africa's participation in the global free market, but it is a fact that the continent has been increasingly marginalized despite the effort to comply with liberalization measures.

What went wrong with the liberalization measures of SAPs is that they aimed primarily to bring about free-market practices with the hope of inducing prosperity by indirectly fighting poverty, hunger, and disease. The whole trickle-down economics comes to mind, and the case of the United States in the Reagan years provides the empirical shortcomings of this approach.

Another element of entrenched structural weakness of Western foreign aid and investment—given that these two areas are in many ways linked, which makes foreign investment part of the quest for economic development and therefore aid—is the expectation for high return and dividends from investors and shareholders, in contrast to Chinese investment and/or aid channeled through a package mode that involves the state. The Chinese operate based on that expectation and not, for instance, on the wish or preference of a host country to see investment channeled into a particular sector that corresponds with its most pressing needs. This explains why physical infrastructure-building, a cornerstone of development as it allows transportation, communication, and circulation of people and goods (a domain in the development process with which China has experience) is still a huge problem on the continent. This structural weakness is been currently addressed by China as we have explored.

Western FDI shies away from projects that do not promise such return. They shy away from politically sensitive regions. They are subject to political decisions in their countries of origin. In the West, this means that whatever political conditionality has been applied to an African country that seeks access to international Western finance is ipso facto a factor with which Western investors have to reckon. When Libya was under the U.S. embargo, U.S. companies were not allowed to do business in the country. Now things have changed, after the courntyr's leader Kadhafi renounced his support for terrorism but they have changed further since his death. .

Sudan is currently under Western embargo and both European and American companies have abstained from the lucrative oil market in that country. Why is this fact an element of the entrenched structural weakness of Western foreign aid? The reason is that it ties both foreign aid and investment to political desiderata of the Western donors, making the economic need of the potential recipient country in Africa subservient to that of the donor.

In the end, the entrenched structural weakness of Western foreign aid has many sources. It has aligned bilateral and multinational bodies of creditors and international finance institutions to a set of principles and has created an intricate network of increasingly complex mechanisms around foreign aid that has contributed to a burdensome regime of aid. As a case in point, we highlight the mechanism designed to address the suffocating effects of debt servicing and the potential eligibility for relief to those African nations that by all economic parameters have fallen too far behind to be viably made accountable and referred to as Highly Indebted Poorest Countries. The program has produced an elaborately intricate and complex mechanism of qualification whereby candidates must pass the decision point after formulating a convincing strategic plan and eventually must reach the completion point after successful performance on key social and structural reforms. This process became in and of itself too burdensome for indebted countries enact.

In the end, foreign aid regimes of loans, debts, and conditionalities designed to bring about economic structures of economic liberalism creates a context wherein developing nations, including those in Africa, have struggled to acquire loans, finance debt, restructure their economies, and face the effects of the dynamics of globalization while having fewer and fewer tools at their disposal to control the process.

THE LIMITS OF THE CHINESE APPROACH

Like any other approach, the Chinese approach to foreign aid, which it couples in a holistic way with trade and investment aimed at inducing economic and social development has its limits. These limits have three origins. The first is the potential of a principal-multiple agent dilemma as described by Reilly and Wu (2007) and alluded to earlier. It is the potential problem of the principal-agents dilemma. With multiple oversight levels, as those we established in Chapter 6 on Chinese enterprises --namely different bureaucratic, political, diplomatic, business interests, and objectives on one side and on the other multiple agents such as the national, provincial, city, and private owners-interests may eventually conflict and collide and potentially undermine the Chinese approach. Reilly and Wu stated, "The combination of multiple oversight bureaucracies, competing companies, and their conflicting interests suggest that Chinese firms are likely to act in ways that undermine the diplomatic objectives of the aid program" (p. 15).

The second limit is areas of similarities with the Western approach. Reilly and Wu (2007) mentioned the fact that Chinese aid, like Western aid, seeks diplomatic and strategic payoffs. Like Western aid, Chinese aid is used to secure access to needed natural resources in Africa. The Chinese use foreign aid to affect the Chinese employment market in China by providing labor for Chinese workers on the African continent as it secures contracts with Chinese firms. The $5 billion made available by the China-Africa Development Fund has tied access to the fund to the purchase of Chinese goods and services, in the same manner as the West.

These similarities beg the question of legitimate expected payoff and that of the potential abuse of the vulnerable position of the borrowing nation by the lender nation. Some degree of payoff is legitimate, as borrowers find themselves in a moral predicament of feeling obligated to return the favor to the lender if the loan has been offered with some degree of facilitation. The quid pro quo becomes questionable if the intent of the lender to lend becomes driven predominantly by the leverage acquired by it or if the expected value of the payoff exceeds the value of the loan. Because we cannot balance the pay off on a tally sheet because of involved elements or interest, such a strategic access cannot be quantified and the balancing must occur in a process of evaluation. Such a process must determine the cost and benefit of involvement in these foreign aid schemes. It should be a process like those conducted by any nation to determine the need to join an international regime, for instance, where its expected payoff must be balanced against the cost of participation in the regime. A pragmatic decision-making process is required as individual nations have particular and multiple interests with different degrees of urgency. These interests must be prioritized and there is, as a result, a hierarchy of preference as to which interests are more valuable to individual states. The decision therefore is individual.

In that sense, some nations have had the courage to reject foreign aid schemes when their conditional terms or quid pro quo undermined some their more valuable interests. In the case of Africa, Botswana in the 1980s and 1990s earned the reputation of independence vis-à-vis such schemes as they were deemed too intrusive and restrictive. Will China avoid maneuvering African nations into such a position or will China manage to steer away from taking advantage of its influential capacity, as has traditionally been the case in international relations? This is the question for which even the Chinese approach will have to account.

The danger of succumbing to the desire to exercise one's power is real. Large and De Oliveira (2008, 158) suggested that Chinese foreign aid "replicates in key ways developed state policies of disadvantageous terms of trade, exploitation of natural resources, oppressive labor regimes and support for authoritarian rulers." Should China succumb to the need to exercise power or provide foreign aid in Western manner, we can expect China's foreign aid to meet the fate of Western foreign aid.

The third origin of the limits to this approach is that China's foreign aid, because it was conceived holistically, tends to focus on countries whose resources are of significant interested to China. The consequence is a concentration of investment, trade, and aid in resource-rich countries. Large and De Oliveira (2008, 158) stated, "China is contributing to an intensification of predominantly extractive economic activity reinforcing the existing unequal geographical distribution based on variable resource endowment." The result, according to Large, is that more than 50 percent of African exports to China come from oil and 85 percent come from five oil and mineral exporting countries.

This concern, however, may not last as China continues to diversify its interests and is practically present in some form or another in every African nation, including those that can offer few mineral and energy resources, such as Rwanda, Burkina Faso, Niger, and so on.

Despite these real or potential limits, the Chinese foreign aid approach may yield results primarily because it operates essentially from a searchers' rather than a planners' perspective, to use Easterly's (2006) terminology. Chinese aid therefore stands a better chance to bring about useful piecemeal changes that have a greater impact to population than the Western planners' approach.

Chapter 9

The Use of Soft Power

Ever since the concept of soft power was pioneered by Joseph Nye (2006), it has resonated as a novelty but more so because the context of international politics has created room for a new analysis beyond the use of hard power. Indeed, the stick (military might), and the carrot (financial incentives) have both shown their limitations as issues of international concern became increasingly complex. The war in Iraq revived the need to question the morality, legality, and effectiveness of sheer use of military might as the United States warned it would do with the use of a military approach called *shock and awe*. This decisive and massive use of power by way of heavy airborne bombardments was the new blitzkrieg of twenty-first century warfare as adopted by a number of military strategists at the Pentagon. Former joint chief of military staff Colin Powell has been its advocate and possibly its most prominent proponent. The sense of triumphalism prevailed since the collapse of the Soviet Union. Hard-liners, called neoconservatives in the Bush administration,got their way. This was the case and the context until the aftermath of the demise of Saddam Hussein from the reins of power in Baghdad. Then, troubles started and soon allusions and then comparisons to the Vietnam War started. The possibility of a civil war in Iraq loomed large. The United States was reminded of the many ways to lose a war after winning battles. The possibility of a new Vietnam was real and with it the reminder that military might is not always the answer. Indeed, if the need to uproot terrorism was the underlying motivation for such an incursion in Iraq, the events on the ground indicated the opposite result and effect. Under these circumstances, voices suggesting change of policy and alternative use of power have been increasingly heard. The concept of soft power, it seemed just an alternative as good as any other to suggest at this point.

Ever since, the concept was part of the discourse that analyzed the best use of power, whether soft or hard, to acquire leverage over new kinds of foes, actors, and issues in the current context of international politics. This new concept found resonance as the international context was itself in a transitional phase in need of a new blueprint in an unraveling need for reconfiguration of players, processes, and structures.

We must ask, however, what is the concept itself about and what does it have to do with China's approach to issues of international concerns to both itself and to the rest of the global players? The concept proposes to attract the very same people whom we seek to influence, which will have the immediate benefit of not having to convince them either by stick or carrot, both of which may require sacrifice such as loss of lives should the use of force become necessary. This preference for the use of soft power contrasts with the use of coercion or hard power. Whereas coercion uses means such as military and other coercive tactics, the use of soft power usually resorts to any means with a potential to generate goodwill, to win the hearts, to convince or persuade that the user of such means is worthy of the trust, the love, and so on. Soft power techniques therefore may be nonmaterial as they seek to win the minds of the addressees. These means may be about convincing them of the appeal, the moral or ethical superiority of the ideals, beliefs, norms, or values of the initiator. They may also be of humanitarian, intellectual, social, cultural, or even of spiritual nature. In other words, diplomacy and positive role modeling are the instruments of soft power rather than threats and bombs. Consequently, such means as diplomacy, tourism, cultural exchange, education, public health care, science/technology, human resources, humanitarian relief, institutional interactions, and other intangibles are areas of predilection to the soft power approach.

These soft power techniques therefore find expression in areas of cooperation wherein the human factor is highly privileged and human contacts are intensive and in the center of processes. These convictions should lead the addressee as a result to open up to the initiator of soft power. A practice that is capable of inducing such a reaction or behavior wins the initiator an ally who is willing to engage freely and cooperate without having to resort to coercive means.

These means are then viewed or ought to be viewed as instruments of power as they are capable of inducing the same effect, which is getting others to act the way one wants them to. It has the same types of benefits that power usually produces but, moreover, it is enduring because it is based on free will in the adherence of an independent entity to the cause of the user of soft power. Soft power engenders good image, sympathy, adherence, and access, which are political capital and indeed can be translated into real currency in helping the soft power user to acquire followers and gain leadership or any other strategic advantage.

This soft approach has historically not necessarily been the forte of the mighty and powerful. Did Rome choose to use the strength of its organizational skills, its engineering genius, the power of its intellectual and literary production to attract the respect and admiration of its neighbor whom it considered barbaric? No. Instead, Rome chose the might of its legionaries to assert its will. The soft power approach is laborious; it requires and implies a long-term commitment. Its results are not instantaneous and therefore not attractive to hard-liners and other militarists. The use of hard power for coercion has the advantage of inducing changes ad hoc and almost instantaneously as a result of fear for retribution. The seamy side of such a quick fix is that because it does not rely on winning over, by convincing the coerced party, its effect lasts as long as the coercion has the capability of containing the coerced party. The order established by a coercive power therefore lives and disintegrates with the power of the hegemon. Emperor Caesar, aware of such repercussions, when privileging coercion to conviction, chose to rely on the fear he had caused in subjugated populations in his various military campaigns and lived with the consequence of their hatred. Reliance on coercion also carries the danger of keeping the mighty and the powerful from seeking transformative solutions to rising issues, because those solutions might erode their standing.

Rising issues in the contemporary world with the potential to lead to conflict have become more and more complex, reflecting an ever more intricate network of actors, interests, space, time, identities, and almost requiring political leaders of the caliber of philosopher-king as once argued and described by Plato in the Republic (360 BCE). Failure to heed these new imperatives of a complex world may easily lead to conflicts with a global dimension.

Such is the context of today's world within which China's rising power will have to maneuver its way to even higher ground. Concrete, visible signs indicate that China is well aware of the implications of carrying a big stick and threatening to use it on one hand and of a humble, friendly, low-key approach on the other hand. This low-key approach favors the tools of soft power, and China has clearly privileged this approach.

CHINA'S PREFERENCE FOR SOFT POWER

China is not a stranger to the use of hard power. In its recent history, China has been involved in matters pertaining to war, namely the Vietnam War in 1963, the Korean War in 1950, and its own defense against the Japanese in 1937. China's involvement in the support of struggles against imperialism and its own revolution, which led Chairman Mao Tze Tung to state that revolution is not a tea party, attests to the country's familiarity with the use of hard power. A shift to a conciliatory tone has been in effect since modernization reforms have dictated a rapprochement with both international finance institutions and the leading free market economies that China until recently preferred to call the capitalist world. Indeed, antagonizing the most important players in that system, which China would soon need for its economic development, would not have been wise. China readjusted its defiant and confrontational tone and even counseled nations still in ideological fervor, such as Marxist parties and revolutionary movements in Africa, to ease up.

Ever since China's economy has, as a matter of fact, taken off, that nation has acquired a legitimate claim to belong to the circle of the powerful and needed to convince and appease those with reason to fear a rising kingdom of the middle. The discourse was about a peaceful rise of China and an emphasis on cooperation and dialogue, win-win cooperation, mutual respect, antihegemonism, international rule of law, and the democratic international system. This approach seems to reflect the value system inherited from Confucian teaching and raises the question of whether we are witnessing a different approach to international relations altogether, a uniquely Asian mode of international behavior. The teaching of Confucianism seems indeed to be echoed in the pronouncements of Chinese foreign policy when officials reiterate, on occasion, that they seek harmonious, peaceful societies that use dialogue to diffuse conflict. This scenario involves respectful societies, which respect even the smallest among them, and are not subject to power stature and status, which condemn of use of force and threats of the use of power.

Confucian ethics always carried a political weight because it is fundamentally political. The influence of Confucian ethics, however, has varied depending on whether those in power preferred Confucian or Buddhist ethics. Thus, throughout the history of China, Confucianism has shared the spotlight with Buddhism. In China's recent history, Confucian ethics have been out of favor since communists took over the reins of power. The ideology does not tolerate any other God or master but Marx, Lenin, and the red book.

Today's China is no longer eager to condemn all things noncommunist. The cultural influence of Confucianism is no longer an enemy. As a matter of fact, China found a use for Confucius as the country has sought to promote its rich history and culture, as articulated in the section later in the chapter on culture.

Naturally this discourse led to the genuine or strategic diplomatic offensive of China throughout the world, propelled by its economic successes to present itself as the trade-seeking partner who also was ready to lend pragmatic assistance to those in need of a helping hand, where and when needed. The context was propitious as Russia was preoccupied with the management of the post-Soviet era, and the United States was preoccupied with the war in Iraq and using the big stick, as Theodore Roosevelt once threatened. This use of the big stick has antagonized many in the international community, and there needed to be an alternative to the U.S. stick. China's gentle, subtle, unthreatening, or, better yet, hands-off approach could not have presented a more contrasting alternative. China has continued to employ the same diplomatic soft approach that has translated into a variety of soft-power operations. Expressions of soft power are indisputably displayed as China simultaneously pursued its primary interests in the continent, namely trade opportunities.

How is China's use of soft power articulated in Africa? China has not left any stone unturned in areas of diplomacy, development aid, tourism, culture, education, public health, humanitarian relief, and science and technology areas that we explore next. In fact, the China-Africa policy paper issued in January 2006 expressed the intent of China's foreign policy in Africa in the exercise of soft power. The entire third part of the document addresses areas we recognize as of the domain of expression for soft power, which we examine in detail in subsequent sections.

DIPLOMACY

Diplomacy is to soft power as the military is to hard power. Diplomacy is the vehicle through which soft power is exercised. Diplomacy utilizes dialogue, a key concept in the Chinese approach, which seeks consultations and resolution of conflict by peaceful means. It is exercised as a means to achieve foreign policy goals. Growing interests have compelled China to an active diplomatic exercise, and we have mentioned the degree to which Chinese diplomacy has matured in a relatively short time, qualitatively rendering itself able to service its growing international economic and strategic objectives. China has recognized the significance of its growing role and realized, according to Chinese Foreign Minister Li Zhaoxing, that

> the central task of Chinese diplomacy is to make best use of such an important period of strategic opportunities and try to lengthen it as much as possible,

> helping to create a favorable external environment
> for china's modernization drive and making as many
> friends as possible for the motherland. ("Another
> Vintage Year" 2005, para. 27)

China has therefore identified the role of its diplomacy as facilitating a swift modernization of its economy on one hand and contributing to world peace on the other hand. The foreign minister added, "Chinese diplomacy will try to make still greater contribution to forming a new world order marked by lasting peace and universally shared prosperity" (para. 28). To achieve just that, Chinese diplomacy has moved "from passive style to an active style," according to Wu Jianmin, a former Chinese ambassador to the Netherlands and France and president of the China Foreign Affairs University (*China Daily*/Xinhua, 11 September 2005, para. 8). As a result, China has multiplied its diplomatic contacts and ultimately its relations with various state-actors from 60 in 1971 to more than 160, which prompted Wu Jianmin to declare this era the golden age of Chinese diplomacy. All this testifies to the mounting great power mentality of China, which is well aware of its new status.

We must understand Chinese diplomacy vis-à-vis Africa in the above-described context. It is, in other words, the preferred vehicle for a China's comprehensive, strategic vision in the twenty-first century.

With respect to Africa, China's foreign policy goals, as mentioned earlier, are twofold: to seek access to raw material and new markets and to improve China's overall strategic position internationally as its interests grow and diversify. These goals are articulated in the fields of international trade and strategic issues. In this context, the diplomat becomes a key player in China's politics. The diplomat is the agent through which foreign policy goals are reached. The presence and visibility of diplomats in specific international fora where China's interests need to be defended also has been noticed and references to China in the United Nations also have increased recently. China, contrary to past experiences, has increasingly found itself directly in the center of international issues with respect, for instance, to Sudan, North Korea, and Myanmar. Noteworthy as well is the fact that China has increasingly worn the mantle of protector of the developing world as it has sided and supported propositions from Africa with respect to UN reforms, by increasing participation in peacekeeping missions of the organization, and with other initiatives, such as debt relief.

The quantity (frequency of visits by Chinese diplomats) and the quality (high-ranking officials) of Chinese diplomatic activity manifest this increased interest in diplomacy and consequently that nation's preference for the use of soft power. Chinese diplomatic successes, as with those of any other nation, can be measured by the number of agreements they have secured in the areas of cooperation, in terms of contracts and bilateral and multilateral memoranda of understandings, which imply successful negotiations.

This soft-power offensive has served as well another Chinese foreign policy goal, which consists of securing the acceptance or allegiance to a one-China policy, to the detriment of the island of Taiwan's wish for independence. As a result, the number of African nations with diplomatic relations with Taiwan has been shrinking. Malawi and Senegal are the last to have backpedaled from recognizing Taiwan's sovereignty.

TOURISM

Just as China was potentially a market for businesses until it became in fact a coveted market, the Chinese people, because of their numbers, also are a huge source of tourism when they develop both the taste and the purchasing power to travel abroad. In fact, this taste and purchasing power have been on the rise as the number of Chinese tourists continues to increase. The proof of this assertion is demonstrated by the increased visible presence of large numbers of Chinese tourists on the streets of Europe's most attractive cities. As in market behavior, tourism is a two-way notion, as people, like goods, can travel from one country into another, as those from other countries can travel the same route from their perspective. Because of that, China itself benefited from opening up the country to tourism. As a matter of fact, the UN World Tourism Organization predicted that around the year 2010, China may very well become the second most popular tourist destination worldwide, behind France, according to Secretary General Francesco Fragialli (Jimog Babatunde, [Lagos, Nigeria] *Vanguard*, 9 February 2007, p. 8). The overall potential of Asian tourism is bound to become full-fledged with increases in both the attraction of tourism and purchasing power in China and India.

With respect to Africa, China has gradually given more and more African countries its approved destination status (ADS), a policy through which China monitors the entries and exits of its own citizens. To date, in 2007, China has granted ADS status to 52 African nations out of a total of 132 worldwide. They are: Algeria, Cape Verde, Cameroon, Rwanda, Gabon, Mali, Benin, Mozambique, Nigeria, South Africa, Namibia, Tanzania, Egypt, Morocco, Madagascar, Angola, Botswana, Central African Republic, Comoros, Congo (DRC), Djibouti, Equatorial Guinea, Ethiopia, Ghana, Guinea-Bissau, Lesotho, Libya, Mauritius, Niger, Seychelles, Somalia, Sudan, Togo, Uganda, Zimbabwe, Benin, Burundi, Chad, Congo (Brazzaville), Cote d'Ivoire , Eritrea, Gabon, Guinea, Kenya, Liberia, Madagascar, Mauritania, Senegal, Sierra Leone, South Africa, Tunisia, and Zambia. The consequence is increased numbers of Chinese tourists on the African continent (see Figure 8). According to China's Exit-Entry Administration Bureau of the Public Security Ministry, in 2005 alone, 110,000 Chinese tourists entered Africa (Jimoh Babatunde, [Lagos, Nigeria] *Vanguard*, 9 February 2007, para. 4). Africa is bound to benefit to some extent from this development as the continent proudly has a number of tourism-worthy sites and attractions.

CULTURE

Culture is seen here as a domain of the artistic, aesthetic, and intellectual production of a people. Culture as an area of societal expression has been a tool to foster exchanges among nations as each nation tends to have its unique, specific inventive genius and expressive connotations and nuances. The distinctiveness of cultures justifies the need for cultural exchange. As such, culture constitutes a venue through which goodwill can be planted and peaceful intentions and amity can be demonstrated. Throughout history, culture as a domain of expression and of manifestation of a people's genius and therefore its identity has, however, accompanied the expanding, conquering, and victorious political power in its quest for more *lebensraum* and resources. These expanding political powers have subjugated others in the course of wars and explain the phenomena of imperialism and colonialism. Conquering nations have imposed in the process their own cultural expressions to the detriment of the vanquished peoples.

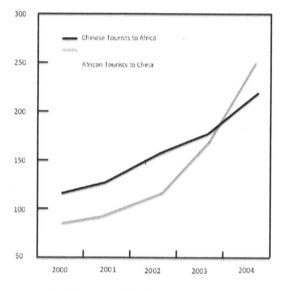

Sources: Yearbook of Tourism Statistics 2006.

Figure 8. Chinese Tourism in Africa

Beyond the context of what is called *cultural imperialism,* a more critical and differentiated look at the rapport between victors and vanquished has been questioned since the 1960s, and a need for recognition of cultural pluralism has slowly emerged. The consensus about the pluralism of cultures is the reckoning among peoples of the planet that each culture is inherently legitimate and self-evidently valid and that cultural imperialism is to be faced with the same resistance as political imperialism. Left to their own devices, without the support of a political power, individual cultures only have the attraction of their genius to spread beyond the arena in which they claim validity. Seen or used in a nondominant-dominated rapport and context, culture is truly another instrument of soft power.

The tool of culture has been used by nations on occasion, and communist nations, like China, are no exception. Communist countries, which have recognized the galvanizing and uniting power capacity of fostering national cohesion and conscious-ness, have made the greatest use of culture as an instrument of propaganda. Communist analysis recognized the galvanizing power of culture but saw it as a product of an historical process that was inherently unjust. Many features of cultural expression therefore reflect and perpetuate established precommunist social structures and contain historically received notions that are deemed corrupt or corrupting. One such corrupt and corrupting notion transported throughout history that has become part of the current culture is the notion of labor. The historic process has alienated labor and created an exploited-exploiters rapport repudiated by communism. Features of cultural expression that function to provide divertissement, relaxation, or enjoyment among communities or people sharing a number of identity-determining factors such as race, ethnicity, religion, geographic space, customs, and so on, were deemed incompatible with the ideology of Marxism and anticommunist in substance.

Deprived of its own historically and tradition-rooted culture, communism has created its own expressions that are rooted in the ideals and teachings of communist theory. This process has cleansed the new cultures of communism from old relics of precommunist societies.

China, a communist country with a long history and civili-zation, has a culture that certainly has many features in which the Chinese, despite their communist identity, can take pride. Under Mao, however, this culture included expressions that were deemed to undermine policy efforts. China, as a result, endeavored to reverse the psychological effects of years of pre-communist culture and customs and replace their content with its own. The Chinese culture has since been impregnated with new content that is designed to support the ideals of the Communist Party. Culture, thereby, became a tool of propaganda.

The cultural revolution of 1968 was such an attempt to root out attitudes inherited from the traditional culture as they did not contribute to the advancement of the communist cause as seen by the party in Beijing. Indeed, the Communist Party had blamed the mishaps of the Great Leap policy initiated by Chairman Mao five years earlier, which was designed to propel China into an industrial era, to the engrained traditional culture and the habits of the establishment and educated elite, professors, artists, teachers, doctors, and professionals whose interests and lifestyle—were not compatible with or even were attacked by the new ideals of communism. It is this bourgeois culture and lifestyle that Mao's communism wanted to purge as it was deemed to sabotage the policy efforts of the regime.

Outside of China, with respect to Africa, China has already instrumentalized culture to cement its relationships. Expressions of the Chinese culture are rich, multiple, and impressive enough to help sell the country to its new friends. Thus, since China first opened official diplomatic relations with African countries, cultural exchanges have been part of activities designed to cement these relations. Egypt is the prime example. under Nasser's leadership, Egypt was the first African nation to engage in diplomatic relations with China and the first African nation with which China signed, in May 1955, a "Summary of Talks on Cultural Cooperation." This modus operandi was soon to be repeated elsewhere. Cultural agreements with African countries have followed the pace of both the rhythm of African countries' access to independence and China's diplomatic successes in postindependent Africa. This was the case throughout the 1960s and 1970s. By 2000, all of the nations with which China had diplomatic relations with cultural and art cooperation agreements expressed this stance.

Indeed, an agreement on culture and artistic cooperation between South Africa and China was signed in April 2000 during the visit of Premier Jiang Zemin. Between China and Africa, there have been more than two hundred cultural delegation visits on each side (China Facts and Figures 2002).

From 1997 to 2000, twenty-eight ministerial-level cultural delegations arrived in Beijing from Africa, and China sent seven governmental cultural delegations on official visits to seventeen African countries (China Facts and Figures 2002). These cultural visits are accompanied by artists, singers, actors, acrobats, drama troupes, dance troupes, and musical and song ensembles that perform or exhibit their craft (including more than a hundred art exhibitions). Visitors from China to Africa have included appearances by the National Ballet of China, the China Oriental Song and Dance Ensemble, the China Acrobatic Troupe, the Wuhan Acrobatic Troupe, the Dalian Art Ensemble, the Sin Kiang Song and Dance Ensemble, and many more. Visits from Africa to China have included the National Dance Ensemble of the Republic of Congo, the Egyptian Folk Art Ensemble, the National Art Ensemble of Mali, the Namibian Art Ensemble, the South African Chorus, and others (China Facts and Figures 2002).

The undertone of these cultural exchanges is the display of cultural diversity, as China often proclaims its respect for the continent of Africa, which, like China, has a long history and tradition; as in China, this African tradition was under attack by the West.

China announced the creation of what it called the Confucius Institute, which renders homage to the eminent thinker in Chinese culture. Here again, France and Germany, with Centre Culturel Français and Goethe Instituten respectively, seem to have served as a model for the Confucius Institute. The intent is as clear as it is noble, namely, as in the case of Germany, using their prominent intellectual figure, these institutes seek to spread the genius of their cultures. By exposing the guest countries to their culture, the Chinese hope to dismantle the proverbial cultural barrier and facilitate the communication that is essential to soft-power usage.

Throughout history, after conquest or commerce, culture has followed. China has been replicating the steps long witnessed in history; only this time, commerce and culture have not been preceded by conquest.

TELECOMMUNICATION

Like any rising power, China also used more modern and high-tech venues to spread its own culture and exerted some degree of control over media outlets and their underlying technology. Diffusion of information is a sensitive issue to all nations, to a lesser degree in open societies and to greater degree in collectivist societies wherein only one ideology reigns supreme. The media therefore are used as a vehicle for feel-good programming or as tool for propaganda and counterpropaganda. Propaganda, however, is not the privilege solely of collectivist societies. China has implemented this control so as not to depend on others or suffer the consequence of their negative, rightly or not, portrayal of its society and realities, as Beijing has long deemed their coverage unfair or inadequate. Furthermore, beyond cementing Chinese relations with its new and old friends and servicing Chinese businesses on the continent, media companies have other interests that are simply utilitarian as they seek sources of investment like any other enterprises.

China has technological capacity in the areas of satellite and spatial technology and know-how and can therefore underline its presence in information generation and broadcasting. China's international news agency is called Xinhua. China created an international broadcast television station called CCTV9 and a radio broadcast station called China Radio International (CRI). These organizations all have global ambitions and all have extended their tentacles and found ramifications on the continent of Africa. These broadcasters have become another source and area of cooperation with African countries and therefore another expression of soft power as China mostly plays supplier, technician, trainer, and provider roles.

An extensive field of what we can call communication aid that consists of Chinese assistance in equipment (e.g., radio materials, transmitters, towers, generators, antennae, technical assistance) has been emerging. The South African Wits journalism program reported on 11 May 2007 the following largesse from China in the area of telecommunication aid: an upgrade of Lesotho television and radio including $4.5 million worth of equipment and technical assistance in 2005; development of a

Malawi radio channel with the help of a 250 million from China; two 2005 grants to Seychelles for $125,000 of multimedia equipment and $50,000 of ICT equipment; Zambia, a country with a long tradition of cooperation with China, received supplies from China to update its short- and medium-wave transmitters and received a grant of $8 million of equipment to upgrade its media sector; Kenya received donations of $150,000 of equipment; and in 2000, the Uganda national television station received from the Chinese news agency Xinhua a satellite station to facilitate reception of news and images emitted by the latter.

Xinhua, a rival in many ways to UPI and Reuters, has established bureaus in more than twenty African nations such as Zimbabwe, South Africa, and Nairobi/Kenya (headquarters). An increasing number of African nations have signed agreements on cooperation or information exchange with states such as Equatorial Guinea, Mali, Djibouti, the Democratic Republic of Congo (Wits Journalism Program, 11 May 2007).

CCTV9 also has entered the West with programs such as the French TV5, British Broadcasting Corporation (BBC), and many others. The Chinese television station is viewed in Africa where courses in Chinese language are offered. Professionals from managers to taxi drivers have become interested in learning the language because of the possible edge it may provide in their lines of duty. Students, anticipating possible study abroad in China, given increased scholarships and cooperation in higher education, learn the language just in case.

CRI – a rival to BBC, Radio France International, Deutsche ell, and Voice of America – broadcasts in more than forty languages, including Chinese, Russian, Portuguese, French, Arabic, English, and African languages such as Hausa, and Kiswahili.

Radio and satellite television broadcasters have been put in place to service the international public in all things Chinese.

China followed in the footsteps of its predecessors with the same interest in projecting a good image and exporting what the Germans refer to as *Kulturegut*.

HUMAN RESOURCES DEVELOPMENT

We established earlier the high intensity of human contact required by soft power use. In the case of China, this has been demonstrated. In all areas of China's involvement in all of the domains we have marked as soft-power areas, that country has established training projects and programs to ensure transfer of knowledge and to some extent a transfer of know-how as a development aid goal that favors Africa. From journalists to technicians, from health care workers to scholarships to African students from fifty African countries to study in Chinese universities, from military personnel assistance to political party exchanges, some 18,000 professionals so far have experienced China's expressions of soft power firsthand. In May 2006, 1,793 African students were studying in China, and China plans to train as many as 10,000 African students every year (Foreign Policy Council 2006).

The benefit of having African students trained in China is obvious as it has been demonstrated time and time again that students educated abroad become the binding glue between their college host countries and their countries of origin. Because these students are expected to hold influential positions and become opinion leaders, they become ipso facto the liaison between their respective nations and China in term of cultural, political, and business communication. The enduring nature of such binding glue is what makes soft power potentially more beneficial than hard power. Rigorous entry requirements for visas to students from Africa into European universities and the disillusionment of many young Africans toward Europe have prompted them to turn toward the United States. However, the United States has, in turn, introduced challenging procedural scrutiny to obtain entry visas since the terrorist attack in September 2001, which has disposed African students to take advantage where advantage was given.

Twenty-seven intercollegiate exchange programs have been established between China and various African countries. These efforts include China sending five hundred teachers as of 2003, according to Chinese officials, to teach Chinese languages, culture, and so on. More than ten intergovernmental agree-

[margin note: Why Africa + China worked]

ments have been signed by China with African countries in areas of scientific and technological cooperation, medicine, biology, and photoelectric technologies (China Facts and Figures 2002). As the main tool for knowledge and technology transfer, human resource development is a key factor in the quest for African economic development. Such a transfer, which has until now not been a key link in developmental efforts, suggests empowerment of humans, which turns them into human capital. In the end, any definition of national power includes the human capital factor. If African development is to be thought out and performed principally by Africans, this empowerment of the African human capital by transfer of knowledge and know-how justifies the importance of human resource development.

PUBLIC HEALTH

Public health is another domain of soft-power expression that China has not hesitated to use with respect to Africa. With a duplicate arsenal of tools (both traditional and Western medicine), and because of its willingness to tackle and confront the most challenging concerns of the African health care crisis (e.g., rural and urban medicine, endemic and epidemic disease), China has the potential to have an impact. Chinese official sources indicate that the Chinese have helped 240 million African patients with medical activity. The same official source noted that three thousand African doctors been trained by their Chinese counterparts to date (2006) (China *Daily* online, 23 June 2006).

As early as 1964, China initiated medical support in Algeria as a tool of soft power diplomacy. Since Algeria, where Chinese teams of medical personnel from doctors to technicians were sent, other medical missions followed, and soon China became active in the areas of clinical, sanitation, pharmaceutical, prevention, health care, and equipment maintenance. Since then, China has had medical missions in forty-seven African nations, a total of 16,000 medical personnel, and until recently, thirty-five Chinese medical teams of young Chinese (aged between 30 and 50) for two years at a time, have been active in thirty-four African nations (*China Daily* online, 20 December 2003).

In Africa, the average life expectancy is forty-nine years. Given the effects of endemic and epidemic diseases and the need to save and protect life itself, the domain of health, next to food and agriculture, is crucial to any economic development effort. Life is both the ultimate reason for economic development and able bodied people are the vessels through which development is made possible. This makes health care issues a most pressing concern to any development effort. China has attempted comprehensively, however limited, to tackle issues relative to health care.

INTANGIBLES

China has openly benefited from some intangibles that have played in its favor. These intangibles originate in a number of domains, including individual, social, cultural, economic, and political. On the individual level, African populations have noticed the capacity of Chinese to adapt to humble African social accommodating facilities that are common in developing nations. Many Chinese workers themselves come from humble social backgrounds and do not demand luxury. This willingness to adapt has bought a sense of proximity that allows a rapport not based on haves and have-nots, superior and subaltern. This in turns allows a lateral integration in a way that the Western presence on the continent has displayed. From that level, China argues that it considers Africans their brothers and that it comes as a friend of the continent. In addition, China claims that it identifies with Africa poverty as a developing nation. China's progress therefore should be seen as an encouraging sign for Africans that there as well things will improve.

This attempt to identify with the history of the African continent has been an intangible parameter used by China since the 1960s as it tried to demarcate itself from both the United States and the former Soviet Union. The Chinese capacity to rub elbows with Africans in their own sphere of existence, in cities and villages, facilitates interactions that Chinese merchant peddlers and small businesses need to engage their African customers in communications. Such communications agree, for instance, with local and traditional practices of informal interpersonal interactions even in business.

Culturally, the Chinese have lived and organized their social value systems based on the teachings of Confucius, which essentially elevated traditional values of the centrality of family and kinship, solidarity, and respect and emphasizes the well-being of the community as superseding that of individuals. They thereby safeguard social harmony and peace. This value system is essentially traditional, as opposed to modern value systems. As such, the value system is not either exclusively or originally Chinese but is common to many premodern societies.

Traditional Africa shares the same value system. The Chinese therefore are not perceived as questioning the intrinsic validity of the African culture and its various expressions. This factor has facilitated what in Senegal is known as the phenomenon of *debarquement*, which causes a minimum of discomfort to locals. This French term, which means landing, alludes to the significant Chinese presence in Dakar. The Chinese do not, for the most part, occupy fancy mansions and have increasingly become part of the African social landscape.

Economically, the spread of China has been further facilitated by the price factor. With products ten times less expensive than their counterparts from the West, Chinese products have resolved the problem of weak African purchasing power. Politically, a mutually beneficial partnership has taken place by building on some additional intangibles. The political intangible is a certain understanding of the concept of power and authority.

The communist concept of power is authoritarian in application despite the intent of Marxism, which explains why Dale Walton (2007) referred to it as the intellectual cousin of fascism. The traditional African concept of power and authority cannot be described simply as authoritarian. Although it comprises such a dimension, it is, however, essentially monarchical, and its exercise of power is mitigated by prerogatives drawn from customs and the adice of influential members of the community based on gerontocratic ranking. Both in China and in Africa, the concept of power as understood in many Western constitutions, based on checks and balances, is foreign.

Since the increasing critics of corrupt governments in the late 1980s resulted in pressure by some Western nations and international finance institutions in demanding good governance, and the 1991 collapse of the Soviet Union bringing a new era, Africa has been undergoing a process of democratization. The process has been, despite drawbacks and shortcomings, fairly successful. However, a trend has been observed since the 2000: old and previously undemocratic regimes have used their entrenched structures and influence to affect elections and acquire ipso facto legitimacy. Omar Bongo of Gabon, Paul Biya of Cameron, and the late, Gnassingbe Eyadema of Togo are examples. Others have profited from their entrenched influential capacity to initiate constitutional amendments to allow the constitution to work in their favor. Robert Mugabe of Zimbabwe and Yoweri Museveni of Uganda are examples of such rulers. Others openly project this willingness to stay in power, not hopefully anticipating a positive result but projecting certainty that the result will be in their favor and of course the unwillingness to contemplate anything else. The election in December 2007 in Kenya, whose outcome ,because it did not validated the entrenched incomebent politial forces, leading to tribal violence, demonstrated the validity of the assertion.

The shape of such a trend can already be identified: emerging regimes can be categorized as dictatorial democracies, where power is exercised under unmitigated prerogative, almost remaining authoritarian despite a democratic constitution. The constitution and limits it exerts upon unlimited exercise are either nonexistent or are tampered with at will. Opposition parties remain for the most part still in need of a legal framework or other viable means to exert pressure on the governing power. Although that is beginning to change, the consequence has been that the parties in power have had quasi-absolute power to decide state affairs. In this context, China has relied on the might of African regimes in power and their capacity to determine policy that China can count on, a practice to which China can relate and with which it has no problem. This has resulted in a certain germane sensitivity to each other's need for noninterference. Here, China's declared policy principle of noninterference has come to strengthen, as an intangible, its rapport with African regimes.

Chapter 10

Tensions on the Ground

The increasing physical presence of both Chinese entre-preneurial businesses (more than 800)[34] and personnel (750,000)[35] on the African continent was bound to generate some kind of reaction. Indeed, there have always been elements of both opportunity and challenge associated with trade. The association of those two elements brings about the notion of trade tension. These tensions are even more directly felt as a result of FDI.

China's presence in Africa represents, according to Moeliski Mbeki, "Both a tantalizing opportunity and a terrifying threat" (Servant 2005, para.17). Indeed China is a special case as it occupies both the supply side and the demand side outside of the commodity sector. China also contributes to the boom of commodity prices but because not all African countries are oil exporters, they suffer from the increases it generates in oil prices (Goldstein et al. 2006).

Opportunities for Africa in trade with China are new demands, new markets, new investments, and the expected spillover effects such as employment, purchasing power increases, and so on. As for the threat, China has highly competitive industry in all sectors such as telecommunication, construction, mining, and so on, as well as a competitive labor force, comparative price advantage, available finances, and others.

Amid all of the possible challenges of trade with China, it has produced so far pockets of tension here and there about specific issues. All things being equal, the reaction to trade with China in Africa has been essentially positive. In general, the Chinese presence in Africa has been welcomed both by official policymakers and the population at large. Official African policymakers have very often publicly declared their delight at the opening of Chinese trade and have confronted issues that no one else even contemplated tackling. These policymakers are enchanted with the efficiency of the Chinese undertaking, their generosity, promptness, cost efficiency, and uncomplicated, unpretentious, smooth rules of engagement. Officials in Sudan, Zimbabwe, and Angola have simply demonstrated an attitude and have spoken words that simply and bluntly spell: Forget the West!

The Cameroonian ambassador in Beijing and dean of African ambassadors, Elieh-Elle Etian, stated in an interview in the *Beijing Review* (Increasing Rapprochement, 8 February 2007, p. 12).

> Concerning the compatibility between our two economies systems [China and Cameroon], I would just like to make a very simple and straightforward comment: The competitive advantage China enjoys over other countries at the similar level of development is that China provides development solutions with developing conditions.

Ethiopian Prime Minister Meles Zenawi proclaimed, "China's exemplary endeavor to ease African countries' debt problem is indeed a true expression of solidarity and commitment" (Eisenman and Kurlantzick 2006).

At the level of the general public, Africans have for the most part welcomed the Chinese trade presence as it is more compatible with the purchasing power of the population than products from, for example, the European Union.

As for pockets of tension, on the businesses side they have reason for complaints. Some African companies, because of the nature of their businesses, have had to compete against Chinese enterprises. These African companies have gotten the short end of the stick due to the highly competitive quality of Chinese enterprises in the textile and construction sectors, for instance.

Here again, in South Africa and Zambia, the influx of Chinese textiles has had a devastating effect on the local industry, leading to the closing of many. Out of thirty four textile companies in Zambia, only eight have remained in business (Grill, 2006, para. 24). Even sharper declarations from official policymakers have been expressed regarding China's danger as a colonizing factor. In Angola, like anywhere else, the reconstruction and recovery effort after years of devastating civil war has seen the local and continental construction companies take a back seat in the contract distribution feast.

The African labor force is another source wherefrom complaints have been voiced. Indeed, negative reactions have been registered as well among Africans in the labor force with respect to employment opportunities that are not provided by Chinese investment. Chinese enterprises generally bring their own labor for their projects. Chinese business officials, according to Chinese Charge d'Affaires Zhou Yuxiao interviewed at China's embassy in South Africa, have explained this practice with arguments such as the following:

> We do sometimes use Chinese technicians because [they] are not available on the local market. Sometimes we use Chinese laborers to make sure our contracts are fulfilled within the [contractual] period because Chinese laborers are hard working and they can do the work according to the plan. If we can be sure the contract will be (completed) in time, then we can use labor from local market. (Eagle 2006, para. 6).

Yuxiao used skills, cultural ethnics, efficiency, communication, and maybe mistrust of local population as the main reasons. His disarmingly honest statement does not beat around the bush by suggesting that Chinese enterprises have no other choice or that even if they wanted to hire African manpower, the timeline to finish the project would have to be long enough for the slower working pace of African labor. Voices of common people

African Commoner vs China

211

on the streets of African cities have reacted to such arguments by Chinese officials both in approbation and in disapprobation. Indeed, Chinese labor has earned a reputation over the years, the world over as a nation with an exceptional pool of laborers. On the other hand, many other complaints have expressed the almost inhuman work conditions observed at various Chinese construction sites in African countries. Starting at dawn and finishing at dusk with a few minutes of lunch break, Chinese labor does not complain and works 24/7 at still competitive wages. Because of that, rumors have circulated that this labor force may be prisoners doing forced labor

China does, however, use local labor, which works under Chinese management and its own ways. In Zambia and Gabon, there have been reports of poor working conditions and lagging wages (Gill and Reilly 2007).

Other instances that have produced tension with some Chinese enterprises have been due to their unacceptable style of doing businesses. Incidents have been registered in Gabon, Zimbabwe, Sudan, Zambia, and the Democratic Republic of Congo, where various deviations from local or international regulations have been noticed, including environmental regulations in Gabon, labor laws (safety and wages issues) in Zambia, and so on.

In the Zambian district of Chambezi, since 2005, there have been resentment and even anti-Chinese sentiments expressed in the aftermath of the explosion in which forty-nine workers were killed at a Chinese-owned Non-Ferrous Corporation copper mine, due to poor safety provisions. The incident triggered subsequent incidents but also provided an opportunity for China and Zambia to address the issues, but not before providing Michael Seta, an opposition leader, an issue on which to rally Zambia (In Africa, China's Expansion Stirs Resentment, *The Wall Street Journal*, 2 February 2007, A16).

Resentments and tensions have arisen as well at the retail level. In many African cities (e.g., Kampala, Dakar, Lusaka, Luanda, Windhuk), an increased number of Chinese retailers have opened *Bahuo* shops whose low cost merchandise has undermined local businesses and entrepreneurship. Chinese retailers seem to have available almost everything, including traditionally African merchandise at lower-costs. This results from the Chinese practices of imitation and even counterfeiting. As a result, Chinese retailers have constituted formidable competition to small, local entrepreneurs who do not take it with ease. The numbers continue to increase and some Chinese have been learning African languages, which suggests their long-term intent.

Another kind of potential tension, which on at least one occasion has already been manifest, is the irreverence of Chinese enterprises for local political conditions. In Nigeria, Chinese workers have been kidnapped just because of the politics of the Delta region, as we have mentioned, where local populations' grievances against the federal regime remain unsolved. In the long run, the association of Chinese businesses with local regimes in power, when contested by the population, may place China on the side of these regimes and alienate the population at large (Gaye 2007).

These tensions ought to be seen as a case of growing pains. China will certainly, alone out of self-preservation instinct, learn to adjust to the reactions generated by its actions. With an historic culture that values harmony and consensus and seeks dialogue, China should be able to defuse these tensions, which are susceptible to becoming full-fledged conflicts, as illustrated by the case of Chambezi in Zambia. In the same situation in Chambezi, the government in China ordered respect of local labor, increased remuneration for their work, and other compensations. In South Africa, where the dispute in the textile industry caused such anger, China voluntarily decided to restrain its exports.

partner in development

Chapter 11

The Critics

The ostensible presence of China on the African continent eventually, this caught the attention of the outside world and most precisely the West since the early 2000s. Both on the European continent and across the Atlantic Ocean, newspaper articles and academic journal articles that reacted to China's engagement in Africa seem to have been characterized by cautious cynicism and criticism. This notice was certainly the result of an observation of China's cumulative, sustained, and accelerating accomplishments. Experts have cautioned about the upcoming war over natural resources and that China was making strides (Council on Foreign Relations 2005; Steingart 2006), and about the strategic repositioning of China and where that would leave the European Union or the United States. In the United States, of course, more than in Europe, the potential strategic repercussions of China's presence in Africa warranted an interest that went beyond economics. Of the literature from the United States, the most significant to date is the 2005 report by the Council on Foreign Relations task force, which cautioned the United States about the resulting strategic advantage that China might acquire and the drafting of Africa into the Chinese zone of influence. This literature therefore has urged a renewal of US policy vis-à-vis Africa on strategic grounds. The criticisms, however, have specifically addressed issues that we examine next.

Main Areas and Ground

The literature criticized the unconditional character of the Chinese engagement and its repercussions in terms of corruption and bad governance on the African continent on the grounds that it emboldens dictators and undermines the efforts of political liberalization and democratization.

The literature criticizes the noninterference principle as it allows China to deal with anybody anywhere, including some regimes deemed unworthy by the United States and the European Union on the grounds that such a policy principle was unethical or irresponsible in that it may encourage regimes to violate human rights.

The charge of unethical behavior also has been formulated not only against the policy itself but also against business practices by a number of Chinese companies ad hoc. This criticism against the practice of some Chinese businesses and Chinese peddlers and small businesses has not specifically been exclusively formulated by Western sources. From Africa, Alfredo Tjiurimo Hengari (2007), for instance, pointed to the involvement by small trader businesses in African cities in counterfeiting and imitation of authentic products that end up pushing African artisans and small entrepreneurs out of the market.

The literature also has charged that the pursuit of China's interests on the African continent would lead to new colonization (Gill, from *Die Zeit*, 19 September 2006, para. 2), and even used the term *yellow colonialism*. Epithets and other adjectives with negative connotations have been used, such as the **Dragon in the Savannah, China's safari in Africa,** "Gelbe Gefahr" (yellow threat), and so on, to suggest that the new Chinese dawn does not presage anything good for Africans, or at least to imply a certain skepticism about the Chinese adventure in Africa.

The literature further criticizes the formal or informal encouragement by China to African regimes to follow its economic model as China officially has sought collaboration in the political sphere by using mutual visits designed to learn about each others' works, bureaucratic and administrative practices and the functioning of their respective institutions, exchange of ideas among officials and politicians, and so on, on the grounds that it curtails overtures by African countries to Western liberal democratic principles.

The literature criticizes the suffocating nature of Chinese economic activity and trade as they demand African natural resources and the structure involved on the ground that it exports back to Africa finished, value-added goods, which causes African economies never to acquire the know-how to process their own raw materials.

COUNTERCRITICISM

China's choice of political system inherently puts it at odds with the West. This is sufficient reason to expect criticism from the latter to the former. The arguments made against Chinese involvement in Africa have often been unable to hold water because of inherent contradictions of many Western policies toward Africa throughout modern history.

On the noninterference charge, China has always seen itself as a potential victim of pro-interfering regimes in international relations. Not only because of the respective divergent ideologies with the United States, for instance, which put them at odds, but also because of concrete incidents such as the Tiananmen Square massacre and the ensuing attempt to marginalize China in international relations; or again the adoption by the United States of a regime-change policy aim, which indirectly implicates China as well. The consequence is that China has openly advocated the principles of the international code of behavior inherited from the Westphalia Treaty. Indeed, one of the elements of the treaty is the recommendation not to interfere in internal affairs. This view makes the central government the sole and unique policymaker, main actor, and enforcer of internal order. This code of international conduct suits China just fine, and that country argues that if such is the law, all nations ought to abide by it. China has repeatedly used the term *respect of international law* to suggest a Western hegemonic deviance from it whenever the West interferes. Other nations are potential victims of hegemonic interference, and China courts those that inherently appear vulnerable.

To prevail in its attempt to drive international relations back to that underlying rule of law, China needs and seeks Africa's support (Taylor 2006).

The issue of noninterference has been questioned when inhumanE, barbaric, and repulsive atrocities have been committed within the confines of national territorial borders, since Germany, during the National Socialist attempt to exterminate the Jewish race. The ensuing holocaust led to recognition of the notion of crime against humanity and gave way to some level of acceptance of interference. The term *genocide* has since had legal imperatives attached to it. After the Nuremberg trial (1945–1949), interference was to become a norm in such cases on moral grounds. The war in Kosovo, a result of the dismantlement of what used to be Yugoslavia, started in 1990. After witnessing the ethnic cleansing and the massacre between orthodox Serbs and Muslim Kosovars and others, French envoy to the region Bernard Kuchner was frustrated by the inability of the international community to provide effective help and support and to stop the killing according to international laws grounded in the noninterference principle. He forced a debate over a right to interfere (*droit à l'ingerence*), as he called it. Subsequently genocide was perpetrated in 1994 in Rwanda by the Hutu against the Tutsi and to some extent retaliation by the latter to the former. Not only was the debate against interference on the table but at the same time, the genocide in Rwanda demonstrated that even when agreed upon, the actuality of a genocide and with the lessons of the Nuremberg judgment as a legal precedent, the involvement by the international community remains selectively applicable. It depends on political expediency and many other factors but not solely on the letter of the international law even when engraved in the African Charta for Democracy in 1990.

This realization begs the question: When is interference in internal affairs acceptable by the international community and when is it not? The answer remains highly political and therefore hazardous. History has shown that such interference is possible given the willingness of a hegemonic power to spearhead the effort. This short history of the interference debate points to

China's perception that it constitutes a potential target, even if it is not as easy to take on as others have been in the past.

On the unconditionality charge, China has argued that the West uses an unfair leverage to keep developing nations in chains. There are currently instances of Western unconditional support and aid to a selected number of nations. The practice also exists in the private sector, which has increasingly risen to become a lender to developing nations (Easterly 2006). Brautigam (2007), referring to Easterly reminded us that the conditionality imposed on African leaders and nations to extract in return good governance or economic growth have not produced results. To continue to impose them begs the question why? Brautigam (2007) provided at least one example of unconditional loans from the West, in the case of Britain's Standard Chartered Bank, Barclays, and Royal Bank of Scotland, which made loans coincidently to Angola. The policies of Western capitals and international institutions have found neither approval, acquiescence, nor usefulness to Africans. In many instances, these policies have failed to produce the result they were designed to achieve. In many other instances, the West has changed some of its policies toward African nations according to political expediency and opportunity—but not Africa. Why should some policies not be questioned as long as the West has not deemed the change necessary? Are all policies right just by virtue of being in place and applied by a given nation? If eventually some policies are indeed changed, does not that suggest the possibility of inherently flawed polices or at least their inefficiency?

On perceived Chinese unethical conduct, although the West's own shortcomings in and of themselves do not constitute *carte blanche* for Chinese perceived immorality, Western criticisms have often come with the taste of sour grapes. Throughout the years, China has had an unpretentious policy formulation with respect to ethical issues. China furthermore sees an ethically derived moral codex in politics as an emanation of a Western Christian civilization and not part of the Christian world, which therefore refutes its universal validity.

Furthermore, there is an inherent incompatibility between the ideologies of communism with respect, for instance, to the role of religion in political life, which further complicates the equation. China has always courted Africa, whose own historical and cultural experience may align better with the Chinese non-Western traditional value system. From its perspective, China has therefore not found unconditionality to be both practically and ethically a liability. The following example illustrates the reality. With increased unrest from the Niger Delta separatist population, which expresses its grievances by using kidnapping, sabotage, and illegal tapping into oil installations, Nigeria sought military support from the United States to help protect oil facilities (*Financial Times* 28 February 2006). The U.S. response was a lukewarm attitude, according to Nigerian Vice President Atiku Abubakar. Regarding the reasons for the U.S. reluctance, observers of Nigerian politics have pointed to concerns about corruption of authority, mistrust of the military, and human rights issues. Nigeria turned to China, which, having interests in the region, reacted and provided support, sending patrol boats to secure the swampy region. China's acceptance was unconditional but also a case of Machiavellian realism. The U.S. conditional refusal is at face value a moral choice but also may have been because that nation did not have any direct stake in the issue at hand. If morality is the underpinning of any conditional policy, however, we should then expect the same moral attitude toward all foreign policy formulations by the United States, which is undoubtedly not the case. This leads to the conclusion that governments, the United States included, selectively apply their foreign policy's moral clauses. In the end, most foreign policy formulations are more Machiavellian than Grotiusian or idealist.

Does this counter-criticism exonerate China? Not necessarily. Out of political realism, China will have to address and respond to the pressure surrounding its neglect of such issues. There are signs that China has started to do just that. The sale of arms to regimes deemed unfavorable to the United States has often been used to accentuate China's immorality. China is just one of all those who export arms to Africa and not even the most successful at that.

On the charges of colonization, the analogy is hard not to use in light of some similarities that can be observed between what motivates China and what motivated the European expansion since the 1500s. Colonization as a paradigm of international processes that characterize nineteenth-century dynamics –namely, the expansion of European economies and their subsequent imperial claims--, has essentially been both a political and an economic endeavor. This colonial attitude was later followed by a cultural dimension –namely, the evangelization of new territories. With this last element, colonization turned into a Westernization process that involved appropriation of these new territories, their subjugation under European political authority, and the subjugation of their inhabitants to both a set of foreign rules and a *modus vivendi* foreign to their historical cultures and customs.

This analogy to colonialism is dictated by the similarities of what has pushed European powers to venture outside: namely, first, the quest for new markets and second, after the industrial revolution, the quest for natural resources. These two motivating factors apply as well to China. In the case of Europe, they have led to colonization but this was possible because, among other things, of the historical state of developmental processes of African societies. Fragmented, and in a pre–nation-state context, the absence of a greater cohesion has contributed to the absence of a sense of national territorial autonomy. For better or for worse, this now exists, and the overall modern context and awareness on behalf of African nations offers a different context for colonization of the kind of that took place in the nineteenth century.

However, there are fundamental differences that defy the use of the analogy. The allusion to colonialism is therefore used by China's detractor, noted Sanusha Naidu (2007, 42): "For China's detractors there is an inherent tendency to use futile dichotomies of the nineteenth century scramble in analyzing and characterizing China's political and economic behavior in the continent as neo-colonialist."

China has not made any territorial claim nor sought any appropriation of land or subjugation of the population to foreign rules of law. The simple fact that China proceeds with the signing of bilateral and multilateral agreements disqualifies this comparison because these agreements imply the recognition of a counterparty, and we dare assume that today's African leaders are more aware of the implications --legal, economic, and political-- of such contracts, and further assume that they are not gatekeepers to foreign interests and act on behalf and in the benefit of their respective states and peoples. When and where these assumptions are wrong it is no longer because Africans are not aware nor have no other choice in the matter. Should they still hand over the resources of the continent, without adequate trade off, to those who seek them, like China; in that case, the culprit will not be Chinese.

By comparing China's presence in Africa to colonization, we essentially refer to the growing economic influence and a growing Chinese population on the continent. Such a comparison may be justified by the influence factor. To have influential capacity, one must not be a colonialist or an imperialist. Influence can be exerted indirectly, and therefore China would not need to control the continent directly physically, legally, or otherwise. Should China succeed in achieving a high degree of influential capacity in African affairs, then the danger of an indirect colonization is possible. Such an influential capacity may result from a growing entanglement of African economic processes with China's capacity to dominate the supply chain, which may very well produce dependency of the former on the latter. From such a dependency, the decision-making processes by African policymakers, as well as African economic institutions and agents, will be influenced, which may erode true power away from African hands and into China's.

China itself remains unphased by these criticisms, mostly because of its own claim that its involvement in Africa is based on a win-win premise, and above all a noninterference principle, which in itself should suffice, as China claims to avoid any attempt to brand it as a colonial power. Furthermore, the entire Chinese involvement in the African continent was driven by the notion of helping Africa to rid itself of colonialism and imperialism. Many have therefore seen this criticism, essentially expressed by the West, and by some in Africa as a sour-grapes reaction by the West. After all, the West has ceased to engage Africa as an equal partner but considers it only a so-called humanitarian basket case, so the reasoning became, why then bother when somebody else takes interest!

On the charge that China's involvement will not serve Africa, China's involvement in the continent, just like the European colonial economic system, will not help Africa develop. Indeed, the state of economic underdevelopment has left Africa the use of its natural resources as almost its only connecting link to the rest of the world economy. Since the infancy of capitalism, cemented by European expansionism, which led to the colonization of the African continent, that link has been structurally implanted in the world capitalist system.

Around the 1960s, when many African countries became independent, the argument of the necessity of their political economies to become integrated in the post–Bretton Woods international trade system, an argument accompanied by the big push and Keynesian progovernmental role policies, was promising enough for Africans to join. Besides, these newly independent African nations had no other choice, given Africa's raw material exporter status, which needed an outlet from which to generate foreign currency that was needed to reboot the stalled modernization. African nations have been stuck in the role of natural resources exporters in the international division of labor, but witnessed how Western economies were growing and the standards of living improving and saw economic development passing them by.

African nations were still stuck in that role when China entered the picture as an expanding economy that is large enough to potentially either cause the same damage as Western colonization or engender hope for a second chance. The worries are about avoiding the mistakes of past involvement of the continent with such growing economies as Europeans in the nineteenth century and Chinese today. The critics contend that China buys raw materials that are shipped to China for processing and end up back in the African continent as value-added processed products. The fact that China sells its products cheaply is in itself part of the equation as it desincentives these developing nations' for developing processing capacity. China's cheap products are competitive enough to suffocate the bourgeoning local manufacturing industry. As a consequence, African economies may not develop their manufacturing sector and wind up with the short end of the commercial stick with China.

The challenge posed by China to economies around the word, not just in Africa, is that it competes using the advantages of developing nations, for instance, in the areas of labor and in the use of industrialized nations' manufacturing capacity. China's low-tech and labor-intensive manufacturing capacity is, however, becoming high tech as China aims at moving up the value chain. Echoing this reality, Engardio (2007, 61) stated, "The assumption has long been that the U.S. and other industrialized nations will keep leading in knowledge-intensive industries while developing nations focus on lower-skill sectors. That is now open to debate."

On the charge that China's approach undermines good governance as Africa may use its support to relapse into bad governance, the charge itself undermines the role of Africans to want, seek, and bring about good governance. The opposition against President Mugabe in Zimbabwe is not alive because of Western instance on good governance. In fact, an argument can be made that the recalcitrance of Mugabe can be explained by his ferocious will to stand against the West as he perceives it to be a version of neocolonialism against which he fought. This could even be characterized as the Castro-U.S. syndrome in which the resistance against reform in Cuba may have ceased to be just that and became identified with the victory of the nearby archenemy. Great Britain has become Mugabe's nemesis, similar to the relationship between the United States and the Castro regime.

Other examples of internally driven democratic movements exist in Africa. Little by little in Ivory Coast, Kenya, and many African nations democratic rule has been gaining a foothold. These movements have essentially existed and have been propelled by Africans. Since the democratization process of the early to mid-1990s, the West has not been as essentially instrumental as one would have expected, in tilting the tide. In many instances, such as in Ivory Coast, Togo, and the Republic of

Congo, France has played a counterdemocratic role. Through-out the cold war, the democratic ideal had never been a foreign policy goal of the West in Africa. Under these circumstances, using the democratic ideal as an argument vis-à-vis China, a proclaimed nonseeker of the democratic ideal, is indeed less potent from the Chinese perspective.

The charge of China's sale of arms to Africa, which consti-tuted up to 10 percent of all conventional arms sales between 1996 and 2003, has been raised as well. Here it suffices to remember that China was neither the first nor the second but the third country exporting arms to Africa. Other criticisms, such as human rights abuses by Africa and by extension China, as well as criticism about corruption, can be addressed in the meantime in more than Africa and China.

This concern, however, is expressed as if China's venture into Africa during the latter's expansion phase of its economy, was way out of line. Henning Melber (2006, 6) echoed the same impression:

> One therefore is tempted to wonder, if the concern expressed is actually not more about the Western interests than about the welfare of the African people, given that what we witness today is anything but new with regard to its forms and effects.

CHINESE UNETHICAL BEHAVIOR?

Although ideals, norms, and values may play a role, foreign policy is essentially driven by concrete interests conceived by relevant actors, and therefore is essentially self-centered and utilitarian by its very nature. There is always the potential of overreaching or overaccentuating one's self-serving utility to the expense of the declared policy partner. In many cases, foreign policy partners are instrumentalized to the very end and very need of the initiating policy party. The balancing act is needed and often empirically difficult to establish because the balance of power, the distribution of resources, and preferred outcome of policy inducers differ. As a consequence, the needed distributive balance in the outcome of foreign policy exercise occurs in favor of one partner and, in the case of a zero-sum game, to the detriment of the other. It takes a superior moral foreign policy actor not to take advantage of the possible gain that one's power status otherwise enables. This requires that the actor voluntarily concede or yield the exercise of power. Realpolitik shows that this speaks against political rationality, and history has yet to be proven wrong.

In its ascendancy, the West has had that advantage, and still has it to some extent, but has not conceded nor yielded the exercise of it. In fact, the entire history of modernity as the contextual paradigm that describes the best the use of Western power status is a product of both its use and abuse. The West has been even immoral in the pursuit of its interests in many instances documented throughout history that we need not regurgitate here. The question is: Is an absolute or relative advantage ontologically immoral? In economics, evidently not, as the premise of liberal economics is built on that notion. In politics, history shows that with an absolute or relative power advantage, abuse can follow.

We must ask, however, how apodictic is such abuse just because one has power? Is capitalizing on one's absolute or relative advantage fundamentally amoral, or are there parameters to be used in determining when it is? Based on their conceived interests, individual state actors may formulate their policies as they please. Some are more realistic than others, some more idealistic than others, and some more aggressive and greedy than others. In a context of empire, the most powerful would just impose their will and usurp power in territories where their interests are best met. In an ideal context of rule of law, consultations, and meetings do take place where different positions are negotiated. Whenever an accord or consensus is reached, agreements can be signed as a result. Here again, however, as taught in the realist perspective in international relations theory, anarchy, power, and asymmetric distribution of capabilities explain the fact that such agreements are not always the fairest solution but rather the expression of respective actors' bargaining powers that therefore they reflect only the distribution of capacity. Such has been the characteristics of the international political and economic order. It has not been essentially either moral or equalitarian. At the risk of sounding Machiavellian, morality has never been the strong suit of politics. If, like Max Weber (1972), we define the exercise of politics as a pursuit of power, we then understand why.

With that in mind, on which ground is or can China's foreign policy exercise be dubbed immoral? Who among political actors are the warrantors or guarantors of political morality? If there are any out there, they will have to have the moral clout, a political saint nimbus on their national flags! Taylor (2007) reminded us the example of a France eager to promote liberty, equality, and fraternity, ideals that were not only not met but not at all pursued. Similar examples are legion!

If China is to be dubbed amoral in its practices, the question must be asked: Has China articulated a moral codex that it failed to live up to? This begs another question: Should China be allowed to have its own codex of morality (the case of moral relativism)? Maybe not; but if not (the case of universality of the moral codex), should not all nations live up to it? Have all other nations done that? If not, dubbing China amoral depicts some nations as more immoral than others. Is China indeed more immoral than others? The injection of the moral dimension in the political discourse has always been problematic. It has been the point of disjunction between ideals and interests. Conquests, imperialism, colonization, slavery, and yes, the entire modern history and the order that it has produced, have been fundamentally based on exercise of power and not on justice, compassion, and humanity, and the like. Whereas idealism and normative principles have been articulated and professed in documents such as the preamble of the French constitutions and the United Nations Charter of Human Rights, they have either been applied and implemented selectively or they have subsided to power interests, as if to reflect the realism of Bismarck who unequivocally saw power trumping rights. The West has been both the locus of liberalism and the notion of inalienable rights and equality and the agent through whom the same norms and values have, in some historical cases, been defied and violated on a larger scale.

These are a number of questions worth exploring but this is not the place nor the context that allows us to argue in that direction. Here these questions only serve the purpose of allowing us to reflect on the accuracy and justification of some criticisms.

All in all, it appears that Western criticism of China is in many ways myopic and occasionally self-serving. This can be illustrated by the criticism of China for not keeping up with environmental standards in Africa, knowing the ecological disaster (oil spillage, gas flaring, groundwater contamination) that Shell has almost irrevocably caused in the Niger Delta.

If China is the new Africa exploiter, it will have to duplicate the hemorrhage of African resources toward Europe during colonial years. That remains to be proven.

CHAPTER 12:

BRACING FOR CHINA

Despite initiatives by Africans and from various bodies of supranational organizations such as the UN and the EU, and their various official development assistance venues, such as USAID, the German Gesellschaft fuer Technische Zusamenarbet, the French cooperation ministry, the British Ministry of Overseas Development, and the international community of donors, as well bilateral provisions and programs of official development assistance and finally their efforts to increase foreign direct investment, Africa was becoming a footnote in the international arena, reduced to a case of humanitarianism and philanthropy. This vision has been changing significantly as China's economic interests in the continent have turned Africa into a strategic field as acknowledged by the Council on Foreign Relations (2005, para.28): "What is necessary is to recognize that the rising economy of China . . . changes the strategic and economic playing field in Africa." Africa indeed is once again seen as a source of natural resources and a terrain wherein China's nascent manufacturing sector could make its mark because of low market-entry competitiveness as mentioned earlier. With this new reality, Africa has been given another chance.

LOOKING AT THE PAST

This, however, is not the only opportunity Africa has had to be the object of interest from those who come from the outside. It is therefore imperative that we look at the following two distinct questions: (1) What has Africa learned from its past involvement with foreign interests? (2) What precautions is Africa taking to insulate itself from exploitation without scruples that is only possible with the complicity of some Africans themselves?

Indeed, the history of the continent has been characterized by foreign infiltrations that have produced the subjugation of African populations culturally, politically, and economically. Africa's traditional fragmentation, which derives from historical cultures of self-governing communities with very few unitary states, has facilitated the infiltration of colonialism, with some resisting exceptions here and there, as with the Hereros in Namibia, the Mau Mau, in Kenya and Shaka Zulu's army in South Africa, to name just a few. The Pan-Africanism movement at the turn of the twentieth century attempted to remedy and reverse the effects of such subjugation and has worked to raise a collective awareness and consciousness of the entire people of African descent. The movement has inspired resistance against colonization. In postcolonial Africa, the movement translated into a dream of an African unity advocated by the Ghanaian Kwame Nkrumah, the fight against apartheid, and the goal of modernization attained by adherence to the paradigm of the moment, that is, the integration of international trade. The creation of the Organization of African Unity (OAU) in 1963 was envisioned to foster, beyond unity, the sense of nationalism needed to emphasize the notion of sovereignty and the independence of new nations. The unity of the continent, however, remained elusive as, paradoxically, the goal of unity collided with that of nationalism of individual states that used it to reaffirm their sovereignty.

The notion of national sovereignty, the persistent dependence on foreign aid and assistance, the cold war in which African states found themselves on different sides of the East-West rivalry or sided with the nonaligned movement, and other factors such as language divisions that constitute a cultural divide within Africa --all have contributed to weakening the Pan-Africanism movement and the OAU. Africa never spoke with one voice, and poverty and dependence have forced these nations into powerlessness and a subordinate role in the international relations arena (Gowan and Gottwald 1975). As a result, the continent was unable to fend off neocolonial policies or to remedy the causes of the distribution conflict.

The 1970s indeed were a period of disillusionment for developing nations in general as that decade failed to bring about a New Economic Order (in Algiers 1973 and in the UN General Assembly, 1974). The disillusionment was real as they seemed trapped by a number of factors that underpin the mechanism of international commerce, such as their vulnerable status in the international division of labor, the lack of real changes to form capital needed for a takeoff phase, and the attempt to force a new international world order.

The 1980s were an era in which the continent faced new challenges. The infamous structural adjustment program, with the consent of the West, which has been leading to mounting debts whose servicing still constrains the budgets of governments, were imposed on the continent. Here again, the continent seemed helpless. Since the 1980s, Africa has attempted to remedy this state of both perceived and real helplessness and sought to induce the necessary changes in its own initiatives: the Lagos Action Plan; the Abuja Treaty in 1991; the Cairo Action Plan in 1993; the Omega Plan conceived by Senegalese President Abdulaye Wade; the Millennium African Recovery Plan coproduced by Bouteflika of Algeria, Obasanjo of Nigeria, and Thabo Mbeki of South Africa; the vision of an African Renaissance invoked by Mbeki; and the subsequent fusion of these by African presidents into the New African Initiative (NAI), which was later renamed NEPAD (New Partnership for Africa's Development), have all had good intentions and programmatic visions aimed at meeting the challenges of the dawn of the twenty-first century and targeting regional integration, improvement of transregional infrastructure and commerce; improving economic conditions, governance, social conditions, management of resources, institutional capacity, education training, health, and agriculture; eradicating poverty; protecting the environment; mobilizing resources; preserving culture;

developing human resources; and obtaining peace, security, democratization, protection of human rights, and so on.

Initiatives from the outside, already mentioned, that address Africa's specific needs have seen the light of day and the conclusions of these initiatives urged a radically revised need to improve the quantity and quality of foreign aid to sub-Saharan Africa. Most of theses have had in common one of the following fates: either they died a good death or have underperformed and yielded meager results inadequate to allow Africa to charter a new course and embark into a new era.

Transformations that occurred in the early 1990s in the aftermath of the collapse of the Soviet Union have enabled the removal of all kinds of obstacles to internal changes on the continent. One of the changes was a bold attack on African authoritarian regimes, which produced the democratization process and was a source of hope for a possible new course and a new era. The hope faded as it was tempered and undermined in 1994 by the effects of the genocide in Rwanda, civil wars in Burundi and the Democratic Republic of the Congo, and with interest and sympathy for diverse warring factions in countries such as Angola, Zimbabwe, and Uganda. Many other civil wars followed, such as in Ivory Coast, which had been until then one of the most stable nations on the continent. As if that were not enough, in January 2008 another short but devastating civil war broke out in Kenya, a consequence of disputed election results between the opposition leader Raila Amollo Odinga and the incumbent Mwai Kibaki Emillio.

The list of incidents, accidents, and negative events continue to pile up, and Africa never seems to catch a break. In the meantime, the majority of African nations' ranking with respect to the Human Development Indicia of 2003 prominently shows African nations at the bottom.

It is in this overall continental context that China's interest and approach soon occurred. As a continent and individual nations within, Africa has realized after gradual and manifestly evident proof of China's influx of economic interest that the presence of the latter was indeed a shift in the fortunes of the continent. We have mentioned that China could not have picked a better time to court Africa. Just as the time was propitious for China, Africa was at a juncture of its history in which many African initiatives and other transformations did not yield the expected harvest.

Revisiting African history, it seems indeed that history keeps repeating itself as Africa has been forced in the past to deal with and to react to historical processes and development from elsewhere. At the peak of their internal dynamism, nations acquire enough resources, capacity, and confidence that quasi-naturally induce the need for expansion. China has not been an exception to that historical fact. Indeed, China after a couple of decades of tasting the waters of the international market eventually launched its Go Out (*zuo ququ*) slogan, which encouraged its firms to seek access to new markets and resources worldwide. That step led China to Africa's doorstep.

HAS AFRICA LEARNED FROM PAST EXPERIENCE?

The awareness that the current situation resembles Africa's is illustrated by following quotation by Eric Chinje, the African Development Bank's director of communication: "Governments hope to avoid repeating mistakes of the past, when African resources were exploited without providing lasting growth" (African Development Bank to Meet in Shanghai AMID Growing Economic Ties, *International Herald Tribune Business*, 23 January 2007, para. 4).

Under these circumstances, African nations, aware of the opportunity, have collectively and individually braced for China's development aid, FDI, and access to China's markets. The proof of such bracing for China was provided at the first interministerial China-Africa Forum in October 2000, attended by more than forty-four African ministers. This bracing for China has been both at the continental level, where Africa's multilateral organizations, such as the African Union, NEPAD, the African Development Bank, and regional organizations, and on bilateral levels at which individual African nations have sought one-on-one, ad hoc agreements that many such as Ethiopia, Gabon, and Zambia have set to monitor with their own action committees.

On the multilateral level, China had, since the year 2000, deliberately cooperated with the African Union, donating 3 million to the organization every year. China likewise provided financial assistance to the African peacekeeping mission in Darfur with a fund of $400,000 since 2005 (Guijin 2006).

What precautions have been taken to ensure a win-win outcome in this China-Africa cooperation? Both continent-wide and bilaterally there is no distinct or coordinated mechanism and effort geared to ensure that an African payoff is proportional to its cost in cooperating with China. Indeed such an attempt depends first and foremost on individual African leaders, negotiators, and their skills; and the capacity, ability, and willingness always to leave the bargaining table with their bottom line secured. Such an outcome has been in the past difficult due to the often weak bargaining power of African negotiators who are desperate for any deal that would breathe life into their situations. Western advanced economies have without scruple taken advantage of that situation as shown by UNCTAD negotiations throughout the 1960s, 1970s, and 1980s, just as African gatekeepers have in many other ways facilitated their tasks.

All in all, on multilateral and bilateral levels, Africa has had intrinsic reasons to explain their difficulties in formulating a concerted and common attitude toward external solicitations. These reasons have been multilaterally intrinsic because of the difficulty of bringing all African nations to a common policy, arising from the fact that each nation has its own priority, levels of necessity, and goals. In addition, Africa has yet to see the emergence of a continental hegemon to help forge such a policy consensus. National sovereignty and distinct and sometimes antagonistic ideologies have always been in the way. As a result, individual African nations have to fend off negative effects of their vulnerable and sensitive status while participating in international trade or other kinds of regimes. Thus they each have to enter into dispute with China on the nonemployment of local labor and workforce, the suffocating effects of the infusion of Chinese textiles on local enterprises, and so on.

The reasons are bilaterally intrinsic because often lone African nations, while dealing with powerful, advanced nations, have gotten the short end of the stick. Structurally there has been an enduring deficiency in Africa's ability to deal with aid. This deficiency is explained by the chronic lack of financial capacity, lack of strong institutions and therefore structure, lack of stability as many African nations have had to deal with ravaging civil wars, and the lack of capacity to deal with donors leading them, according to Zimmermann (2005, para. 11), to "take aid however it is given."

There are cases in Africa in which individual governments have been fending off attempts by China to cut corners to the detriment of host countries. The unrest in Zambia, as mentioned earlier, is one such example of popular expression of frustration as limits were overstated by China. On an official level, there are cases of national authorities expressing their willingness to resist any abusive manifestation of Chinese operational sites. The earlier-mentioned case of China having been admonished by Gabonese authorities is a further example.

In the Democratic Republic of the Congo, President Kabila required that the state-owned company Gecamine be taken as a joint venture partner to Chinese mining operations in the southeastern region of Katanga. Local officials did hesitate to demand readjustment or even sanction of Chinese companies whenever violations, such as abuse of environmental or labor laws (Congo Has Something China Wants, and Vice Versa, *The Economist*, 12–15 March 2008, p. 14).

Underlying the argument, Chris Alden (2007, 77) stated,

> The fact remains, however, that at the regional and multilateral levels African reactions to Beijing have been basically lacking in any strategic approach, as well as being fundamentally uncoordinated, reflecting the underlying bilateral structure of China-Africa relations.

However, nation-states see it as their prerogative to be the sole entity to engage government officials and the depository of their last word in the decision-making process. In the modern era, they have been reluctant to turn over some of their prerogative to supranational bodies. The poignancy of that perspective, however, has been receding as the repercussions of globalization and its giant players have proven to be too powerful for individual nations to handle the privilege. The process of regional integration has been reaping the benefits.

The late Thomas Sankara of Burkina Faso long ago deplored Africa's isolated dealings with the most powerful nations against which individual Africans nations cannot succeed to break through. The enthusiasm for regional regrouping has caused that phenomenon to start to proliferate throughout Africa. Indeed, based often on geographic proximity, these regional organizations have had to deal with the issue of how much distance to the core is allowed, as illustrated by Rwanda's application to belong to the East African Community (EAC). Furthermore, the most successful organizations tend to attract more members even though at a distance. Criticisms have been expressed against such a trend, arguing that it would undermine the need for continental cohesion and the efficacy of the African Union.

The African Union has in fact acknowledged the potentially counterproductive proliferation of regional groupings. These regional organizations do not always imply improvement on the regional needs that justify their creation in the first place. Like any other institutions, they are subject to structural and functional efficiency, financing, competent personnel, and overall effectiveness in servicing the needs. With respect to efficiency, the African Union itself was audited by a panel of competent and respected African figures, such as Dr. Adebayo Adedeji. The report in December 2008 cited among other things structural and functional weakness and lack of communication.

However, the relative success of some African regional organizations argues in favor of their contribution to the improvement of overall conditions on the continent. The Economic Community of West African States (ECOWAS) has proven with various degrees of success the possibilities of a regional organization in Africa to intervene and play an active role in issues that encompass trade, common security, the promotion of multinational projects, and even the attempt to develop common policy in key areas. The Southern African

Development Community (SADC) has been making progress in playing the same role in southern Africa.

Other regional organizations have been less effective or have had a near-zero impact on their respective regions. Some have even found themselves in the middle of political conflicts or disputes between the members that have rendered the regional organizations irrelevant. Such were the cases of the Economic Community of Central African States (ECCAS)[34] and the Conservation of Private Grazing Lands (CPGL) organization's regrouping of the Democratic Republic of the Congo, Rwanda, and Burundi in the 1980s. Others, such as the EAC (which regrouped Kenya, Uganda, and Tanzania, with Rwanda and Burundi having since been admitted), have dealt with either the fear of a regional hegemon, Kenya, or the regional hegemon has resisted carrying along the poorer members (Mungomba 1978).

The EAC, a regional organization created in 1977, collapsed in 1984 and was revived in 1996. It then took the current appellation a year later and has since been slowly recovering, though not without an infusion from China. Indeed, Tanzania's old ties to China, Uganda's active courting of China, and most important, the geographic attractiveness, stability and relative prosperity of Kenya, despite the unrest that erupted as a result of contested elections in early 2008, have become cornerstones of Chinese market-entry strategy for the eastern region. India, with old ties in the region, has shown signs of following right behind China. As a result, the EAC has been revived.

Others, such as the ECCAS, have suffered from lack of leadership. All, however, seem to have been reinvigorated and have been active in seeking support for regional projects and therefore need the influx of financing from external sources. China here again has demonstrated greater readiness to cooperate with African regional organizations.

China's support to regional organizations in Africa is real. In 2005, China appointed a representative to the African Union. The same year, it did the same with the Common Market for Eastern and Southern Africa (COMESA)[35], SADC[36] and ECOWAS.[37] On 25–28 March 2008, the first China-West African Summit was held.

With respect to NEPAD, since the creation of the initiative, after the Lagos Plan of Action in 1980 and its adoption in 2002, China has been calling for a new supportive partnership with the international community under the chairmanship of Jiang Zemin, who pledged to cooperate with it. Indeed, the objectives of NEPAD address not only the overall needs of the continent but also areas in which China has targeted with impact on the continent. These are: regional infrastructure programs, transportation, energy, water, sanitation, food security and agricultural development programs in subregions, market access, debt relief, and attainment of Millennium Development Goals in areas of health and education. Those needs are in the sectors that China has been willing to target from its own perspective. There is therefore a complementarity of purpose between China's Africa strategy and NEPAD's own wish list. As a consequence, coordination and mutual support between these actors was in order.

China donated $500,000 in 2006 to the NEPAD secretariat based in Midrand, South Africa. China's support of NEPAD from the point of view that it was an African-centered and African-dominated development strategy differs from the West, which pledges its support on the basis of the initiative's compatibility with liberalization. China's tangible support can be measured, however, in the various investment projects, development aid packages, cooperation programs, and increased trade volume, all of which reflects China's expectations of NEPAD. The congruence of goals and the complementary interests between the China-Africa Forum and NEPAD call for a bridging of these two programs. Addressing just that, Wenping (2006, para. 9) stated,

> During the past, the two programs seemed to work independently and separately. Even though they share lots in common in terms of goals and sectoral priorities, the collaborative projects and exchange of ideas on time seems not enough at all.

That has started to change since 15 March 2006, when the secretary general of the Forum Follow-up Committee, Madame Xu Jinghu, met the chief secretary general of the NEPAD secretariat for the first time (Wenping 2006).

The African Development Bank was bracing as well for China, taking advantage of the boom in the oil sector by exporting countries and most generally of improved terms of trade for commodities with the increase in demand by emerging markets. As oil and other commodities markets improves, so do investment opportunities, which attract funds, new partners, shareholders (altogether, twenty-four non-African partners), and investors. The continental bank has seen its financial capacity increase. By doing what banks usually do, namely being a depository of funds, lending and financing projects such as the Millennium Development Goals, the bank has contributed to fueling the economic growth of the continent. Although China was part of this infusion of funds and lending and financing projects as early as the 1950s, involvement with the African Development Bank, which itself was created in 1964, became a reality only in 1985. In 2004, China had 24,021 shares with a voting power of 1.12 percent.

In mid-1985, as mentioned previously, Africa experienced an era of change in the role that China saw for Africa in the midst of its own transformation. As a foreign partner, China has become more directly involved in the work of the African Development Bank by donating financial support to various bank projects.

China has further enjoyed the benefit of cementing its growing role by hosting the 42nd meeting of the bank's council of governors and the 33rd African Development Funds council of governors in June 2007 in Shanghai.

A concerted effort between improved terms of trade, increased financial capacity of the bank, and improved economic policy tools in many African nations has resulted in an overall improvement of economic indicators, which explains the economic growth on the continent. The activity has allowed the bank to improve its financial capacity and to play the role that banks usually play. As a result, the African Development Bank has improved its credit rating internationally. Under this conceptual framework, it was only logical to associate these organizations and existing structures if China were to contribute to an effort of development redefined by Africans since 2001 in an effort to revitalize the continent.

Africa has been bracing to profit from China in the areas articulated in the second meeting of the forum in Addis Ababa in 2003, such as benefiting from the support of regional integration, support of the African Development Bank, technical transfer, increased trade agreements, and from the 10.5 billion ren min bi (RMB, the currency of the People's Republic of China, equal to $1.3 billion) debt cancellation to thirty-one African nations, which became a reality at the subsequent forum in November 2006.

The third China-Africa Forum in November 2006 in Beijing was a coup de force by China. China has asserted its presence and received the appropriate recognition in an impressive gathering of more than forty-eight African states, represented by at least thirty African leaders and other high ranking officials, which gained notice around the world.

Africa and Foreign Solicitations

It is an historical fact that communities, cultures, and civilizations eventually meet others as a result of conquest and/or trade and often spread the religion of the conquerors and traders. It is also a fact that communities and cultures that expand as they seek conquests and trade are usually those at the peak of their dynamism. The result has been that communities and cultures that are less prepared to encounter others, have paid the price. The price has been in the worse cases, conquests and domination if not subjugation of the least prepared communities or cultures. This domination or subjugation has taken various forms and expressions. It has been economic and political and led to serfdom, occupation, slavery, and colonization, and it has been cultural and led to the imposition by conquering newcomers of expressions of their cultures, languages, religions, school curricula, and so on. Africa has historically been successively a victim of various expanding civilizations. The Arabs in the aftermath of the death of Mohammad, the caliphate of Omar, reached the northern part of the African continent in 644 C.E. Ever since, Africa has become familiar with Islam and other features of the Arab culture that originated the religion of the Prophet. Today's Swahili, next to Islam, remains the most prominent witnesses of this era.

In the early 1400s, Portugal spearheaded a mercantilist European expansion intended to access the Asian market and began a new venture that led to colonization. Indeed, Europe, since the Crusades, has gotten wind of the flourishing Asian trade between China, India, and Japan. The quality and variety of goods, silk, porcelains, spices, and so on were an irresistible opportunity. The flow of these goods encompassed all of Eurasia after the conquest of Baghdad by the Mongols in 1258. Europeans, however, were not free to travel across Asia under the successive control of the Mongols and the Ottoman Turks. To circumvent that obstacle to reach the Far East, Portugal and other European nations, soon to be colonial powers, needed to deal with Africa as well, a continent that already had a reputation of possessing gold deposits, as Europeans learned from Islamic sources such as Ibn Khaldum and Batuta.

Both Islamic and Western civilizations became the most influential foreign powers on the African continent. Although the influence of Islam precedes that of the West, the former has been entirely trade- and religion-driven. Islam as a religion has had as well the reputation of accommodating indigenous cultures of newcomers by not requesting that new believers entirely abandon their customs as they adhere to the Islamic faith. This facilitated adhesion has not altered fundamentally in substance and in process the historical cultures of new believers in Africa. Islam's code of ethics, the *Sharia*, and features such as the acceptance of polygamy and so on were not drastically foreign or strange to Africans.

Both the religion of Islam and Arab culture blended in the traditional social structure and order of Africans. J.C. Froehlich (1962, 19) wrote that Islam has practiced

> *la tolerance des paiens, permit aux musulmans de s'enfoncer profondement de long des pistes caravanieres jusqu'aux lisieres de la foret et d'y porter des produits manufactures en provenance du Maghreb ou Egypte.*[38]

The consequence is that the impact of Islam is diametrically different from that of the West that was soon to occur.

Indeed, European expansion into Africa had covered the entire continent, contrary to Islam, which had geographical limitations. Furthermore, the West has been intrusive, demanding and forcing changes in the historical traditional social sector such that Africa had to learn to operate and function under new societal paradigms. These alterations included expropriations of land, wage-producing labor, the introduction of poll and hut taxes, market economy, currency, and so on, which forced African populations to abandon their traditional subsistence economic system and more into proletarianization, rural exodus, urbanization, and to different degrees of labor specialization, professionalization, and education.

These changes brought about what we call a societal paradigm shift as colonization became classical. This classical colonization goes beyond the settling of a new territory by colonizers to imply political management of the occupied territory. After political claims were made on specific territories since 1885, the exploitation of the land to the sole profit of the European metropolises soon was deemed inappropriate amid increased criticism of the colonial adventure. The burden of the white man and the limits of the colonial state exposed during both world wars have forced a second colonization, to use the terminology of Bill Freund (1998). This second colonization was about transforming countries into viable modern nations. Africa was to become modern. This colonization therefore introduced Africa to the structure of modern societies.

Modernization is one of the successive foreign paradigms that Africa has had to embrace. This paradigm is called *foreign* because it was not the result of historical processes, emerging from the endogenous societal transformations as a result of a dynamic culture. Colonization-led modernization aimed at transforming African societies from traditional to modern societies. Modern societies are structurally functional systems, as described by functionalist sociologists such as Talcott Parsons (1971), with subsystems (political, social, economic, and cultural) that interact and function rationally to meet the needs that various institutions are created to serve. This functional scheme, however, is the result of a process of modernization that is enabled only by a process of industrialization. Indeed, traditional societies cease to be traditional when the traditional mindset has subsided as a result of imperatives of industrial societies to the benefit of a rational culture. Industrial societies as a matter of fact impose their rhythms on society. This rhythm is rational and affects the culture of those who function under it.

This rational culture therefore is a characteristic of modern societies. There cannot be therefore a modernization of a society without industrialization. African colonization as practiced by European powers has introduced modernization but without industrialization. European colonial powers have created a colonial political economy whose features were about servicing the economies of metropolises in Europe where the processing sector was located. This colonial political economy has been about colonial states specializing in one or two products for export purposes, leading to mono-exportation, a feature, among many others, from which postcolonial African economies suffered.

The consequence of this industry-less modernization of Africa by colonization is that African modernity has suffered this congenital malaise. Of course, colonization is long gone and one now addresses the questions to Africans themselves, namely What have they done to remedy and rectify the wrong done by colonization? Here as well the answer is not simple, as there is plenty of blame to go around. One goes once again to African political and other leadership, which does not seem to take control. The other answer addresses exactly the issue of control and has pointed to the limits set on African political leadership due to the nature of the international system that has ways to undermine African initiatives if they do not fit a certain mold prescribed by the most influential members of the current international system and order. The SAPs implemented in the 1980s come to mind.

The malaise engendered by this state of affairs is expressed in the tension between the traditional value system and the imperatives of modernity. As modernity has only partially penetrated the African social fabric and because of lack of industrialization and its capacity to absorb traditional populations into modernity, this population often finds itself trapped between the application of material rationality criteria as required by modern institutions and traditional reflexes that are driven by a different set of expectations such as customary practices and ethnic solidarity.

Expressions of the malaise of modernity in Africa can be observed in many ways and instances. Often the reaction ends up being a preference of one over the other of these two reference sources (i.e., modern rationality or traditional reflexes). Franz Nuschler and Klaus Ziemmer (1980) used the term *Montesquieu complex* to denote the preference of modern rationality over traditional value systems and explained the complex as an attitude of considering as intrinsically good that which is modern and introduced by Europeans and by inference everything African as less valuable. On the other hand, many Africans still do not recognize themselves in many of the rational formulations of modern institutions perceived to reduce the human experience to a functional experience, and find themselves detached from them.

This notion of foreign paradigms in Africa is relevant here insofar as the continent has to negotiate their implications. Stalled African economic development has been explained for the most part by the vicious cycle of being unable to form capital, from which investment can be made, which will increase productivity and revenues and therefore savings, from which more investment could derive, and so on and so forth. The result has been a continent still facing numerous existential problems and still depending on handouts from the outside, from development aid to humanitarian relief. This dependency has kept Africa in bondage as those who lend their support to Africa always find ways to make their aid and loans work for them in ways that keep limiting the independence of the continent.

Other foreign paradigms followed and Africa had to deal with them. The next in line was the Cold War. Just as most African nations achieved their independence around 1960, the international order entered in the mid-1980s in the aftermath of World War II, a new era and a new paradigm of international politics based on ideological positioning in favor of either the capitalist, democratic West or the communist East, respectively led by the United States and the former Soviet empire. In the midst of negotiating its postindependence era, African nations soon had to choose camps. Negotiating with this new paradigm of international politics has meant that Africa must divert attention and political capital to matters of international security against a possible nuclear holocaust. This era also meant for Africa the freezing of any internal initiatives as long as they were not sanctioned by the leading nations to which African nations were clients. Political Africa has never debated its social contract with its peoples. Africa has never discussed the place of its own worldview and value system in the modern context, the role of ethnic identity, and so on. Instead, political Africa was eager to define itself in rapport with Marxism-Leninism or the West whose democratic system was conveniently avoided even by those African leaders who lauded their preference for the West.

This time of freezing of any Africa-based and induced dynamics of political and economic transformation in favor of the masses has had as a side effect the entrenchment of African dictatorships. The oppressive, repressive, suppressive, and exclusive nature of these dictatorial regimes explains the numerous coups d'état as the only means to induce a change of the status quo. These coups produced a constant switch from Marxist to capitalist regimes depending on whether the CIA or the KGB was successful in helping their proxies to victory.

This era lasted until the collapse of the Soviet empire in 1991. The freezing of any Africa-based and induced dynamics of political and economic change also unfroze at that time. Indeed, the collapse of the Soviet empire brought about the beginning of the democratization process in Africa, enabled after African dictatorships lost their support from the West and the East. Emboldened by the weakening of African dictatorial regimes, various opposition parties and movements that until then were clandestine or operated from the outside forced their way into the African political scene.

COLD WAR EFFECTS ON AFRICA

The end of the Cold War constituted a paradigm shift in international processes and principally had two effective repercussions in Africa. The first was the emergence or revival of multiparty-system subsequent to the demise of authoritarianism and the beginning of a democratization process in Africa. Africans themselves have been since the late 1980s pressing for democratic reforms and the rule of law. They have reclaimed the preponderant role of the people in African politics. At the Arusha Conference of 12–16 February 1990, they formulated an African Charta for Democracy, which was adopted in July of that year. Democratization became a matter for African themselves to carry out, which they did. It was an opportunity to get rid of dictators that clouded their skies, in a Leviathanian kind of way. In Benin, demonstrations under the headline "*front du refus*" were organized to support political changes. In the Democratic Republic of Congo, populations and students from high schools to university campuses marched in Kinshasa to encourage the national conference. In Ivory Coast, students and urban citizens did the same. The democratic momentum was evident through the mid-1990s.

African political and intellectual elites actively joined the movement at the Dakar Conference under the auspices of the current Senegalese president Abdulaye Wade and Ibrahim Badamassi Bandanyida of Nigeria, whose communiqué demanded the return of all opposition leaders in exile, the depolitization of national armies, the deculpabilization of ethnic conscience, the establishment of constitutional state, and so on.

Soon after, the effort showed results. Old African statesmen such as Julius Nyerere of Tanzania, Leopold Sedar Sengor of Senegal, and Amadou Ahijo of Cameroon, who voluntarily gave up power, gave a necessary push. They demonstrated that it was possible for political succession in Africa to proceed peacefully, and that it did not need to occur with bloodshed.

Such overall conditions of pressure, coupled with the end of the Cold War, rendered African authoritarian regime leaders dispensable, and they became the first casualties of the paradigm shift. Weakened, they embarked on the democratic course by organizing national conferences during which the terms of a new beginning were to be designed. African Marxist regimes, the first to lose support and moral backbone, were also the first to initiate political reforms. Indeed, in December 1989, Mathieu Kerekou of Benin organized a conference during which he distanced himself from Marxism. In February 1990, he organized a national conference to decide the political future of the nation. The conference agreed to create and introduce a multiparty system. This conference lasted twelve days and culminated with Kerekou losing the presidency of his country. In January 1990, Mozambique, under the leadership of Joaquim Chissano, signed an ordinance that authorized the separation of state from party.

A series of national conferences continued to occur in Africa, signaling the willingness of African regimes to comply with the new changes. In March and April 1990, Gabon introduced multipartism. In April–June 1990, the Democratic Republic of the Congo (known then as Zaire) organized a national conference. Ivory Coast did the same in April/May, Nigeria in May, and Zambia in June/July. Angola decided to revise its constitution in June of the same year, followed by Cameroon. In July, more nations followed the path of national conferences, including Burkina Faso, Congo-Brazzaville, Somalia, and finally Togo, Tanzania, Cap Verde, and the Central African Republic.

Because old habits die hard, military resistance to the democratic order as a nostalgic remnant of the old African pretorianism still tempted some officers. Such was the case in Nigeria with General Sani Abacha, who reversed the outcome of the elections won by Chief Moshood Abiola. The outcry and pressure, both internal and external, forced the Nigerian military junta to give up power. The election of March 1999 produced the presidency of Olesegun Obassanjo. In Burundi, Melchior Ndadaye was democratically elected in October 1993, only to be overthrown by Major General Buyoya in July 1996, killing at least 250,000 people. In Congo-Brazzaville, Joseph Lissouba was elected and shortly thereafter was forced to give up power by an armed rebellion that was led by Denis Sassou Ngouesso and favored by France for economic reasons. Indeed, Lissouba was in the process of restructuring the contract practices of oil corporations in Congo-Brazzaville in favor of a more openly competitive basis. French oil companies, then and now in charge of major Congolese oil exploitation, resented the move. In Sierra Leone, the election of Ahmed Tejan Kabbah was contested as well.

In other countries such as Gabon and Togo, democratic elections were held and resulted in a reproduction of the status quo. Opposition in those countries learned to cooperate to dethrone old and still governing guards. Elections to come promised to produce different results. All in all, although the process of democratization is still on course, most African nations have become democratic. Democratic elections have become part of political practice and landscape, and the population has been experiencing the test of empowerment. Democracy is, according to Claude Ake (1990, 2), "not just a consummatory value but also an instrumental one." With this new democratic instrument, African populations have a tool to engage and contribute to the transformation and manufacture of their societies. Democratization in Africa represents a second independence of the continent. Modern Africa has welcomed this new phase of its sociopolitical history. Africa should use this opportunity to negotiate better than it did with independence. Neuradine Delwa Kassive Coumakoye wrote (in *Africa International*, February 12, 1993, 37), "*Il ne faudra pas qu'elle rate le tournant democratique car elle a raté le virage des independences.*"[39]

Even if this democratic development cannot achieve a miracle, it does have the advantage of encouraging competition of ideas and projects, political discourse around the issues of accountability, and so on, a context that has never been part of the African political landscape since independence.

A New Pardigm of Globalization

The end of the Soviet empire coincided with a number of other events and processes that together ushered in the new paradigm of globalization. As a new paradigm, globalization describes the state of the evolving international processes. It serves as a road map that reflects current realities. Globalization, however, is seen here as a foreign paradigm as it reflects better the stage of developmental processes that are spearheaded by nations outside of Africa. As a result, Africa once again has had to deal and cope with the repercussions and imperatives of this new paradigm.

The post–Cold War era war provided an unprecedented opportunity for the dynamics of the free market to reign without geographic boundaries. The era's quest for market is now global and dictated by liberal economic principles, supported by the infrastructural architecture of international institutions and regimes. In this new paradigm, the ubiquitous presence of resources, labor, capital, and entrepreneurs optimize the synergy. The scope of new technological progress --a new political landscape wherein ideologies no longer pose barriers to market dynamism-- have led to a market that is truly global. This globalization of the free market has sparked a series of repositioning moves by entities with global ambition. Nations have changed policy stances, seeking to maximize the welfare of their populations. Regions have formed trading zones, and multinational companies have made strategic moves to survive and/or capitalize on new markets. Bernard Esambert (1992, 242) compared global enterprises to armies and their chef executive officers to army generals in the economic war:

> Dans le nouverau champs de bataille de cette fin du 20ieme siecle, qui abolit le temps et l'espace, la conquete des marches et des technologies a pris la place des anciennes conquetes territoriales et colonials. Nous vivons desormais en Etat de guerre economique mondiale et il ne s'agit pas seulement la d'une recuperation du vocabulaire militaire. Le conflit est reel, et ses lignes de force orientent l'action des nations et la vie des individus. L'objet de cette guerre est, pour chaque nation, de creer chez elle des employs et des revenues croissants au detriment de ceux de ses voisins. . . . C'est en exportant plus de produits, des services, d'invisibles, que chaque nation essaie de gagner cette guerre d'un nouveau genre, dont les enterprises forment les armies et les consommatuers les victims.[40]

The nonprofit sector also has learned to operate globally, speaking on behalf of those interest areas, underserved areas that are not on the agenda of businesses and politicians. This new configuration of structure and process and the new dynamics of interaction are what we call the paradigm of globalization.

The global market's synergy better accommodates those nations and economic actors who have competitive capacity and contributes to their increase of wealth better than the others. As a piece of the global and international puzzle, Africa has historically been incorporated in the world capitalist system. Africa has not yet been able to take advantage of this global market. In fact, as far as globalization is concerned, Palan et al. (1996, 184) wrote, "African countries can be classified in our terms as being out of the competitive game in the global economy." As a result, this stage of the globalization process produced the success of some nations and the marginalization of many others. Greider (1997, 188) stated, "In this new world, developing nations that lack multinational corporations of their own may become the new equivalent of colonies, assigned to subordinating roles in the global production system." Echoing the same thought, Palan et al. (1996, 84) stated, "Unless there is fundamental reform or revolutionary change the plight of these countries is likely to remain forlorn reinforcing their peripheral nature in the global political economy."

This current stage is in itself a paradox, as globalization implies inclusion (in one global free market system), but carries at the same time the dangers of marginalization of those entities that are unable to sustain the forces of a free-market system. This marginalization seems to be the effect of a competition-based market system and a global economic system that still has problems in accommodating less competitive nations without changing the rules of the game. The nature of competition implies casualties. The global economic system, therefore, strives to reconcile and address the antinomy of competitive cooperation. This antinomy seems to explain a number of conflicts in international trade, among them the distribution conflict. Development assistance, which was thought to address the question, has done nothing but bandage the casualties of the free-market system.

However, globalization is a dynamic phenomenon. Many nations have learned to reposition themselves to take better advantage of the new global economic constellation. The Asian tigers --Malaysia, South Korea, Singapore, and Thailand-- were the first to demonstrate the power of proactive national economic reform prior to globalization and flourished during that process. China implemented the same proactive reform in the midst of globalization, and many others, such as India and Vietnam, have been following the trend, each using its advantages to the fullest. For the first time since the mid-nineteenth century, the best-performing economies have been those of non-Western nations, which have experienced economic growth averaging 10 percent yearly. This development allowed the rise of China, and as China rose, its expansion reached Africa. As part of the global reality, Africa has had to deal with the implications of the globalization paradigm.

In reacting to such imperatives, Africa found itself in the margins of global trade with insignificant trade volume in and out of the continent. This state of affairs, however, is not set in stone and could reform to better take advantage of the global market, just as many other nations have done or are doing currently.

AFRICA'S POTENTIAL

Africa surely has global credentials. Africa is the last non-conquered market surface. As mentioned previously, from a population of more than 700 million[41], currently only 50 million are considered world customers. The majority of its population is under thirty years of age and is in possession of 20 percent of the cultivatable land of the world, and with only 13 percent of the world population. Most of Africa's innumerable natural resources are still mostly unexploited:, a one-quarter of the world's copper reserves in Zambia and Congo, 90 percent of the world's cobalt, with important uranium reserves, gold in West and East Africa, more and more discoveries of gas and petroleum, newly discovered colombite and tantalum, and even more still unknown resources, Africa has a lot to offer to the world.

Such world credentials are the reason that, despite all of its difficulties, Africa has attracted the interest of China, to name the most aggressive investor. China can be that lifeline support to Africa in the midst of the continent's dealing with another foreign paradigm. However, Africans will have to recognize that the responsibility of the destiny of African people is incumbent upon Africa and Africans themselves. There is a need for a bolder Africa that must critically discern and analyze the demands of the intertwined external world, reclaim its sovereignty and primary responsibility of the conduct of its affairs, and engage the international community without surrendering its prerogatives. In Africa, Botswana, as mentioned, demonstrated this kind of boldness vis-a-vis international aid donors. The need to trade, the need for capital, and the need to cooperate must not be a remedy that is not only hard to swallow but also comes with hardship harsher than the malady it proposes to cure. The needs of a developing economy with infant industry are different from those of advanced economies. The consensus to adhere to a free-market system ought not necessarily to imply adhesion to laissez-faire economics. There are different levels at which capitalism can be practiced. South Korea has exemplified the kind of impact governments can have in leading the economy toward the path of market economy without antagonizing the free market. China has been opening its economic structure to the path of the free-market system at its own pace. Not long ago, European economies, such as France, were and still are applying socially proactive economic policies within the context of a market economy.

Every paradigm in use has a referential validity but not an ontological one. A theoretical assumption should then be allowed, which supposes a failure of liberalism to engage successfully the objective situation and reality in Africa. In case of such a failure, a change of paradigm should follow. This possibility is not utopian. As a matter of fact, works have been written about the imperfection of the free-market system promoted unconditionally by liberal economics, which may account for such a possibility, at least for some nations. Indeed, some nations use and take advantages of, or resist, such imperfection better than others. The asymmetry of political power and economic wealth is the ground upon which this game is won or lost. Because of such an imperfection, Africa should learn to protect itself, as others will do should it come down to it. Liberalism is not and should not be a religion. Even in advanced economies, voices in favor of protectionism are heard without any shame, as increasingly little about the current stage of globalization is in favor of once powerful pro–free-market economy advocates.

This also leads us to affirm that it is not up to African nations to deliver on liberal economics, after they have signed onto SAPs, for instance, but the other way around. In other words, it should not be up to African nations to vindicate liberal economics but rather that liberal economics must vindicate itself in the African case. Africa therefore should undertake to deal with China in a way that satisfies a certain orthodoxy of a religiously and rigidly applied laissez-faire but also in a way that satisfies the fundamental needs of the people and their nations.

UNTIL THE NEXT SOLICITATION?

It is inherent in human nature and societies to be inquisitive of both social and physical environments. This nature has produced modernity. Modern societies have consequently pushed natural limits in their constant quest for new ways. Modernity is essentially antifatalistic. Its attitude is that we do not have to accept as given and final any of these realities that seem to limit human expression. The successes of human minds and the evolution of civilizations in their intellectual and material manifestations have acted as an encouragement in that quest. There is no telling where the generations to come will take the universe, what they will be able to do, how they will live their lives, and organize societies. This openness of modernity, which Karl Popper (1971) rightly considered to be the essential characteristic of modern societies, constantly produces changes and new ways to navigate or negotiate them. These changes are what we have called *paradigms*.

Globalization is the paradigm of the moment, and is in itself such a dynamic concept that it constantly forces adjustments in the way actors within relate to it. Nation-states, social individuals, and businesses and organizations almost every other season readjust their game plans and figure out how to position themselves favorably.

In this constant motion of repositioning, a *perpetus mobile*, the paradigm exhausts its possibilities to accommodate evolving ideas, inventions, and technologies. If and when that happens, we have a new challenge that calls for a new paradigm. With the emergence of a new paradigm, the same game starts over again. Some in the area of futurology, in studying how necessary and sufficient elements interact and predict the kinds of changes they would produce, tend to anticipate future conditions. The fact is that there are just too many factors, both known variables and unknown and accidental variables, that can influence the course of events in the world of humans. It is, therefore, an audacious endeavor to attempt to imagine or figure out what the next paradigm will be or the domain in which it will derive and what its driving engine will be.

Africa has been at the receiving end of these international paradigms, as opposed to the initiating end. The African challenge has been to navigate successfully through them, when they have been unstoppable, or initiate those that fit its mode and realities. There is a need for a much more courageous, bold, and demanding Africa, as opposed to an Africa that has been too timid, too respectful, and too insecure to carve through stone. Authentic, visionary, and adept leaders must accept and assume such a responsibility.

CHAPTER 13

WILL CHINA SUCCEED WHERE OTHERS HAVE FAILED?

Give China five decades—the time the West has had to assist Africa—and we will have more ground to answer the question whether it has been comparatively successful. Whatever the outcome, the pace of accomplishments by, and the approach of, China seem to have, without a doubt, produced impressive results to date (2007). Visible, palpable, and concrete accomplishments can already be seen when visiting African cities and some remote areas. These accomplishments are of a physical nature, which seems to be the place to start in a continent where the most basic elements of supportive infrastructure for a functional economy are for the most part still missing.

One of the advantages of China in the matter is the holistic approach, the targeting of sectors that are key and essential to the developmental project, a sentiment of respect that Chinese project toward Africans, and a searcher rather than a planner attitude, which brings the promise of efficiency. It is exactly the apparent inefficiency, justified by the fact that Western planners themselves are not affected by the results and not accouncountable to anyone (Easterly 2006), and by the fact that Western planners' operational procedures require schemes in which time is made functional, bureaucratic procedures are cumbersome, and there is an orthodoxy that when confronted with empirical bumps usually present no flexible alternative. Kenneth King (2006, 13) illustrated the point with following example: "One of the problems about the G8 agreement in July of 2005 to double aid to Africa was that there was no mechanism or time-line set up for monitoring this commitment."

The Chinese approach may, however, dissipate before it has evenhandedly shown what it can accomplish on its own. Indeed, this Chinese approach has been criticized in the West by Western governments over Sudan and by international institutions such as the IMF over Angola and the Congo. China has asked to become a responsible stakeholder in the international system by IMF President Robert Zoellick in 2005. The OECD has sought to bring under its codex of international donors' behavior, for instance, getting China to abide by the Extractive Industry Transparency Initiative or describing and defining its operations according to so-called international norms, and so on, as explored in Chapter 11 on the critics of China's involvement in Africa. Other forms of pressures have been exerted on China to resemble and to align with the modus operandi of the current international community of donors. The European Union has actively made steps to achieve a realignment of its approach with that of China with *A Mutual Partnership: Shared Interest and Challenges in EU-China Relation* (2003).

China seems to have recognized the need to work with previously established structures. In 2005, China and the UN Development Program established the China-Africa Business Council with the purpose of promoting private Chinese business in some African nations (e.g., Cameroon, Ghana, Mozambique, Nigeria, Tanzania, and South Africa).

There also are signs that China has been listening. In May 2007, a Memorandum of Understanding was signed between China and the World Bank to improve cooperation (J.Y. Wang 2007). China accepted in December 2007 the joint development aid projects in Africa (China's Quest for Resources, *The Economist*, 15–21 March 2008, p. 14). Should China eventually render compatible its approach to the finance and credit market system with the traditional system of aid disbursement, we may never find out to what degree China singlehandedly would have impacted the African quest for economic development.

However, no externally conceived development aid program will ever induce the economic progress of a given people. The successive suggestions of remedy and their failure in all areas of societal develpmental scholarship, constitutes vivid proof. These suggestions range from focusing on specific mechanical steps such as the five steps by Rustow (1990) or big-push by Paul Rosenstein-Rodan (1943), or laissez-faire of liberalism, or economistsor state interventionism by other classical economists. There has been dissociation suggested by economists of dependency school, to institutionalism and legalism by political scientists, from focusing on social differentiations by sociologists to the emphasis on cultural stimuli by sociopsychologists. The notion of how societies develop is indeed complex as it encompasses all of these elements, some of which allow quantifiable, mathematizable variables and some others that are elusive and nonmaterial and therefore simply not mechanically or intellectually malleable.

All of these fields and their focuses contribute to the elucidation of aspects of a whole. Each considered alone has not produced commendable final results. The development of a nation is a complex endeavor that requires a congruence of clearly formulated goals and means and the coordination of inputs from all elements of a social fabric in a realistic setting and using actual resources at hand and at the same time dealing with the eventualities of history. The many and pragmatic elements required by development efforts have been the source of difficulties for many theories. It is simply difficult to assert and weigh all relevant elements, their values and significance, their possible impact on each other and overall, and to formulate a theory that accommodates them all. As a result, empirically grounded models are recommended. They have inspired the progress of those societies we consider advanced. Newly industrialized nations in the 1980s and emerging nations in the 2000s illustrate such models of development that are conceived, driven, and carried out by concerned people.

WILL CHINA MAKE THE DIFFERENCE?

The enthusiasm of China's involvement in Africa also has led to the question of whether China's activities have had the chance to lift Africa out of poverty at last or at least induce Rostow's famous takeoff phase. China will make a difference because a number of factors suggest a greater potential for impact. These factors are: the sheer manpower of the Chinese and their capacity to materialize sizable physical infrastructural projects, the increasing financial capability to finance projects that otherwise would not see the light of day because either the African nation in question does not have the funds or the traditional lenders such as the IMF did not approve of them. We have mentioned the flexibility of the Chinese approach, which is instrumental in possibly making the difference. China seems genuine in its pronouncement that it wants to contribute to the economic development of the continent, and it has demonstrated its willingness in concrete projects that target public health, agriculture, personnel training, and so on. China's chance to make the difference lies in the fact that it targets entire sectors, such as mining, power, telecommunications, and transportation with tangible instantaneous benefits and lasting impact. Traditional development aid focuses on isolated, individual projects with no multiplying effect.

The bigger question is whether that difference will be enough to allow an internally driven dynamics of economic development. Such dynamics are possible only if Africans themselves take the reins of their economic processes in following ways. First, policymakers ought to formulate concrete visions and societal projects that seem to be at the basis of every development. No development occurs randomly, as a result of unguided market exchanges. Reforms and a vision that links together resources, entrepreneurs, policy, populations, and finance must be formulated by Africans. Second, there must be an effort to ensure formation of capital and transfer of technology if Africa is to escape its fate in terms of agricultural products and raw materials exports. A chronic lack of capital has plagued the continent since independence and the vicious cycle of lack of finance, lack of production, lack of saving, lack of investment, and lack of productivity has been the hallmark of African economies. The booming prices of commodities and raw materials that have improved the terms of trade in favor of African exporters must be taken advantage of to obtain the goal of capital accumulation. With improved finances, investment is possible, and from investment the acquisition of means of production and technology is possible. Such acquisition may allow the structural transformation necessary for economic development as it facilitates the transition from an agriculture-dominated economy to manufacturing and thereby leads to mass consumption.

The end result is the modernization of African societies, which implies mass employment and mass income, generating purchasing power. This process seems to be a rite of passage, the condition sine qu non for moving away from mass poverty into mass consumption. All other political, ideological, cultural, and intellectual debates must subside to this imperative.

The international aid regime and bilateral and multilateral venues to economic development have created a system whose functionality has become an end in and by itself and the true finality, that of development, subject to policy papers, policy tools, and policy instruments such that their workability, not their accountability vis-à-vis misery, is the measure by which they are judged. Any deviation from existing models deserves a shot at the projection of economic development in Africa by virtue at least of being something different that might just work.

Will China make the difference? Maybe it suffices for China to do what it can within the limits of its intentions and policy goals and for Africa to capitalize on this interest. The question therefore ought to be, Will Africa capitalize on this interest from China in a way that future international developments and their paradigms (e.g., slavery, colonization, globalization) will not find the continent passive but rather the main actor in its own destiny?

THE ROLE OF AFRICA

Africa has no choice but to be at the core of any conceptualization and materialization effort to induce the very process described by Rostow. This responsibility implies the closing of all sources of sabotage (e.g., rent-seeking, gatekeeping, patrimonialism) in favor of strong institutions, constitutional state systems, and law enforcement, all of which contribute to an environment that is conducive to sound pursuit of collective and individual happiness in both sound policy choices and individual entrepreneurship.

Many Africans and Africanists in general find themselves forced to engage in academic discussions and debates in which they are asked to explain the cause of underdevelopment and stalling economic development in Africa. These discussions usually produce all kinds of causally constructed answers that at the end of the day seem not to render justice to the scope of the problems. This reminds me of a conversation I had on a train going from Copenhagen, Denmark, to Frankfurt, Germany, in which a passenger seated next to me having a coffee in the train restaurant, after hearing that I was from Africa, told me the story of his trip to Kenya, where he went to visit his sister. He stated that he could not understand why people were living in such poverty compared to life in Denmark, in a country such as Kenya with such a climate that allows the growth of almost everything, and where he saw people simply spending the entire morning relaxing. To such questions, sometimes there is no rationalization to explain the suggestion that it is incumbent upon Africans to make things happen and that whatever is not working is primarily their own responsibility, as they are primarily the ones who suffer the consequences.

Keith Richburg, for one, a Washington Post bureau chief based in Nairobi, found the situation far gone enough to call African leaders and their people to responsibility. In his book entitled *Out of Africa* (1997), Richburg explicitly laid blame primarily on Africans and did not shy away from the harsh criticism of Africa that tends to elicit a racist bias. In fact, he found the fear of such criticism to be part of the problem. As an American of African descent, he broke away from the malaise and tension felt by many of the African Diaspora, namely that between the need to criticize the state of affairs in African politics and the affinity felt from belonging to the same race and the identification tendency it otherwise implies. He wrote,

It is an ugly truth, but it needs to be laid out here, because for too long now Africa's failings have been hidden behind a veil of excuses and apologies. I realize that I'm on explosive ground here, and so I'll tread carefully. It's too easy to stumble onto the pitfall of old racial stereotypes—that Africans are lazy, that Asians are simply smarter, that Blacks still possess a more savage primitive side. But I am Black, though not an African, and so I am going to pull ahead here, mindful of the dangers, knowing full well that some will say I am doing a disservice to my race by pointing out these painful realties. But we have come too far now to pull back; the greater disservice now, I think, would be to leave the rest unsaid. (p. 171)

Africans must recognize the embarrassing state of affairs on the continent to raise the level of conscientiousness and at some level, shame, which is, according to Karl Marx, the beginning of the any revolution. Shame has a cultural dimension, as both individuals and societies feel the need for respect and recognition from peers and foes alike. The desire for recognition, according to Richard Appingnanesi (2006), is an integral part of human nature. When humans fail, they experience absence of recognition, which may produce frustration, despair, anger, and yes, shame. The same desire produces pride, respect, self-esteem, and prestige when we succeed both individually and socially or politically. Africans, both as individuals and political entities, are not indifferent or insensitive to the need for recognition and respect they would command in light of grandiose accomplishments.

Because civilizations, cultures, and progress are expressions of their respective visions, as they inform practical and efficient solutions to practical questions, studies (e.g., that of David McClelland, 1961) have questioned cultural factors that may or may not encourage and stimulate the drive to succeed. In the quest for better ways to organize society and production or to prevent and cure diseases, societies rely on their respective know-how. This know-how drives the paradigm of progress. Its differentiated levels among societies constitute a parameter or an indication by which to scrutinize the different vision, path, and pace to progress. Throughout history, traditional societies have had to embark eventually on the path to modernization to carry out progress. China is currently demonstrating what the West started in 1500 and Japan emulated in 1886. The Islamic world was well on course during the golden age of Islam, between the ninth and thirteenth centuries, and eventually shifted back in favor of the centrality of religion.

As for Africa, societies have remained traditional until the fundamental transformation implemented by colonization in the context of exploitation of resources, which produced expropriations, proletarianization, rural exoduses, poll and hut taxes, currency, and so on—in brief, a disruption of traditional subsistence economy based on the family as unit of production. The result for Africa was that it embarked on a process of modernization that unfortunately remained partially entrenched as the entire continent was not fully incorporated in modernity. This congenital handicap to African modernity, which explains the concept of dualism and leads to a parallel economy, parallel society that functionally influence each other negatively, has been one of the root causes of stalled economic development on the continent, as progress, by definition, constantly challenges the status quo whereas traditional societies hold on and nurture the status quo.

Because societies that develop later usually and generally benefit from accomplishments of those that developed earlier, Africa is deemed to take advantage of effective solutions proposed by others, by way of technology transfer, tapping into their markets, development of human capital, and so on. This capacity to learn, profit, use, and appropriate what has already worked elsewhere and adapt it to the continent's own empirical conditions, and possibly add value and build on it, has hindered African progress. The consequence of this failure has been the tendency to expect a handout in the form of foreign aid.

Just as development models conceived, driven, and carried out by concerned people have a better chance to succeed, today's foreign aid programs seem to have failed as they seem to be seen by concerned peoples as foreign bodies in their organisms. China's effort to help Africa therefore should be seen just as that: a help. Its impact has the potential to be significant if, as claimed by China's Premier Wen Jiabao. "We do not seek to export our own values and development models to Africa." China's approach promises better results simply because it goes where the West never went or has ceased to go in its official development assistance and investments.

CHAPTER 14

CONCLUSION

The economic and strategic ramifications of what has become of China since the reform initiative in 1978 have sparked the interest in that nation. That interest was further defined and it became clear that as many inquiries look into the global geopolitical ramifications, we should focus on Africa. One reason that justifies this perspective is the limited amount of scholarship with a non-Western perspective in the field of international affairs. This was made clear to me in conversations with fellow faculty members that some have not found any point nor substance and not enough material to warrant academic exploration of the topic. The examination of the literature has revealed the limited amount and scope of research, which further justifies my intent.

As I proceeded with the exploration of the topic at hand, it became apparent that in a relatively short period of time, since the reforms were implemented in the late 1970s and since China's aid policy vis-à-vis Africa shifted in the mid-1980s and evidently since the exhortation to go out for Chinese enterprises in the early 2000, that China has become prolific and involved almost ubiquitously, both geographically and in the sectors of economic activity. Although China's aid, trade, and FDI volume in Africa has been growing steadily, they remain behind the combined volume of those from the West.

One thing generated by China's offensive in Africa is the revival of a continent that was only seen since the collapse of the Soviet Union as a humanitarian cause, as a recipient of foreign aid, and was increasingly marginalized in all issues of crucial global strategic and economic pertinence. Africa's resources were no longer crucial for the economies of its traditional Western suitors, which had increasingly achieved a structural transformation that led them into the era of the service industry.

Along came the economic ascent of China. Next to China, India was emerging on the horizon, and both have justified a renewed interest in the remaining commodities and resources of Africa. Because of the sheer size of these new emerging global players, they have the peculiarity of expressing demand in respectable volume. With respect to energy, these latecomers needed a place at the table but could not get fed to their satisfaction. Africa became an imperative. The result has been increased competition for commodities, and resources and consequently increased interest in Africa as the locus where demand could be satisfied. China has since contributed to the improvement of the terms of trade for products from Africa and in the process contributed to increased economic growth of African nations with demand in energy, minerals, and commodities as well as by sparking economic activity with trade venues, FDI, and various projects in progress.

China alone is not responsible for Africa's economic renaissance. Good economic performance in Africa has been the product of good economic policy in a number of African nations (Botswana, Namibia., Mauritius, Ghana, Uganda, Tunisia, Mozambique, and Gabon). The impact of the works of the humanitarian relief organizations and multiple aid projects in this context in Africa has been difficult to evaluate. Whereas it is undeniable that many such projects help support conditions that otherwise would be desperate, the overall, big-picture impact has been questioned, considering that they have been in practice for decades and seem not to improve the underlying conditions of poverty but rather assist the conditions of poverty.

This book has spent a reasonable amount of interest in the examination of the apparent failure of so-called foreign aid. China's approach was therefore scrutinized in light of its potential to generate a different result. We have pointed to indications and evidence that that may indeed materialize. It remains potential because China's approach has only recently been implemented at full speed in Africa.

Criticism against China's approach has been revealed not to have substantive merit—at least not enough to necessitate or force a change of approach. African governments and public officials have shown that they understand the potential for China to ignite sustained economic growth at least until such a time as China's economic structure might no longer necessitate massive involvement on the continent.

China's involvement in Africa in this era of globalization is still in process, and the account we make of it is only partial and suggestive of what is still to come. It is still early to dare formulate one way or the other a conclusive judgment about China's approach to dealing with Africa.

China's Africa Policy

Foreword

The first few years of the new century witness a continuation of complex and profound changes in the international situation and further advance of globalization. Peace and development remain the main themes of our times. Safeguarding peace, promoting development and enhancing cooperation, which are the common desire of all peoples, represent the irresistible historical trend. On the other hand, destabilizing factors and uncertainties in the international situation are on the rise. Security issues of various kinds are interwoven. Peace remains evasive and development more pressing.

China, the largest developing country in the world, follows the path of peaceful development and pursues an independent foreign policy of peace. China stands ready to develop friendly relations and cooperation with all countries on the basis of the Five Principles of Peaceful Coexistence so as to contribute to peace, stability and common prosperity around the world.

The African continent, which encompasses the largest number of developing countries, is an important force for world peace and development. China-Africa traditional friendly relations face fresh opportunities under the new circumstances. With this African Policy Paper, the Chinese Government wishes to present to the world the objectives of China policy toward Africa and the measures to achieve them, and its proposals for cooperation in various fields in the coming years, with a view of promoting the steady growth of China-Africa relations in the long term and bringing the mutually-beneficial cooperation to a new stage.

PART I: AFRICA'S POSITION AND ROLE

Africa has a long history, vast expanse of land, rich natural resources and huge potential for development. After long years of struggle, the African people freed themselves from colonial rule, wiped out apartheid, won independence and emancipation, thus making significant contribution to the progress of civilization.

Following their independence, countries in Africa have been conscientiously exploring a road to development suited to their national conditions and seeking peace, stability and development by joint efforts. Thanks to the concerted efforts of African countries and the Organization of African Unity (OAU)/the African Union (AU), the political situation in Africa has been stable on the whole, regional conflicts are being gradually resolved and economy has been growing for years. The New Partnership for Africa's Development (NEPAD) has drawn up an encouraging picture of African rejuvenation and development. African countries have actively participated in the South-South cooperation and worked for the North-South dialogue. They are playing an increasingly important role in international affairs.

Africa still faces many challenges on its road of development. However, with the persistent efforts of African countries and the continuous support of the international community, Africa will surely surmount difficulties and achieve rejuvenation in the new century.

PART II: CHINA'S RELATIONS WITH AFRICA

China-Africa friendship is embedded in the long history of interchange. Sharing similar historical experience, China and Africa have all along sympathized with and supported each other in the struggle for national liberation and forged a profound friendship.

The founding of the People's Republic of China and the independence of African countries ushered in a new era in China-

Africa relations. For over half a century, the two sides have enjoyed close political ties and frequent exchanges of high-level visits and people-to-people contacts. Bilateral trade and economic cooperation have grown rapidly; cooperation in other fields has yielded good results; and consultation and coordination in international affairs have been intensified. China has provided assistance to the best of its ability to African countries, while African countries have also rendered strong support to China on many occasions.

Sincerity, equality and mutual benefit, solidarity and common development – these are the principles guiding China-Africa exchanges and cooperation and the driving force to lasting China-Africa relations.

PART III: CHINA'S AFRICAN POLICY

Enhancing solidarity and cooperation with African countries has always been an important component of China's independent foreign policy of peace. China will unswervingly carry forward the tradition of China-Africa friendship. Proceeding from the fundamental interests of both the Chinese and African peoples, China will establish and develop a new type of strategic partnership with Africa which features political equality and mutual trust, economic win-win cooperation and cultural exchange. The general principles and objectives of China's African policy are as follows:

- Sincerity, friendship, and equality. China adheres to the Five Principles of Peaceful Coexistence, respects African countries' independent choice of the road of development and supports African countries' efforts to grow stronger through unity.
- Mutual benefit, reciprocity, and common prosperity. China supports African countries' endeavor for economic development and nation building, carries out cooperation in various forms in the economic and social development, and promotes common prosperity of China and Africa.
- Mutual support, and close coordination. China will strengthen cooperation with Africa in the United

Nations and other multilateral systems by supporting each other's just demand and reasonable propositions and continue to appeal to the international community to give more attention to questions concerning peace and development in Africa.

- Learning from each other and seeking common development. China and Africa will learn from and draw upon each other's experience in governance and development, strengthen exchanges and cooperation in education, science, culture and health. Supporting African countries' efforts to enhance capacity building, China will work together with Africa in the exploration of the road of sustainable development.

The one-China principle is the political foundation for the establishment and development of China's relations with African countries and regional organizations. The Chinese Government appreciates the fact that the overwhelming majority of African countries abide by the one-China principle, refuse to have official relations and contacts with Taiwan and support China's great cause of reunification. China stands ready to establish and develop state-to-state relations with countries that have not yet established diplomatic ties with China on the basis of the one-China principle.

PART IV: ENHANCING ALL-ROUND COOPERATION BETWEEN CHINA AND AFRICA

1. THE POLITICAL FIELD

(1) High-level visits

China will maintain the momentum of mutual visits and dialogues between Chinese and African leaders, with a view of facilitating communication, deepening friendship and promoting mutual understanding and trust.

(2) Exchanges between legislative bodies

China favors increased multilevel and multichannel friendly exchanges on the basis of mutual respect between China's National People's Congress (NPC) and parliaments of African countries and the Pan-African Parliament of the AU, for the purpose of deepening understanding and cooperation.

(3) Exchanges between political parties

The Communist Party of China (CPC) develops exchanges of various forms with friendly political parties and organizations of African countries on the basis of the principles of independence, equality, mutual respect and noninterference in each other's internal affairs. The purpose of such exchanges is to increase understanding and friendship and seek trust and cooperation.

(4) Consultation mechanisms

Mechanisms such as national bilateral committees between China and African countries, political consultation between foreign ministries, joint (mixed) committees on trade and economic cooperation and mixed committees on science and technology should be established and improved, so as to institutionalize dialogue and consultation in a flexible and pragmatic manner.

(5) Cooperation in international affairs

China will continue to strengthen solidarity and cooperation with African countries in the international arena, conduct regular exchange of views, coordinate positions on major international and regional issues and stand for mutual support on major issues concerning state sovereignty, territorial integrity, national dignity, and human rights. China supports African nations' desire to be an equal partner in international affairs. China is devoted, as are African nations, to making the United Nations play a greater role, defending the purposes and principles of the UN Charter, establishing a new international political and economic order featuring justice, rationality, equality, and mutual benefit, promoting more democratic international relationship and rule of law in international affairs, and safeguarding the legitimate rights and interests of developing countries.

(6) Exchanges between local governments

China's Central Government attaches importance to the exchanges between local governments of China and African countries, vigorously supports twin province/state and twin city relationship aimed at facilitating bilateral exchanges and cooperation in local development and administration.

2. THE ECONOMIC FIELD

(1) Trade

The Chinese Government will adopt more effective measures to facilitate African commodities' access to the Chinese market and fulfill its promise to grant duty-free treatment to some goods from the least developed African countries, with a view of expanding and balancing bilateral trade and optimizing trade structure. It intends to settle trade disputes and frictions properly through bilateral or multilateral friendly consultation, mutual understanding and mutual accommodation. Efforts will be made to encourage business communities on both sides to set up China-Africa Joint Chamber of Commerce and Industry. When conditions are ripe, China is willing to negotiate Free Trade Agreement (FTA) with African countries and African regional organizations.

(2) Investment

The Chinese Government encourages and supports Chinese enterprises' investment and business in Africa, and will continue to provide preferential loans and buyer credits to this end. The Chinese Government is ready to explore new channels and new ways for promoting investment cooperation with African countries, and will continue to formulate and improve relevant policies, provide guidance, and service and offer convenience. African countries are welcome to make investment in China. The Chinese Government will continue to negotiate, conclude, and implement the Agreement on Bilateral Facilitation and Protection of Investment and the Agreement on Avoidance of Double Taxation with African Countries. The two sides should work together to create a favorable environment for investment and cooperation and protect the legitimate rights and interests of investors from both sides.

(3) Financial cooperation

To further develop China-Africa cooperation in the area of finance, the Chinese Government will support the effort of Chinese financial institutions to increase exchanges and cooperation with their counterparts in African countries as well as regional financial institutions in Africa.

(4) Agricultural cooperation

China intends to further promote its agricultural cooperation and exchanges with African nations at various levels, through multiple channels and in various forms. Focus will be laid on the cooperation in land development, agricultural plantation, breeding technologies, food security, agricultural machinery, and the processing of agricultural and side-line products. China will intensify cooperation in agricultural technology, organize training courses of practical agricultural technologies, carry out experimental and demonstrative agricultural technology projects in Africa, and speed up the formulation of China-Africa Agricultural Cooperation Program.

(5) Infrastructure

The Chinese Government will step up China-Africa cooperation in transportation, telecommunications, water conservancy, electricity and other types of infrastructure. It will vigorously encourage Chinese enterprises to participate in the building of infrastructure in African countries, scale up their contracts, and gradually establish multilateral and bilateral mechanisms on contractual projects. Efforts will be made to strengthen technology and management cooperation, focusing on the capacity-building of African nations.

(6) Resources cooperation

The Chinese Government facilitates information sharing and cooperation with Africa in resources areas. It encourages and supports competent Chinese enterprises to cooperate with African nations in various ways on the basis of the principle of mutual benefit and common development, to develop and exploit rationally their resources, with a view of helping African countries to translate their advantages in resources to competitive strength, and realize sustainable development in their own countries and the continent as a whole.

(7) Tourism cooperation

China will implement the program of Chinese citizens' group tours to some African nations and grant more African countries, as they wish and as far as feasible, Approved Destination Status for out-bound Chinese tourist groups. China welcomes citizens from African nations for a tour of the country.

(8) Debt reduction and relief

China is ready to continue friendly consultation with some African countries to seek a solution to, or reduction of, the debts they owe to China. It will urge the international community, developed countries in particular, to take more substantial action on the issue of debt reduction and relief for African nations.

(9) Economic assistance

In light of its own financial capacity and economic situation, China will do its best to provide and gradually increase assistance to African nations with no political strings attached.

(10) Multilateral cooperation

China is ready to enhance consultation and coordination with Africa within multilateral trade systems and financial institutions and work together to urge the United Nations and other international organizations to pay more attention to the question of economic development, promote South-South cooperation, push forward the establishment of a just and rational multilateral trade system, and make the voices of developing countries heard in the decision-making of international financial affairs. It will step up cooperation with other countries and international organizations to support the development of Africa and help realize Millennium Development Goals in Africa.

3. *EDUCATION, SCIENCE, CULTURE, HEALTH AND SOCIAL ASPECTS*

(1) Cooperation in human resources development and education

The Chinese Government will give full play to the role of its African Human Resources Development Foundation in training African personnel. It will identify priority areas, expand areas of cooperation and provide more input according to the needs of African countries so as to achieve greater results.

Exchange of students between China and Africa will continue. China will increase the number of government scholarships as it sees fit, continue to send teachers to help African countries in Chinese language teaching and carry out educational assistance projects to help develop Africa's weak disciplines. It intends to strengthen cooperation in such fields as vocational education and distance learning while encouraging exchanges and cooperation between educational and academic institutions of both sides.

(2) Science and technology cooperation

Following the principles of mutual respect, complementarity, and sharing benefits, China will promote its cooperation with Africa in the fields of applied research, technological development, and transfer, speed up scientific and technological cooperation in the fields of common interest, such as bio-agriculture, solar energy utilization, geological survey, mining, and the R&D of new medicines. It will continue its training programs in applied technologies for African countries, carry out demonstration programs of technical assistance, and actively help disseminate and utilize Chinese scientific and technological achievements and advanced technologies applicable in Africa.

(3) Cultural exchanges

China will implement agreements of cultural cooperation and relevant implementation plans reached with African countries, maintain regular contacts with their cultural departments, and increase exchanges of artists and athletes. It will guide and promote cultural exchanges in diverse forms between people's organizations and institutions in line with bilateral cultural exchange programs and market demand.

(4) Medical and health cooperation

China is ready to enhance medical personnel and information exchanges with Africa. It will continue to send medical teams and provide medicines and medical materials to African countries, and help them establish and improve medical facilities and train medical personnel. China will increase its exchanges and cooperation with African countries in the prevention and treatment of infectious diseases including HIV/AIDS and malaria and other diseases, research and application of traditional medicin,e and experience concerning mechanism for public health emergencies.

(5) Media cooperation

China wishes to encourage multitiered and multiformed exchanges and cooperation between the media on both sides, so as to enhance mutual understanding and enable objective and balanced media coverage of each other. It will facilitate the communication and contacts between relevant government departments for the purpose of sharing experiences on ways to handle the relations with media both domestic and foreign, and guiding and facilitating media exchanges.

(6) Administrative cooperation

China will carry out exchanges and cooperation with African countries in civil service system building, public administration reform, and training of government personnel. The two sides may study the feasibility of setting up a mechanism for personnel and administrative cooperation.

(7) Consular cooperation

China will hold regular/irregular consular consultations with African countries during which the two sides may have amicable discussions on urgent problems or questions of common interest in bilateral or multilateral consular relations in order to improve understanding and expand cooperation. The Chinese side will work with Africa to facilitate personnel flow and ensure the safety of their nationals.

(8) People-to-people exchanges

China will encourage and facilitate the exchanges between people's organizations of China and Africa, especially the youth and women, with a view of increasing the understanding, trust and cooperation of people on both sides. It will encourage and guide Chinese volunteers to serve in African countries.

(9) Environmental cooperation

China will actively promote China-Africa cooperation in climate change, water resources conservation, antidesertification, biodiversity and other areas of environmental protection by facilitating technological exchanges.

(10) Disaster reduction, relief and humanitarian assistance

China will actively carry out personnel exchange, training, and technological cooperation in the fields of disaster reduction and relief. It will respond quickly to African countries' requests for urgent humanitarian aid, encourage and support exchanges and cooperation between the Red Cross Society of China and other

NGOs on the one side and their African counterparts on the other side.

4. PEACE AND SECURITY

(1) Military cooperation

China will promote high-level military exchanges between the two sides and actively carry out military-related technological exchanges and cooperation. It will continue to help train African military personnel and support defense and army building of African countries for their own security.

(2) Conflict settlement and peacekeeping operations

China supports the positive efforts by the AU and other African regional organizations and African countries concerned to settle regional conflicts and will provide assistance within our own capacity. It will urge the UN Security Council to pay attention to and help resolve regional conflicts in Africa. It will continue its support to and participation in UN peacekeeping operations in Africa.

(3) Judicial and police cooperation

China is prepared to promote the exchanges and cooperation between Chinese and African judicial and law enforcement departments. The two sides may learn from each other in legal system building and judicial reform so as to be better able to prevent, investigate, and crack down on crimes. China will work together with African countries to combat transnational organized crimes and corruption, and intensify cooperation on matters concerning judicial assistance, extradition, and repatriation of criminal suspects.

China will cooperate closely with immigration departments of African countries in tackling the problem of illegal migration, improve exchange of immigration control information, and set up an unimpeded and efficient channel for intelligence and information exchange.

(4) Non-traditional security areas

In order to enhance the ability of both sides to address nontraditional security threats, it is necessary to increase intelligence exchange, explore more effective ways and means for closer cooperation in combating terrorism, small arms smuggling, drug trafficking, transnational economic crimes, etc.

PART V: FORUM ON CHINA-AFRICA COOPERATION AND ITS FOLLOW-UP ACTIONS

Launched in 2000, the Forum on China-Africa Cooperation has become an effective mechanism for the collective dialogue and multilateral cooperation between China and Africa and put in place an important framework and platform for a new type of China-Africa partnership featuring long-term stability, equality, and mutual benefit.

China attaches importance to the positive role of the Forum on China-Africa Cooperation in strengthening political consultation and pragmatic cooperation between China and Africa, and stands ready to work with African countries to conscientiously implement the Beijing Declaration of the Forum on China-Africa Cooperation, the Program for China-Africa Cooperation in Economic and Social Development, and the Forum on China-Africa Cooperation-Addis Ababa Action Plan (2004-2006) and its follow-up action plans. China will work with African countries within the framework of the Forum to explore new ways to enhance mutual political trust, promote the comprehensive development of pragmatic cooperation, further improve the mechanism of the forum, and try to find the best way for furthering cooperation between the Forum and the NEPAD.

PART VI: CHINA'S RELATIONS WITH AFRICAN REGIONAL ORGANIZATIONS

China appreciates the significant role of the AU in safeguarding peace and stability in the region and promoting African solidarity and development. China values its friendly cooperation with the AU in all fields, supports its positive role in regional and international affairs, and stands ready to provide the AU assistance to the best of its capacity.

China appreciates and supports the positive role of Africa's subregional organizations in promoting political stability, economic development and integration in their own regions and stands ready to enhance its amicable cooperation with those organizations.

JANUARY 2006

Appendix B

Asia-Africa Summit Communiqué

We, the Heads of State, Government and delegation of the People's Republic of China and 48 African countries, met in Beijing from 4 to 5 November 2006 for the Summit of the Forum on China-Africa Cooperation.

We applaud the Summit held on the occasion of the 50th anniversary of the inauguration of diplomatic relations between the People's Republic of China and the African countries.

For the purpose of promoting "friendship, peace, cooperation and development," we have reviewed the sincere friendship, solidarity, and cooperation between China and Africa over the past half century, and had fruitful discussions on the common goals and direction for growing China-Africa cooperation in the new era.

Conscious of the fact that thanks to the concerted efforts of both sides, the Forum on China-Africa Cooperation founded in 2000 has become an important platform for collective dialogue and an effective mechanism for pragmatic cooperation between the two sides, we have decided to enhance the role of the Forum and to this end, reaffirmed our commitment to the purposes and objectives set forth in the documents adopted by the Forum.

We hold that the world today is undergoing complex and profound changes, that human society is becoming increasingly interdependent, and that the pursuit of peace, development, and cooperation has become the trend of the times and the priority of all countries.

We declare that the development of our friendly relations and cooperation are in accordance with the Five Principles of Peaceful Coexistence as well as all the international principles that promote multilateralism and democracy in international relations. We urge that diversity of the world should be respected and upheld, that all countries in the world, big or small, rich or poor, strong or weak, should respect each other, treat each other as equals and live in peace and amity with each other and that different civilizations and modes of development should draw on each other's experience, promote each other and coexist in harmony.

Faced with the growing trend of economic globalization, we call for enhancing South-South cooperation and North-South dialogue and call on the World Trade Organization to resume the Doha Round of negotiations to promote balanced, coordinated and sustainable development of the global economy to enable all countries to share its benefits, and realize common development and prosperity.

We call for reform of the United Nations and other multilateral international institutions to make them better meet the need of all members of the international community. Through reform, the United Nations should strengthen its role, give full scope to the function of the UN General Assembly, and pay greater attention to the issue of development. Priority should be given to increasing the representation and full participation of African countries in the UN Security Council and other UN agencies.

We hold that the adherence of China, the world's largest developing country, to peaceful development and the commitment of Africa, a continent with the largest number of developing countries, to stability, development and renaissance are in themselves significant contribution to world peace and development.

The African countries are greatly inspired by China's rapid economic development. They extend congratulations to China and wish China even greater achievements in its development endeavors. They reiterate that they adhere to the one- China policy and support China's peaceful reunification.

China commends Africa's progress in safeguarding regional peace, promoting regional cooperation, and accelerating economic and social development; appreciates the active role played by the African countries, the African Union, and other regional and subregional organizations in this regard, reaffirms its support for the African countries in their efforts to strengthen themselves through unity and independently resolve African problems; supports the African regional and subregional organizations in their efforts to promote economic integration; and supports the African countries in implementing the New Partnership for Africa's Development (NEPAD) programs.

We call on the international community to encourage and support Africa's efforts to pursue peace and development and provide greater assistance to African countries in peaceful resolution of conflicts and postwar reconstruction. In particular, we urge the developed countries to increase official development assistance and honor their commitments to opening market and debt relief, and call on the related international organizations to provide more financial and technical assistance to enhance Africa's capacity in poverty and disaster reduction and prevention and control of desertification, and help Africa realize the UN Millennium Development Goals[43] solemnly declared in September of 2000. Greater attention should be paid to the issue of development facing the least developed countries and the heavily indebted poor countries as well as the small island and landlocked countries in Africa.

We point out that China and Africa enjoy traditional solidarity and cooperation and have always treated each other with sincerity and shared weal and woe. Having stood the test of time and changing international environment, China-Africa friendship is flourishing and enjoys immense popular support.

We maintain that in the new era, China and Africa have common development goals and converging interests that offer a broad prospect for cooperation. In the new century, China and the African countries should enhance their traditional friendship and expand mutually beneficial cooperation to achieve common development and prosperity.

We hereby solemnly proclaim the establishment of a new type of strategic partnership between China and Africa featuring political equality and mutual trust, economic win-win cooperation and cultural exchanges. For this purpose, we will:

- Increase high-level visits, conduct strategic dialogue, enhance mutual political trust, and promote enduring friendship;
- Deepen and broaden mutually beneficial cooperation, encourage and promote two-way trade and investment, explore new modes of cooperation, and give top priority to cooperation in agriculture, infrastructure, industry, fishery, IT, public health, and personnel training to draw on each other strengths for the benefit of our peoples;
- Increase exchange of views on governance and development to learn from each other, make common progress, and enhance our respective capacity for self-development;
- Increase dialogue between different cultures, promote people-to-people exchanges and interaction, particularly those between the young people, and boost exchanges and cooperation in such areas as culture, science and technology, education, sports, the environment, tourism, and women's affairs;
- Enhance international cooperation to jointly address global security threats and non-traditional security challenges, and uphold the common interests of the developing world in the spirit of mutual trust, mutual benefit, equality, and coordination;
- Enhance the Forum on China-Africa Cooperation, strengthen collective dialogue, and increase coordination and cooperation of the Action Plan with NEPAD and the social and economic development plans of African countries; and

- Properly handle issues and challenges that may arise in the course of cooperation through friendly consultation in keeping with China-Africa friendship and the long-term interests of the two sides

We hold that the establishment of a new type of strategic partnership is both the shared desire and independent choice of China and Africa, serves our common interests, and will help enhance solidarity, mutual support, and assistance, and unity of the developing countries and will contribute to durable peace and harmonious development in the world.

We have, in the spirit of this Declaration, formulated and adopted the Beijing Action Plan of the Forum on China-Africa Cooperation (2007–2009).

We commend the Ministers participating in the Third Ministerial Conference of the Forum on China-Africa Cooperation for their dedicated efforts and outstanding work, applaud the outcome of the High-Level Dialogue between Chinese and African Leaders and Business Representatives, and express our congratulations on the full success of the Summit.[44]

Appendix C

Zhou Enlai's Eight Principles Governing Chinese Foreign Aid

1. In the assistance it furnishes to other countries, the Chinese government constantly observes the principle of equality and mutual benefit. It never considers this assistance as a type of unilateral charity but rather as mutual aid. Thanks to the assistance, friendly and newly independent countries can progressively develop their national economies, free themselves from colonial control, and consolidate world anti-imperialist forces.

2. In furnishing aid to other countries, the Chinese government strictly respects the sovereignty of the recipient states. It never asks for any privilege and never poses conditions.

3. The Chinese government furnishes its economic assistance in the form of loans exempt from interest or at a minimum rate of interest and provides long periods for their repayment, so as to reduce to a minimum the burden carried by the recipient countries.

4. In furnishing economic aid to foreign countries, the Chinese government does not seek to place the recipients in a state of dependency on China but rather to aid

them to move forward, step by step, on the pathway of self-sufficiency.

5. Projects that the Chinese government helps the recipient countries to realize are, as much as possible, those capable of yielding rapid results for a minimum investment. This makes it possible for the recipient governments to increase their revenue and accumulate capital.

6. The Chinese government furnishes the best material manufactured by its own plants at prices prevalent on the international markets. If the material proves not to be in conformance with the norms and the quality desired, it promises to replace it.

7. To be sure that personnel of the recipient country have fully assimilated the necessary knowledge to use its technical aid, the Chinese government offers them the appropriate professional training.

8. The experts that the Chinese government sends to recipient countries to aid them in their tasks of construction have the same standard of living as the experts of these countries. Chinese experts are forbidden to formulate any special demands or to benefit from special advantages.

Notes

1. In French: *Quand la Chine s'eveillera le monde tremblera.*

2. Deng Xiaop Ping: 3rd Plenun of the 11th National Party Congress Central Committtee.

3. In French: *La China s'est enfin reveille.*

4. Sima Qin: Historical Records (Shi Ji). Chinaknowledge.de/literature/historiography/shi Ji.html.

5. Author's translation from French: "A political or economic mobilization, depending on the era, of an intelligent, docile, courageous, industrious, and laborious population tends to amalgamate conviction and conformity.".

6. At the signing of the "Rapport de la Rochelle.".

7. Zheng Bijian is president of the Forum for ChinaReform and vice president of the Chinese Communist Party. The speech was entitled (translated):"The New Way of the Peaceful Rise of China and the Future of Asia".

8. *Gelbe Gefahr* in German or le *peril jaune* in French expressing more a fear of a steam- rolling Chinese economic machine (cheap labor, cheap export products, beneficiary of delocalization, and killer of the European employment market).

9. Goldstein (2003, 58) used the term to denote the position in which China find's itself today, which is similar to that of Germany in the late nineteenth century.

10. These are nations profoundly separating from the West and linking their long-term welfare to China through entrenched agreements, as opposed to traditional friendships expressed through friendly policy articulation.

11. Africa has 8percent of world known oil reserves and a consensus on more sites yet to be discovered.

12. For the Chinese embassy list, see Larkin (1971, 66).

13. Malawi was the last, on 14 January 2008, to switch diplomatic allegiance to China.

14. For participants, see CEMIS, Gamorta paper.

15. Subject of an upcoming manuscript by this author entitled:: Shifting Balance: The Unraveling of Western Grip on International Politics", whose synopsis has been presented in International Studies Association conference in Odense, Denmark, 23–25 May 2007.

16. Dutch disease describes a resource curse; a case where exploitation of resources leads to raise of currency value, making a nation's manufacturing good less competitive, causing increase of import good to the detriment of export and may produce desindustrialization.

17. Export buyers' credit is disbursed to foreign borrowers to support the Chinese export market.

18. Export, sellers' credit is disbursed to Chinese businesses in the export industry.

19. International Monetary Fund/World Bank: Amendments to the Guidelines for Public Debt Management. Novemeber 25, 2003.

20. Peter Navarro referring to his book: The Coming China Wars, during an appearance on C-SPAN2, Books Series, 18 July 2007.

21. Those who have yet to adhere to the one-China policy: Burkina Faso, Swaziland, Malawi, Gambia, and São-Tomé and Principe.

22. Not much attention was payed to.

23. In addition to the two visits in 2001 and 2005, there was an initial visit by President Olesegun Obasanjo in April of 1999.

24. BBC News: China and Nigeria Agree Oil Deal.. April 26, 2006.

25 For example, the advocacy group 50 Years Enough, based in Washington, DC.

26. UN stastistics often entail figures that tell the story of families in least developed countries, living on an income that they would practically not survive on. The question therefore arises: How do these families yet survive?.

27. Max Weber in: The Protestant Ethic and the Spirit of Capitalism, Emanuel Kan in: Critics of Pure Reason, and Francis Bacon in: Novum Organon.

28. Noam Chomsky who, in may of his prouncements, has repeatedly argued against the many expressions of Western dominance.

29. Drop of water on a hot wooden plate.

30. They are (nations and total debt relief in $ million and percentage of total outstanding debt): Benin ($460, 31%), Bolivia ($2,060, 44%), Burkina Faso ($700, 54%), Honduras ($900, 18%), Mali ($870, 37%), Mauritania ($1,100, 50%), Mozambique ($4,300, 72%), Senegal ($850, %$%), Uganda ($1,950, 57%), Cameroon ($2,700, 30%), Chad ($250, 27%), Ethiopia ($1,300, 23%), Guinea ($1,150, 34%), Guinea Bissau ($600, 66%), Guyana ($4,100, 24%), Malawi ($1,100, 43%), Nicaragua ($5000, 66%), Rwanda ($800, 71%), Zambia ($4,500, 62). Source: World Bank (2002). As for the breakdown of the rest: Latin America 13%, Europe 7% (most of it from Russia, Africa 7%, Asia Pacific, and North America, 4%. Source: *The Economist* (2001).

31. A coalition of adi groups, churches, unons etc. organization and initiatives around the debt crisis in the 1990s, leading a movement and a campaign for HIPC debt forgiveness.

32. For instance: Nigeria borrowed $48 billion, paid $16 billion as of 2003, and still owes $32 billion (as of 2008).

33. Titled: African Alternative Framework to Structural Adjustment Program for Socio-Economic Recovery and Transformation (Addis-Ababa: ECA, 1989).

34. China.org.cn (Xinhua News Agency, May 16, 2007).

35. BBC News: 29 Nomber, 2007,17:49 GMT.

36. This organization comprises Angola, Burundi, Cameroon, Central African Republic, Chad, Congo (Brazzaville), the Democratic Republic of the Congo, Equatorial Guinea, Gabon, São Tome, and Principe.

37. COMESA comprises Angola, Burundi, Comoros, the Democratic Republic of the Congo, Djibouti, Egypt, Eritrea, Ethiopia, Kenya, Libya, Madagascar, Malawi, Mauritius, Rwanda, Seychelles, Sudan, Uganda, Zambia, and Zimbabwe.

38. SADC comprises Angola, Botswana, Democratic Republic of the Congo, Lesotho, Madagascar, Malawi, Mauritius, Mozam-

bique, Namibia, Seychelles, South Africa, Swaziland, Tanzania, Zambia, and Zimbabwe.

39 ECOWAS comprises Benin, Burkina Faso, Cap Verde, Gambia, Ghana, Guinea, Guinea Bissau, Ivory Coast, Liberia, Mali, Niger, Nigeria, Senegal, Sierra Leone, and Togo.

40. Translated by the author: "Pagan tolerance has allowed Muslims to venture deep into the heart of the forest following the trace of the caravans to carry manufactured products from the Maghreb and Egypt."

41. Translated by the author: Africa should not miss the opportunity for democratic rule as she has already missed the one for independence.

42. Translated by the author: "In the new battlefield of the twenty-first century, which abolishes the notion of time and space, the conquest of markets and new technologies has replaced old conquests of colonial territories. We now live in a state of economic war, and this is not simply a recuperation of military vocabulary. The conflict is real, and its imperatives dictate the action of nations and the lives of individuals. The aim of this war is, for each nation, to create for itself revenues and employments to the detriment of that of its neighbors. . . . In exporting more product, services, intangibles, each nation tries to win this new kind of war, in which enterprises make up the armies and customers constitute its victims."

43. Grew sicne to reach 1 billion.

44. In a statement made while visiting South Africa, at a press conference in Cape Town, 10 December 2007.

45. Eight goals have been established: eradicate extreme poverty and hunger; achieve universal primary education; promote gender equality and empower women; reduce child mortality; improve maternal health; combat HIV/AIDS, malaria, and other diseases; ensure environmental sustainability; and develop global partnership for development.

46. Department of Policy Planning, Ministry of Foreign Affairs, People's Republic of China. *China's Foreign Affairs: 2007 Edition.* World Affairs Press, Beijing. 2007), 668–71.

References

Adeola, Fola. 2004, 23 September. Commission for Africa: China-Africa Cooperation from an African Perspective. Keynote address presented at seminar, Supporting Africa's Development: Sharing Experiences to Reduce Poverty, Beijing, China.

Ake, Claude. 1990, 23–25 March. The Case for Democracy. In *African Governance in the 1990s: Objectives, Resources, and Constraints.* Working Papers from the Second Annual Seminar of the African Governance Program, Atlanta, Georgia, Carter Center of Emory University.

Alden, Chris. 2007. *China in Africa.* London and New York: Zed Books.

Alvater, Elmar, and Birgit Mahnkopf. 2007. *Konkurrenz fuer das Empire: Die Zukunft der Europaeische Union in der Globalisierten Welt* [Competition for the Empire: The Future of the European Union in the Globalized World]. Muenster, Germany: Westfaelische Dampfboot.

Angola-China: An Example of South-South Cooperation. 2004, 26 March. Embassy of Angola, Luanda.

Another Vintage Year for Chinese Diplomacy, *China Daily*, 23 December 2005 Retrieved from Sohu.com, http://english.sohu.com/20051223/n227694561.shtml.

AnnualPartnership: Shared Interest and Chanllenegs in EU-Cina Relations. 2009.

Aphorism and Suspicions: China's World Order. *The Economist*, 19-25, November, 2005, p. 24.

Atkinson, Jeff. 1994, September. GATT: What Do the Poor Get? Background Report no. 5, Fitzroy, Australia.

Appingnanesi, Richard, ed. *Introducing Hegel*. Singapore: Tien Wah Press, 2006.

Badiane, Ousmane. 1997. *Africultural Recovery and Structural Transformation in African Countries*. Washington DC: International Food Policy Research Institute.

Bajpaee, Chietigj. 2005, 10 July. Sino-US Energy Competition in Africa. Retrieved from Power and Interest News Report Web Site, www.pinr.com/report.php?ac=view_report&report_id=378&language_id=1.

Barnett, Thomas. 2005. *Blueprint for Action: A Future Worth Creating*. New York: Penguin Group.

Bate, Roger. 2006. *The Trouble with USAID*. Washington DC: American Enterprise Institute.

BB News: China and Nigeria Oil Deal, April, 2006.

Beijing Review 50, no. 6 (8 February 2007).

Bergsten C. Fred, Gill Bates, Lardy R. Nicholas, and Mitchell Derek. 2006. *China: The Balance Sheet What the World Needs to Know About the Emerging Superpower*. New York: BBC Public Affairs.

Bijian, Zheng. 2003, October. *"The New Way of the Peaceful Rise of China and the Future of Asia".* Speech delivered at the Asian Forum Annual Meeting at Bo Ao, Hainan.

Bloomfield, Steve. 2007. Chinese Cheques-Dar es Salaam, Nairobi and Luanda. *Monocle* 1, no. 1: 078-086.

Braud, Pierre Antoine. 2005, October. *La Chine en Afrique: Anatomie d'une Nouvelle Strategie Chinoise* [La Chine in Africa: Anatomy of a New Chinese Strategy]. Retrieved from the Analysis Web site at www.iss.eu.org.

Brautigam, Deborah. 2007, February 20. *Discussant in online debate: Is Chinese Investment Good for Africa?* Washington, DC: Council on Foreign Relations.

Broadman, Harry G. 2007. *Africa's Silk Road: China and India's New Economic Frontier.* Washington, DC: The World Bank.

Brookes, Peter, and Ji Hye Shin. 2006, February *China's Influence in Africa: Implication for the United States.* Heritage Foundation Web Site, Research/Asia and the Pacific, Backgrounder #1916, retrieved from www.heritage.org/Research/Asissndthepacific/bg1916.cfm.

Browne, Robert S. 1996. The World Bank Versus the Economic Commission of Africa: Is This Really a Conflict as to Development Strategy. In *Prospects for Recovery and Sustainable Development in Africa.* edited by Aguibou Y. Yansane. London: Greenwood Press.

Brzezinsky, Zbigniew. 2004. *The Choice: Global Domination or Global Leadership.* New York: Basic Books.

Centre for Chinese Studies, Stellenbosch University, 2006, October 17. China's Interest and Activity in Africa's Construction and Infrastructure Sectors. Retrieved from http://www.dfid.gov.uk/countries.asia/China/partners.asp.

China Facts and Figures 2002. Retrieved from China.org.cn.

China Grows its Role in Africa's Media. 2007, 11 May. Wits Journalism Program. Retrieved from Journalism.co.za. www.journalism.co.za/insight/chin-grows-its-role-in-africa-media-2.html.

Collette, Elise, and Gilles Yabi. 2004, January 25. Chic, les Chinois Reviennent. Retrieved from http://www.cameroon-info.net/cmForumNG/viewtopic.php?t= 7581&sid=21b19fb1a 72af49cfd7aa14412d6b1d0, originally pubulished at http://www.jeuneafrique.com/article.php ?idarticle=LIN25014c hicltnenne0.

Congo Has Something China Wants, and Vice Versa, *The Economist*, March 2008: 14.

Cooley, J. 1965. *East Wind over Africa: Red China's Africa Offensive.* New York: Walker.

Corden, M. W., and P. J. Neary. 1982. Booming Sector and De-Industrialization in a Small Open Economy. *Economic Journal* 92, no. 368: 825–845.

Council on Foreign Relations. 2005. *More than Humanitarianism: A Strategic US Approach Toward Africa.* Report of the Independent Task Force sponsored by the Council on Foreign Relations. Retrieved from http://www.cfr.org/ publication.

Council on Foreign Relations. 2006, 12 January. Retrieved from www.cfr.org/publication/9557china_and_oil.html.

Davies, Martyn et al. 2008. *How China Delivers Development Assistance to Africa.* Stellenbosch, South Africa: Center for Chinese Studies.

Davis, Anthony. 2000. Blue-Water Ambitions: Beijing is building up its navy to project power. *AsiaWeek* 26, no. 11. http://www-cgi.cnn.com/ASIANOW/asiaweek/ magazine/2000/0324/nat.2china.navy.html.

De Saint-Paul, Marc Aicardi. 2004. *La Chine et l'Afrique entre engagement et interet* [China and Africa Between Engagement and Interest]. Retrieved from Geopolitique Africaine Web Site, http://www.African-geopolitics.org /show. aspx?ArticleId=3726.

Department of Policy Planning, Ministry of Foreign Affairs, People's Republic of China. 2007. *China's Foreign Affairs 2007 Edition.* Beijing: World Affairs Press.

Dugger, Celia W. 2007, October 15. World Neglects African Farming, Study Says. *The New York Times.* Retrieved from www.nytimes.com/ 2007/10/15/world/africa15worldbank. html.

_____. 2008, December 7. US Agency's Slow Pace Endangers Foreign Aid. *The New York Times,* retrieved from www. nytimes.com/2007/12/07/world/africa/07millennium. html.

Eagle, William. 2006, May 16. China Defends Its Economic Policies in Africa. *Voice of America,* retrived from http:// www.voanews.com/english/archive/2006-05/2006-05-16-

voa26.cfm?CFID=127930582&CFTOKEN=83434806&jse ssionid=de301 9f2e09d363a3df5541a3c386dbe1de6.

Easterly, William. 2006. *The White Man's Burden. Why the West's Efforts to Aid the Rest Have Done So Much Ill and So Little Good.* New York: The Penguin Press.

Eisenman, Joshua. 2005. Zimbabwe: China's Africa Ally. *China Brief* 5, no. 15: 1–4.

_____ and Joshua Kurlantzick. 2006, May. China's Africa Strategy. *Current History: The American Foreign Policy Council*: 219–24.

Elliot, Michael. 2007, January 11. China Takes on the World. *Time Magazine*, retrieved from http://www.time.com/time/magazine/article/0,9171,1576831,00.html.

Ellis, Linden J. 2007, March 22. *China Exim Bank in Africa.* Washington, DC: Woodrow Wilson International Center for Scholars.

Engardio, Peter, ed. 2007. *Chindia: How China and India Are Revolutionized Global Business.* New York: McGraw-Hill.

Esambert, Bernard. 1992. *L'Etat et l'Entreprise* [The State and the Company]. In *Ou Va l'Etat* [Where the State Goes], ed. by Rene Lenior. Paris: Le Monde Editions.

European Parliament Council Commission. 2006, 24 February. *Official Journal of the European Union*, no. 2006/C: 1–46.

Firozi, Manji, and Stephen Mark, eds. 2007. *African Perspectives on China in Africa.* Fahamu, Nairobi: Oxford.

Fisher-Thomson, Jim. 2006. Washington Forum Examines Chinese Trade Trends on Continent. Retrieved from http://www.USinfo.state.gov/xarchives/display.html?p=washfile-english&y=2006&m=November.

Freund, Bill. 1998. *The Making of Contemporary Africa: The Development of African Society Since 1800,* 2nd edition. Boulder, CO.: Lynne Rienner Publishers.

Friedman L. Thomas. 2005. *The World Is Flat: A Brief History of the Twenty-First Century.* New York: Farrar, Strauss and Giroux.

Frankfurter Rundshcau. 2007, 1 June, no. 125.

Froehlich, J. C. 1962. *Les Musulmans d'Afrique Noire* [The Muslims of Black Africa]. Paris: L'Orante cop.

Galtung, Johan. 1998. *Frieden mit Friedlechen Mittlen: Frieden und Konflikt, Ent-wicklund und Kultur* [Peace with Peaceful Means: Peace and Conflict, Development and Culture]. Opladen, Germany: Leske & Budrich.

Gattamorta, Martia Egiza. 2004, Spring. Africa-China: Winning South-South Cooperation for the Third Millennium. *CeMISS Quarterly* 2, no. 1, pp. 77–88.

Gaye, Adam. 2007. *China-Africa: The Dragon and the Ostrich*. Paris: L'Harmattan.

George, Susan, and Fabrizio Sabelli. 1994. *Faith and Credit: The World Bank's Secular Empire*. Boulder, CO: Westview Press.

German Development Institute. 2005. *How Much Aid Is Good foR Africa?A Big Push as a Way Out of the "Poverty Trap"* Briefing Paper 4/2005.

Gill, Bates, and James Reilly. 2007. The Tenuous Hold of China Inc. in Africa. *The Washington Quarterly* 30, no. 3: 37–52.

Goldman Sachs Report. 2003, October 1. *Dreaming with BRICs: The Path to 2050*. Paper No. 99. New York, Goldman Sachs Group.

Goldstein, Andrea, Nicolas Pinaud, Helmut Reisen, and Xiaobao Chen. 2006. *The Rise of China and India: What's in it for Africa?* Paris: Development Centre Studies, OECD Publication.

Goldstein, Avery. 2003. An Emerging China's Emerging Grand Strategy: A Neo Bismarckian Turn? In *International Relations Theory and the Asia-Pacific,* edited by G. John Ikenberry and Micheal Mastanduno. New York: Columbia University Press.

Greider, William. 1996. *One World Ready or Not: The Manic Logic of Global Capitalism*. New York: Simon and Schuster.

Grill, Bartholomaeus. 2006, 14 September. *Die neuen Kolonial-herren* [The New Colonial Masters]. *Die Zeit* 38, retrieved from http://www.zeit.de/2006/38/China-Afrika?page=all.

Guijin, Liu. 2005, 15 February. Chinese Ambassador to South Africa. Retrieved from Za.Chineseambassy.org.

_____. 2006, October 16. China in Africa in the 21st Century. Retrieved from Za.Chineseambassy.org.

Guixuan, Liang. 2005. Perspective on China-Africa Trade and Economic Cooperation. Retrieved from http://www. Chinese embassyorg.za.

Hare, Paul. 2006, 8 November. China in Angola: An Emerging Energy Partnership. China Brief. *Jamestown Foundation* 6, no. 22, retrieved from http://www.jamestown.org/programs/chinabrief/single/?tx_ttnews%5Btt_news%5D=3997&tx_ttnews%5BbackPid%5D=196&no_cache=1.

Hengari, Alfredo Tjiurimo. 2007, 19 January. China Must Give Its Africa Policy Ethical Content. *The Namibian*, retrieved from www.namibian.com.na/2007/January / columns/076EAFB900.html.

Hertsgaard, Mark. 2000, 26 April. A Global Green Deal. *Time Magazine Online*. Retrieved from http://www.time.com/time/magazine/article/0,9171,996756-1,00.html.

Hilsum, Lindsey. 2005, 4 July. We Love China. *Granta Magazine* online. Retrieved from www.granta.com/extracts/2616.

Hu, W., G. Chan, and D. Zha, eds. 2000. *China's International Relations in the 21st Century*. Lanham, MD: University Press of America.

Human Rights Watch. 1998. Global Trade, Local Impact, Arms Transfers to all Sides in the Civil War in Sudan. *Human Rights Watch* 10, no. 4(a): 28–29.

Huntington, Samuel. 1996. *The Clash of Civilizations and the Remaking of World Order*. New York: Simon and Schuster.

Independent Task Force Report. 2005, 4 December. Council on Foreign Relations. Retrieved from www.cfr.org/publication.

International Herald Tribune Business. 23 January 2007.

International Mononetary Fund and The World Bank: Amendments to the Guidelines for Public Debt Management. Novemebr 25, 2003.

International Monetary Fund. 2004. Direction of Trade Statistics. Statistics Department. *Yearbook, 2004.* Washington, DC: International Monetary Fund.

Jan, Michel. 2006, May. Point de Vue sur la Chine Contemporaine [Point of View on Contemporary China]. *Equations Chinoises*, nos. 26–27: 1–218.

Kabou, Axelle. 1991. *Si l'Afrique Refusait le Development?* [If Africa Refuses Development?]. Paris: L'Harmattan.

Keohane, Robert, and Joseph Nye. 1973. Power and Interdependence. *Survival* 15, no. 4: 158–165.

Khadiagala M. Gilbert, and Lyons Terrence, eds. 2001. *African Foreign Policies: Power and Process.* Boulder, Colo: Lynne Rienner Publishers.

Kim, Samuel S. 1997, September. China as a Great Power. *Current History: A Journal of Contemporary World Affairs* 96, no. 611: 246–51. Beijing.

King, Kenneth. 2006. Aid Within the Wider China-Africa Partnership: A View from the Beijing Summit. Comparative Education Research Center. Originally published in K. King and P. Rose, eds., International and National Targets for Education: Help or Hindrance, *International Journal of Educational Development* 25, no. 4, Special Issue: 1–19.

———. 2007, Multilateral Agencies and the Construction of the Global Agenda on Education Special Issue of *Comparative Education*, vol. 47, no. 3, August.

———. 2006b. China in Africa: A New Lens on Development Cooperation, with a Focus on Human Resources. Special Issue of *West Asia and Africa* (Institute of West Asian and African Studies, CASS, Beijing) on Comparative Culture and Education in African and Asian Societies.

_____. 2006c. China's partnership discourse with Africa Paper to Conference on China in Africa in the 21st century: Preparing for the Forum on China-Africa Cooperation organized by the Royal African Society, the South African Institute of International Affairs, and the Secretariat of NEPAD (the New Partnership for Africa's Development), 16-17 October, Muldersdrift, near Johannesburg.

Kitissou, Marcel, ed. 2007. *Africa in China's Global Strategy*. London: Adonis Abbey Publishers Ltd.

_____. 2007. China's Corporate Engagement in Africa. In *Africa in China's Global Strategy*, London: Adonis Abbey Publishers.

Kornberg F. Judith, and John Faust R. 2005. *China in World Politics Policies, Processes, Prospects*. 2nd edition. Boulder, CO: Lynne Rienner Publishers.

Large, Daniel. 2006. As the Beginning Ends: China's Return to Africa. In *African Perspectives on China in Africa*, Edited by Firoze Manji and Stephen Marks.. Oxford, Capetown, Nairobi: Fahamu Books.

_____ and Daniel, and Ricardo De Oliveira. 2007. *China Returns to Africa: A Superpower and a Continent Embrace*. London: C. Hurst and Co. Publisher,.

Larkin, B. 1971. *China and Africa: 1949–1970*. Berkeley: University of California Press.

Leonard, Mark. 2005. *Why Europe will Run the 21st Century*. New York: Public Affairs Books.

Le Pere, Garth, and Garth Shelton. 2007. *China, Africa and South Africa: South-South Co-operation in a Global Era*. Cape Town, South Africa: ABC Press.

Lyman, Princeton N. 2005, 21 July. China's Rising Role in Africa. Retrieved from Council for Foreign Relations Web site at www.cfr.org/publication8436/chinas_rising_role_in_africa. html?breadcrumb=crumb=default.

Mazrui, Ali. 1985. *Africa Eden Garden in Decay* [film series].

Mbaku, John Mukum. 2004. *Institutions and Development in Africa.* Trenton, NJ: Africa World Press.

McClelland, David C. 1961. *The Achieving Society.* Princeton, NJ: D. Van Nostrand Company.

McKinlay, R. D., and R. Little. 2006. A Foreign-Policy Model of the Distribution of British Bilateral Aid, 1960–70. *British Journal of Political Science* 8, no. 3: 313–332.

Melber, Henning. 2007. The (Not So) New Kid on the Block: China and the Scramble for Africa's Resources. *China in Africa: Current African Issues*, no. 35: 6–9.

Michel, Serge. 2008, May/June. When China Met Africa. *Foreign Policy*: 41.

Mischler, Walter. 1988. *Weissbuch Afrika.* Johann Henrich Wilhelm Dietz. Bonn.

Mkulo, Mustafa H. M. 1994. The Impact of Structural Adjustment Programs on Social Security in Eastern and Southern African Countries. *Social Security Documentation*, no. 15: 1–12.

Morin-Allory, Ronan. 2005. *Echanges Multipliés par Trois en Quatre Ans* [Trade increased threefolds in four years]. Retrieved from JeuneAfrique.com/jeune_afrique/article_jeune_africque.asp?art_cle=LIN28095e.

Morrison, Kevin. 1999. Understand Debt Relief. Retrieved from www.dc.org/commentary/ibaug99.html2.

Mungomba, Agrippah T. 1978. Regional Organizations and African Underdevelopment: The Collapse of the East African Community. *Journal of Modern African Studies* 16, no. 2: 263.

Naidu, Sanusha. 2007. China-Africa Relations in the 21st Century: A "Win-Win" Relationship. *China in Africa: Current African Issues*, no. 35: 41– 46.

Navarro, Peter. 2007. *The Coming China Wars: Where They Will Be Fought and How They Can Be Won.* Upper Saddle River, NJ: Financial Times Press.

Nuschler, Franz. 1994. *Lern-und Arbeitsbuch Entwicklungs-Politik* [Didactic and Working Manual on Development Politcs]. Bonn: Verlag Neue Gesellschaft.

_____ and Klaus Ziemmer. 1980. *Politische Herrschaft in Schwarzafrika* [Political Rule in Black Africa]. Munich: C. H. Beck.

Nye, Joseph. 2006, March 1. Think Again: Soft Power. *Foreign Policy.* Retrieved from YaleGlobal Online, www.yaleglobal.edu/display.article?id-7059.

OAU. 1980. Lagos Plan of Action for the Economic Development of Africa 1980–2000. Addis-Ababa, Ethiopia: OAU; Geneva, Switzerland: International Institute for Labour Studies, 1981.

Ogunsanwo, Alaba. 1974. China's Policy in Africa 1958–71. Cambridge, UK: University Press.

Palan, Ronen, Jason Abbot, and Phil Deans. 1996. *State Strategies in the Global Political Economy.* New York: Pinter Publishers.

Pan, Esther. 2005, September/October. China's Global Hunt for Energy. *Foreign Affairs* 84, no. 5: 25–38.

_____. 2006, 12 January. *China-Africa Oil.* Washington, D.C.: Council on Foreign Relations.

Payer, Cheryl. 1975. *The Debt Trap.* New York: Monthly Review Press.

Pedde, Nicola. 2004, spring. Between Energy Security and Insecurity in the Wake of the Chinese Market. *CEMISS Quarterly,* 91–103.

Petromatrix GmbH Report. 2006. Zug, Switzerland, retrived from http://www.petromatrix.com/IEA%20Review%20Dec13%20 2006.pdf.

Peyrefitte, Alain. 1973. *Quand la Chine s'Eveillera, le Monde Tremlera* (When China Wakens, the World Will Tremble). Paris: Fayard.

_____. 1996. *La Chine s'Est Eveillee* [China Is Awake]. Paris: Fayard.

Plato: The Republic, Hackett Pubishing, Cambridge , Massachusetts, 1992.

Prebish, Raul. 1950. *The Economic Development of Latin America and its Principal Problems*. Lake Success, New York: United Nations Economic Commission for Latin America.

Popper, Karl. 1971. *Open Society and its Enemies*. Princeton, NJ: Princeton University Press.

Reilly, James, and Wu Na. 2007. China's Corporate Engagement in Africa. In *Africa in China's Global Strategy*, edited by Marcel Kitissou. London: Adonis Abbey Publishers.

Richburg, Keith. 1997. *Out of Africa: A Black Man Confronts Africa*. New York: Harper Collins.

Rosenstein-Rodan, Paul N. 1943, June–September. Problems of Industrialization of Eastern and South Eastern Europe. *Quarterly Journal of the Royal Economic Society* 53, nos. 210–211: 202–211.

Rostow, W. W. 1990. *The Stages of Economic Growth*. New York: Cambridge University Press.

Sachs, Jeffrey et al. 2004. Ending Africa's Poverty Trap. *Brookings Paper on Economic Activity*, no. 1/2004, 117-240.

Seligson, Mitchell, and John Passé-Smith, eds. 1998. *The Confucian Ethics and Economic Growth in: Development and Underdevelopment*, 2nd ed. Boulder, Colo.: Lynne Rienner.

Serraux, Albert. 1927. *La Mise en Valeur des Colonies Françaises* [The Exploitation of French Colonies]. Paris: Payot.

Servant, Jean-Christoph. 2005, May. China's Trade Safari in Africa. *Le Monde Diplomatique* (English edition retrieved from mondediplo.com).

Shaopeng, Gong. 2006, May. *La Chine Dans le Monde* [China in the World]. *Equations Chinoises*, no. 26–27: 21–28.

Shichor, Yitzhak. 2005, October 13. Sudan: China's Outpost in Africa. *China Brief, The Jamestown Foundation* 5, no. 21: 1–4.

Shuffield, Robin [Director]. 2006. *Thomas Sankara: The Upright Man*, A Documentary Film.

Singer, H. 1950. The Distribution of Gain between Investing and Borrowing Countries. *American Economic Review* 40, no. 3: 473–83.

Simons R. Matthew. 2005. *Twilight in the Desert: The Coming Saudi Oil Shock and the World Economy.* Hoboken, NJ: John Wiley and Sons.

Song, Xinning, and Gerald Chan. 2000. International Relations Theory in China. In: *China's International Relations Theory in the 21ˢᵗ Century: Dynamics of Paradigm Shifts.*, edited by Weixing Hu, Gerard Chan, Daoiong Zha, Lanham, MD: University Press of America.

Sriram, Chandra Lekha. 2007, 30 January. China, Human Rights, and the Sudan. *Jurist: Legal New and Research.*

Steinfeld, Edward S. 2002, November. Chinese Enterprises Development and the Challenge of Global Integration. The Future of Growth. Prepared as a background paper for World Bank Study *Innovative East Asia: The Future of Growth.* Paris, France.

Steingart, Gabor. 2006. *Weltkrieg um Wohlstand: Wie Macht und Reichtum New Verteil Warden* [World War on Wealth]. Munich: Piper.

Traub, James: China-African Adventure. The New York Times November 19, 2006.

Parsons, Talcott: The Modern Society. Prentice Hall, New Jersey, 1971.

Taylor, Ian. 2006. *China and in Africa: Engagement and Compromise.* New York: Routledge.

_____. 2007. Unpacking China's Resource Diplomacy in Africa. *Current African Issues*, no. 35: 15.

Timberg, Craig. 2007, February 11. Inventive South Africa Firms Thrive in Booming China: Companies Apply Lessons Learned in Expanding to Poor, Complex Markets on Their Own Continent. *The Washington Post*, p. A25.

UNDP: Human Development Report, 2000.

Wallerstein, Emmanuel. 1974. *The Modern World-System I: Capitalist Agriculture and the Origins of the European World-Economy in the Sixteenth Century*. Burlington, MA: Academic Press.

Walton, C. Dale. 2007. *Geopolitics and the Great Powers in the Twenty-first Century: Multipolarity and the Revolution in Strategic Perspective*. New York: Routledge.

Wang, Hongying. 2000. Multilateralism in Chinese Foreign Policy: The Limits of Socialization. In China's International Relations in the 21st Century. Edited by: Weixing Hu, Gerald Chan, and Daojiong Zha. Lanham, Md.: University Press of America.

Wang, Jian-Ye. 2008, October. What Drives China's Growing Role in Africa? Africa Department *IMF Working Paper* WP/07/211.

Weber, Max. 1972. *Wirtschaft und Gesselschaft* [Economy and Society]. Tuebingen, Germany: J.C.B. Mohr.

Wenping, He. 2006, October 16–17. Engaging with NEPAD: A View from China. For the Conference: China in Africa in the 21st Century: Charting the Future, Johannesburg, South Africa.

Wild, Leni, and David Mepham. 2008. The New Sinosphere. *China in Africa*: 1–72.

Williamson, John. 1993. Democracy and the "Washington Consensus." *World Development* 21, no. 8: 1329–36.

World Bank. 1997. *World Development Report: The State in a Changing World*. Oxford, UK: Oxford University Press, World Bank.

_____. 2002. *African Development Indicators, 2002*. Oxford, UK: Oxford University Press, World Bank.

Xinhua, November, 2006: President Hu: Beijing Summit to be a milestone in China-Africa relations. English.gov.cn/2006-11/content_430255.htm.

Yu, George T. 1988. Africa in Chinese Foreign Policy in JSTOR. *Asian Survey* 28, no. 8: 849–862.

Yuanying, Pei. 2004, 30 July. The Five Principles of Peaceful Coexistence and Theory and Practice of China's Diplomacy in the New Era. China Institute of International Studies. Retrieved from http://www.ciis.org.cn/en/index.asp.

Zimmermann, Felix. 2005. The International Aid System: A Question of Perspective. *Policy Insight*, no. 12. Retrieved from www.OECD.org.

INDEX